A THEORY OF
THE MULTIPRODUCT FIRM

STUDIES
IN MATHEMATICAL AND MANAGERIAL ECONOMICS

Editors

HENRI THEIL
HERBERT GLEJSER

VOLUME 28

NORTH-HOLLAND PUBLISHING COMPANY
AMSTERDAM – NEW YORK – OXFORD

A THEORY OF THE MULTIPRODUCT FIRM

KENNETH LAITINEN
University of Chicago

1980
NORTH-HOLLAND PUBLISHING COMPANY
AMSTERDAM – NEW YORK – OXFORD

ISBN 0 444 85495 9

PUBLISHERS:

NORTH-HOLLAND PUBLISHING COMPANY
AMSTERDAM · NEW YORK · OXFORD

DISTRIBUTORS FOR THE U.S.A. AND CANADA:

ELSEVIER NORTH-HOLLAND, INC.
52 VANDERBILT AVENUE
NEW YORK, N.Y. 10017

Library of Congress Cataloging in Publication Data

Laitinen, Kenneth.
A theory of the multiproduct firm.

(Studies in mathematical and managerial economics ; 28)
Based on the author's thesis, University of Chicago, 1979.
Bibliography: p.
1. Industrial management--Mathematical models.
2. Conglomerate corporations--Management--Mathematical models. 3. Microeconomics. I. Title. II. Series.
HD30.25.L34 338.5'01'51 80-13339
ISBN 0-444-85495-9

PRINTED IN THE NETHERLANDS

Introduction to the series

This is a series of books concerned with the quantitative approach to problems in the social and administrative sciences. The studies are in particular in the overlapping areas of mathematical economics, econometrics, operational research, and management science. Also, the mathematical and statistical techniques which belong to the apparatus of modern social and administrative sciences have their place in this series. A well-balanced mixture of pure theory and practical applications is envisaged, which ought to be useful for universities and for research workers in business and government.

The Editors hope that the volumes of this series, all of which relate to such a young and vigorous field of research activity, will contribute to the exchange of scientific information at a truly international level.

The Editors

Preface

A cursory look at the world of actual firms suggests that many – and most large firms – supply multiple products to the market. A similar look at the world of economic theory of the firm suggests that the single product firm is predominant.

It appears that there are two reasons for this discrepancy between theory and observation. One is that greater mathematical sophistication is required in order to analyze the multiproduct firm. The other is that it is only recently that econometrics has advanced to the point where measurement of the multiproduct firm's economic behavior can be contemplated.

Two recent developments in the mathematical treatment of economic theory have combined to eliminate the first reason. The first of these is duality theory, originated by Shephard [70, 71], which permits easier analysis of many aspects of the firm. The second is the emergence of the differential approach to microeconomic theory, an approach which is a rather modest extension of Hicks's [40] technique.

The purpose of this volume is to apply the differential approach to the multiproduct firm. Some of the material which appears here has appeared previously in other places. The basic theory of profit maximization, which is the major part of Chapters 3 and 4, together with the application of the theory of rational random behavior to the multiproduct firm in Chapter 7, has appeared both in Laitinen and Theil [50] and in Theil [80]. The derivation of the output homogeneous production function has also appeared in Laitinen and Theil [50]. Chapters 5 and 6, which are concerned with revenue maximization and its relation to cost minimization and profit maximization, consist almost entirely of new material. Chapters 8 and 9 are also new: these chapters treat the development of an econometric model, estimation and hypothesis testing techniques, and an application of this model to hypothetical data.

Although the theory presented in this volume is generally applicable, I have also considered the implications of a number of special cases. Among these are input–output separability, homotheticity, input independence, and output independence. There are three reasons for including these special cases. First, many existing studies apply to firms for which one or more of these specialized assumptions hold: it is therefore of interest to see how limiting these assumptions are. Second, several of these assumptions have considerable theoretical interest. The third reason is that econometricians are necessarily interested in any sensible assumptions which can be made to simplify the models they estimate: in the world of small samples it is wise to avoid large or complex models as far as this is possible.

I have presented this material in a slightly unconventional manner. One disadvantage of the differential approach is that it typically involves a great deal of clumsy algebraic derivation. It is necessary to present this material in order that the interested reader can follow the argument in detail. However, the level of detail required is so great that it distracts from the main line of the argument; this is as true for the reader who is ultimately interested in these details as it is for one who is mainly interested in results.

My approach has been to place such detailed arguments in the Appendices and to replace them in the main body of the work with brief verbal descriptions of the lines these arguments follow. My hope is that this will make the main body more readable. I recommend that even those readers who are interested in these details defer reading the Appendices until they have become acquainted with the more interesting material.

Acknowledgements

This book is a slightly revised version of the dissertation which I submitted in 1979 to the Graduate School of Business at the

University of Chicago. Any work of this magnitude has been improved by the comments and suggestions of people other than the author. This work is no exception. I wish particularly to acknowledge the contributions made by my dissertation committee. These long-suffering individuals, each of whom read at least two drafts of this volume, were (in alphabetical order): Kenneth Clements, John Gould, Roger Kormendi, Albert Madansky, Linus Schrage, and Henri Theil.

In addition to these, I wish to thank Barry Plotkin of the Dean's office in the Business School and Gerry Ketterson for helping me to keep my balance while I was doing this work. Margaret Gorodes and Marilyn Bowie typed drafts and the final version, and their cheerful competence was extremely helpful. I have to give special thanks to Kenneth Clements for various conversations and comments which made me think more deeply about the subject.

Most of all, however, I have to thank Professor Henri Theil, my advisor, whose contribution is best described as follows: without his aid, encouragement, and support this volume would never have been completed.

This work was partly supported by NSF grant SOC 76-82718.

In spite of all that I owe to others, the usual disclaimer applies: I alone am responsible for any errors which remain. In particular, the contents of this book are in no way the responsibility of Bell Laboratories, by whom I am now employed.

Murray Hill, N.J., February 1980 Kenneth Laitinen

Contents

List of tables

List of figures

CHAPTER 1

The problem of the multiproduct firm

Any elementary textbook on price theory includes a substantial section on the theory of the firm. The firm which is typically analyzed combines variable amounts of several inputs or factors of production in order to produce some amount of output. Implicitly, the output of the firm is taken to be homogeneous, or at least approximately so; by this is meant two different things. First, it is assumed that the output of the firm is not lumpy, i.e., that the amount of output produced by the firm can be changed infinitesimally. Second, it is also assumed that the units of output produced are interchangeable.[1]

Both of these assumptions appear at first glance to be violated by firms in the real world. For example, General Motors' Electromotive Division produces locomotives, an extremely lumpy commodity. Other divisions of General Motors produce automobiles ranging from Chevrolet compacts to Cadillacs. It does not seem very fruitful to argue either that it is worthwhile for General Motors to produce a tenth of a locomotive or that, say, ten Chevettes are interchangeable with that tenth of a locomotive.

The first of these arguments is naive, since it ignores the fact that production is a flow. Although it makes no sense to manufacture a tenth of a locomotive, it is quite sensible to

[1]Curiously, these assumptions are seldom stated explicitly for the firm, although the corresponding assumptions for consumption goods usually are. The same assumptions, of course, are also made for each of the inputs.

consider manufacturing a tenth (or nine-hundredths or eleven-hundredths) of a locomotive per day. Thus, it is perfectly defensible to assume that output, interpreted as output flow, is not lumpy.

The other assumption is not so easily justified. It is no more the case that ten Chevettes per day is equivalent to a tenth of a locomotive per day than that the objects themselves are equivalent. In fact, it appears that for many firms it is desirable to distinguish several different output flows. We shall call such a firm a *multiproduct firm*, and assume that each output (and each input) is not lumpy and consists of interchangeable units.

1.1. A survey of existing work

The idea of the multiproduct firm is hardly new. One reason why such firms should be expected to exist is the existence of *jointness of production*. This concept has been discussed in many textbooks, e.g., Stigler [74, pp. 162–165]. Hotelling [42], Reder [65], Weldon [87], Clemens [24], and Bailey [6] have each discussed the question of how the multiproduct firm will choose its output levels.[2] Hotelling's paper is the most mathematically oriented among these; he appears to have been the first to note the symmetry of price effects among outputs in the multiproduct firm. Reder has described a diagrammatic method for determining how much of each of two outputs to produce. Weldon's paper describes an accounting-oriented way of handling the same problem.

[2]Since we are concerned here with the static behavior of the multiproduct firm, there is no reason to be explicit about the fact that the outputs are defined as flows. There appears to be almost no literature on the dynamic behavior of the multiproduct firm. However, Makower and Baumol [52] developed a model of the multiperiod, multiproduct firm whose capital resources are limited, which leads to an income component of the utility maximizing entrepreneur's decisions. Graaff [34] has presented a similar model without the multiperiod aspect. Reder [65] has pointed out that a single product firm whose production is dynamic can be considered a multiproduct firm.

Clemens and Bailey each considered the extension of the same problem to the firm which faces downward sloping demand curves for its products. Later work of a more general nature was done by Mauer and Naylor [53] who considered situations where the multiproduct firm is monopolistic, monopsonistic, or both. Baumol [10], Baumol, Bailey and Willig [11], Panzar and Willig [58, 59], and Sharkey and Telser [69] have considered various aspects of the question of when the multiproduct firm is a natural monopoly.

The earliest general analysis of the competitive multiproduct firm was given by Hicks [40, pp. 85–98, 319–323], whose discussion has also been reported by Allen [1, pp. 613–618] and Henderson and Quandt [39, pp. 89–98]. These treatments are all very brief, and it should be noted that Henderson and Quandt devoted more than half of their attention to the analysis of the two output, one input case. Carlson [20] earlier gave a less general but more detailed analysis of the two output case. One conclusion reached by these authors amounts to the equation of output and input prices with marginal costs and values of marginal products, respectively. This result has also been derived by Mauer and Naylor [53] and by Hasenkamp [37]. However, these later authors have not used the second-order conditions to show that the multiproduct firm has symmetric price effects among all inputs and outputs. This result, an extension of Hotelling's (and ultimately of Slutsky's for the consumer), was reported by Hicks, Allen, and Henderson and Quandt. A conclusion corresponding to Slutsky negativity for the consumer was also derived in each of these sources.

More recently, Sakai [66] extended Hicks's model by considering cost minimization and revenue maximization as well as profit maximization. His paper is probably the best currently in existence, but it is extremely condensed; Sakai is aware of many of the derivative properties of the multiproduct firm and states his conclusions exclusively in terms of such properties.

Hicks's analysis was partly in the context of general equilibrium theory. Arrow and Hahn [5, ch. 3] have performed a similar analysis in a more general mathematical context;

however, their emphasis was much more strongly on general equilibrium, and consequently they had less to say about the firm as such.

Samuelson [67] has described a different version of general equilibrium theory in the context of international trade theory. His production functions were for industries rather than firms, and were explicitly separate (no joint production) and homogeneous of degree one. These differences appear to remove this work from the sphere of the multiproduct firm. However, he later (Samuelson [68]) pointed out that a multiproduct production function need not exhibit jointness of production and gave conditions under which this will occur. This work was extended by Hirota and Kuga [41] and by Burmeister and Turnovsky [19].

Another body of literature which treats the multiproduct firm in a very general way is that of duality theory. This was initiated in 1953 by Shephard [70] for the single product firm, and has since been extended to the multiproduct firm by Shephard [71], McFadden [54], Lau [51], Jorgenson and Lau [45] and others. The most important result in this literature is that under certain rather general circumstances the firm's cost, revenue, and profit functions are all equivalent to the production function as descriptions of the firm's technology.[3] As an example of the fruitfulness of this result, we can cite Hall [35] who proved that the condition (mentioned in the last paragraph) for nonjointness of production can be stated extremely simply using the cost function. An unfortunate aspect of duality theory is that it requires a high degree of mathematical sophistication and is therefore not always easily accessible to economists. This is reflected in the literature by an unfortunate emphasis on mathematical generality rather than economic interpretation.

Pfouts [60] and later Ferguson [31] have analyzed a short-run model of a multiproduct firm which involves individual production functions for each product. They tied these individual production functions together by assuming that some of the inputs are fixed for the firm in the short run and must therefore

[3]This duality principle will be described more explicitly in section 2.3.

be allocated among the outputs.[4] This is a very limiting assumption since in the long run there can then be no jointness in production of the various outputs.[5] This model has been extended in various directions by Pfouts [61, 62], Naylor [56], and Hughes [44].

Frisch [33, pp. 269–289] presented an idiosyncratic treatment of "multiware" production in which more than one production constraint is permitted. This approach permits a much more detailed model of the internal structure of production, and hence the firm, but sacrifices generality to gain this end.

Various authors have contributed to the theory of the multiproduct firm in more specific ways. Thus, Hanoch [36] extended Shephard's [70] definition of homotheticity to the multiproduct firm. Powell and Gruen [63] have defined the *elasticity of transformation* between two outputs in a manner analogous to the usual definition of the elasticity of substitution between two inputs. Dhrymes [28] and Blair and Heggestad [15] considered cases where the output prices faced by the multiproduct firm are random functions of output, but their assumptions are not very general. Mundlak [55] considered variations on Cobb–Douglas production functions, but his major contribution was a simple demonstration that it is not possible to convert the multiproduct firm to a single product firm whose output is measured by revenue.[6]

The earliest empirical study of the multiproduct firm appears to have been reported by Klein [46, 47] in 1947.[7] He used

[4]It is assumed that these inputs are the services of machines. An additional element is the assumption that there is a cost for switching these machines from one use to another. This additional cost may add to the realism of the model, but it appears to add little to the analysis.

[5]Pfouts and Ferguson reached opposite conclusions as to the significance of their results; Ferguson's view, that there is little difference between the multiproduct firm presented by them and a single product firm, is probably more supportable.

[6]However, see Chapter 4 where the aggregated *change* in output is measured by the volume component of the *change* in revenue.

[7]As a historical note, Crum [26] used the same sources to obtain a cross section of cost data for U.S. railroads. He used this data in 1926 to estimate, in a very crude way, the marginal costs of passenger and freight service.

cross-sectional data for American railroads to estimate the parameters of the production function

$$z_1 z_2^{\alpha} = [\text{Cobb–Douglas function of inputs}], \tag{1.1}$$

where z_1 (ton-miles of freight carried) and z_2 (passenger miles) are two outputs.[8]

Later, Hasenkamp [37, 38] considered the case where the production function takes the form

$$[\text{function of outputs}] = [\text{function of inputs}]. \tag{1.2}$$

He then used Klein's data to estimate several combinations of specific input and output functions.

Another type of data which has been analyzed is farm data. Beringer [13] has used cross-sectional data to explore the production functions of farms, but the value of his work is questionable because of the way he specified the problem. Weaver [86] has recently estimated a translog cost function (see below) using aggregate time series data.

Production functions of the form (1.2), of which (1.1) is a specific example, are known as *input–output separable*. In (1.2) the functions on the left and right can be regarded as aggregating functions for the outputs and inputs, respectively. With this kind of production function the firm can choose its allocation of outputs independently of its allocation of inputs, so there can be no specific interaction between any particular output and any particular input. While this may be a realistic assumption in certain cases, it is important to recognize that there is no necessity for the multiproduct production function to take this form.

A similar specialization has been used by Clements [25], who

[8]This production function is not suitable for profit maximization, but is suitable for cost minimization. Since American railroading is a regulated industry, this may be appropriate. Nerlove [57, pp. 72–82] also discusses this model.

has developed a short-run model based on a production function of the form

$$[\text{function of outputs and variable inputs}]$$
$$= [\text{function of fixed inputs}]. \qquad (1.3)$$

The restriction imposed by this type of production function is similar to that imposed by input–output separability: here there can be no specific interaction between any of the fixed inputs and either the outputs or the variable inputs.[9]

Another empirically oriented approach which does not involve the restrictions described above is based on *translog* production and cost functions.[10] The difficulty with this approach from a theoretical viewpoint is that such functions cannot satisfy the convexity and concavity conditions which the duality theorists have proven must be satisfied. The justification for using such functions in empirical work is that they can be regarded as local approximations of the true functions. This is true enough, but Theil [80, section 13.1] has pointed out that these approximations in actual use are only linear and therefore are not necessarily very good ones.

1.2. The purpose of this research

The literature survey in the previous section is not meant to be complete; its purpose is rather to give an impression of the

[9] It should be noted that, aside from the restriction mentioned, Clements' approach is similar to the one which will be described here. The two lines of research were begun independently.

[10] Most of this research involves highly aggregated production. The original paper by Christensen, Jorgenson and Lau [23] involves two outputs, but later papers, for example, Berndt and Christensen [14], Burgess [17], and Christensen and Greene [22], do not. It is well known (see, for example, Burgess [18] or Applebaum [4]) that translog production and cost functions do not specify the same technology. Vinod [85] has used a translog production function in connection with an idiosyncratic estimation technique which he calls the "canonical ridge model".

general state of knowledge about the multiproduct firm. Much of the work cited is very recent. This has led to a situation where many authors do not seem to be aware of the work of others. There is no general consensus about the nature of the problem: many authors deal with special cases (e.g., firms whose technologies are input–output separable), and are not fully aware of the limitations they have imposed.

An extreme example of this is provided by Vinod [84] who, in addition to making statistical errors (pointed out by Chetty [21], Dhrymes and Mitchell [29], and Rao [64]), also specified the technology of the multiproduct firm by setting *each* output equal to its own Cobb–Douglas function of all inputs used by the firm. Such a formulation severely limits the possibility of substitution among outputs, since this can be achieved only by changing input combinations.

The model used by Pfouts [60–62], Naylor [56], Ferguson [31], and Hughes [44] is another case. These authors seem, to varying degrees, to be unaware of the relationship of this model to the one pioneered by Hicks [40]. The latter model, which is the one we will explore in more detail in this volume, is a long-run model, while Pfouts's model is short-run because some inputs are fixed. If Pfouts's model is extended to the long run, production becomes nonjoint (see section 4.6), while if Hicks's is converted to a short-run model by holding some inputs constant, it becomes a generalization of Pfouts's model.

One of the main aims of this volume is to provide a comprehensive discussion of the long-run behavior of the multiproduct firm in competitive circumstances. Since this was the problem addressed by Hicks [40] and Sakai [66], it might seem that this is a redundant effort; however, their discussions of the multiproduct firm were too brief to include many interesting results. Hicks considered the profit maximizing behavior of the firm: his conclusions were all drawn from the fact that the matrix of derivatives of quantities (with inputs considered negative outputs) with respect to prices is symmetric and positive semidefinite. Sakai extended these results to cost minimization and revenue maximization, but the nature of the conclusions he drew is similar.

Here we shall examine the same problems more closely. We shall consider each of the three problems of cost minimization, profit maximization, and revenue maximization in considerably more detail than Sakai, paying particular attention to the relationships among the behaviors of the firm in different circumstances. We shall draw heavily on the results of duality theory in this process.

Of particular interest will be the implications of specialized assumptions about the firm: we shall study in detail the implications of input–output separability, homotheticity, and nonjointness of production, and also extend Theil's [79] definition of input independence to the multiproduct firm. One reason for doing this is to assess how limiting assumptions of this sort are; since so many theoretical and econometric studies rely on such assumptions, this is clearly of interest.

A second reason for considering the implications of specialized assumptions is that such assumptions frequently lead to economically interesting restrictions which can be tested and imposed on an econometric model. The procedure (to be described in section 1.3) which we use to analyze the multiproduct firm, leads in a natural way to a family of econometric models which we describe as an extension of the theory of the multiproduct firm. These models are nonlinear in their parameters; consequently, we also describe procedures for estimating them and for testing various economically interesting hypotheses. These procedures have been used with hypothetical data; the results indicate that their application is useful and yields meaningful results.

Another extension of the theory of the multiproduct firm which has econometric implications is the application of Theil's [80] theory of rational random behavior. This theory predicts that because information about prices is costly, the firm will make random errors in its optimizing behavior. Under certain circumstances the predicted error distribution is highly regular and can be used to sharpen the precision of estimates.

1.3. The differential approach

The purpose of my research is to provide a relatively comprehensive analysis of the static behavior of the multiproduct firm in competitive circumstances. The approach I use is very similar to that used by Theil for consumption theory [78] and the single product firm [79]. This can conveniently be called the *differential approach* to microeconomic theory. It is a relatively recent development, although its roots go back at least fifty years to Divisia [30].

To describe this approach it is convenient for concreteness to consider the case of consumption theory. The usual approach is to assume that the consumer acts in such a way as to maximize a utility function which describes his tastes. It is assumed that the maximum level of total expenditure and the prices of the goods he can buy are not under his control; what he can control are the amounts of each good which he buys, subject, of course, to the constraint on total expenditure. This amounts mathematically to a constrained optimization problem: the economic agent (consumer) varies his controlled variables (quantities of goods consumed) so as to maximize his criterion function (utility) subject to a constraint (the budget constraint) for given values of his uncontrolled variables (prices and total expenditure). The problem is analyzed by setting up a Lagrangian function and then differentiating. This yields first- and second-order conditions which must be satisfied by the solution. Analysis of these conditions then makes it possible to describe what happens when the uncontrolled variables, prices and total expenditure, change.

This analysis is known as *comparative statics*; the results which are obtained are ordinarily regarded as qualitative in nature. An example in consumption theory is Slutsky negativity: if the price of one good increases and a compensating increase in total expenditure occurs simultaneously so that the consumer can reach the same indifference curve, then he will consume less of the good whose price has increased.

It is in the analysis of comparative statics that the differential approach differs from the usual one. Using the former approach, the first-order conditions, including the constraint, are differentiated with respect to the uncontrolled variables. This can be done because the first-order conditions must hold both before and after a change in the uncontrolled variables. The resulting equations can then be combined in the form of a matrix equation. This matrix equation, called by Barten [9] the *fundamental matrix equation* for the consumer, can then be solved, by exploiting the second-order condition, for the matrix of derivatives of the controlled variables and the Lagrange multiplier with respect to the uncontrolled variables. Finally, it is noted that the optimal level of each controlled variable is a function of the uncontrolled ones. Thus, it is possible to take the total differential of each controlled variable and substitute the derivatives obtained from the fundamental matrix equation to obtain a set of equations in differential form.

The resulting set of equations is interesting in several ways. First, it amounts to a quantitative (although not necessarily a numeric) expression of the comparative statics results described above. Second, it is possible to write these equations in such a way that the coefficients have definite economic interpretations. Third, many comparative statics results which are not readily stated in qualitative terms are displayed obviously in these equations. An example of this in consumption theory is Slutsky symmetry, which amounts in the differential approach to the symmetry of a square matrix of price coefficients. Another example is the necessity in consumption theory for two distinct price indexes, one to deflate income and the other to deflate prices.

A fourth characteristic of this set of equations is that it can be regarded as describing the behavior of the entire system of controlled variables, a point Theil [80] has made by calling this a *system-wide* approach. Fifth, depending on the nature of the controlled variables, the equations can be interpreted as demand or supply equations which describe the *change* in demand or supply in response to changes in the uncontrolled variables. Sixth, it is relatively simple to convert these equations to an econometrically estimable system. An example is the Rotterdam model of consumer demand described by Theil [78]. Seventh, it is not difficult to trace the implications of specializing assumptions; this makes it relatively easy to assess how restrictive such assumptions are.

All of the points outlined above are advantages of the differential approach and indicate that it leads to rich results. It is fair to note that there are disadvantages too, although these are relatively minor in scope. One disadvantage is that for some results slightly stronger second-order conditions than are strictly necessary have to be assumed. A second is that it is difficult, when using this approach, to deal with either corner solutions or the interchange of inputs and outputs. This makes it difficult to analyze general equilibrium models using formulations like that of Arrow and Hahn [5]. A third disadvantage is that since each equation is a total differential, it holds exactly only for infinitesimal changes in the uncontrolled variables. This is no great disadvantage from a theoretical point of view, but it must be taken into account when data are to be analyzed.

CHAPTER 2

The technology of production

An intuitive view of a firm is as an entity which combines inputs or factors of production to produce outputs or products. A price is associated with each input and output so that revenue is determined by the amount of each output produced, and cost by the amount of each input used.

Clearly, the amount of each output produced must be related in some way to the amounts of inputs the firm uses. We shall refer to this relation as the firm's technology of production. This technology can be represented in various ways, and the purpose of this chapter is to describe some of these representations.

Much of the material here is drawn from McFadden [54] and Shephard [70, 71], and will consequently be stated without proof. The generalization of the concept of the distance function and subsequent definition of the output homogeneous production function in section 2.2 was originated by Laitinen and Theil [50] and is crucial to the theory developed later. Section 2.1 and the first part of section 2.2 are intended to place this definition in context. Section 2.3 presents certain basic duality results which will also be important. Section 2.4 introduces several simplifying assumptions about the firm's technology, the implications of which will be of interest.

2.1. Production functions

We begin with a single product firm which uses n inputs whose quantity vector is $\boldsymbol{q} = (q_1, \ldots, q_n)'$ to produce a scalar output z, where each input quantity and the output quantity are positive. Then the technology of this firm can be represented by a production function

$$z = h_a(q_1, \dots, q_n) = h_a(\boldsymbol{q}), \tag{2.1}$$

which is interpreted as the maximum amount of output which can be produced by the firm using amounts $q_1, \dots, q_n$ of the inputs. For single product firms this is the traditional way to represent production technology.

For the case of the multiproduct firm we replace the single output z with a vector of m outputs $\boldsymbol{z} = (z_1, \dots, z_m)'$. Now we can represent the firm's technology implicitly by

$$h_b(q_1, \dots, q_n, z_1, \dots, z_m) = h_b(\boldsymbol{q}, \boldsymbol{z}) = 0. \tag{2.2}$$

By solving (2.2) for (say) z_r, we can write the production relation as

$$z_r = h_{dr}(q_1, \dots, q_n, z_1, \dots, z_{r-1}, z_{r+1}, \dots, z_m), \tag{2.3}$$

which is similar to (2.1) and can be interpreted similarly as the maximum amount of the rth product which can be produced by the firm using amounts $q_1, \dots, q_n$ of the inputs when it also produces $z_1, \dots, z_{r-1}, z_{r+1}, \dots, z_m$ of the other outputs.

However, (2.3) has the disadvantage that it treats the products of the firm asymmetrically, unlike (2.1) and (2.2). Thus, although some economists[1] have specified technological relationships in the form (2.3), we will retain the more symmetric form (2.2).

Variously weak or strong assumptions about the technology can be embodied in assumptions about the production function. For our purposes we will use the relatively strong neoclassical assumption that (2.2), or (2.1) where a single product firm is discussed, has continuous derivatives of the first and second

[1]E.g., Samuelson [68]. It might also be noted that he uses the term *production possibility frontier* while others use *transformation function* to mean production function as we use it.

order for positive $z_1, \ldots, z_m$ and $q_1, \ldots, q_n$. We also assume that the first derivatives of (2.2) have positive signs for the first n arguments and negative signs for the last m. This assumption means that an increase in the production of any product requires an increase in some input, and that a decrease in any input requires a decrease in some output.

We also assume that (2.2) can be solved for each product as in (2.3) with the interpretation given below (2.3), and in addition that it can be solved for any input,

$$q_i = h_{ei}(q_1, \ldots, q_{i-1}, q_{i+1}, \ldots, q_n, z_1, \ldots, z_m), \tag{2.4}$$

with the corresponding interpretation as the smallest amount of q_i which can be used to produce $z_1, \ldots, z_m$ when amounts $q_1, \ldots, q_{i-1}, q_{i+1}, \ldots, q_n$ of the other inputs are also used.

Certain assumptions about the second derivatives of (2.2) will also be needed at various points to ensure the existence of solutions of optimization problems. These can be more easily described when they are needed, so their statement will be deferred to Chapters 3, 4, and 5.

2.2. Distance functions and homogeneous production functions

Although the implicit production function (2.2) is similar to (2.1) for the single product firm in that it treats the products symmetrically, it has a serious disadvantage in that it is not unique. Thus, suppose we take any single-valued, twice continuously differentiable function $s(\cdot)$ which satisfies $s(0)=0$, $s'(0)>0$. Then $s(h_b(\boldsymbol{q}, \boldsymbol{z}))=0$ is also a perfectly satisfactory representation of the firm's technology.[2] This nonuniqueness may seem a

[2]This should be compared to the similar situation in consumption theory with regard to the utility function (see, for example, Theil [78, section 2.5]). The two situations are not identical, however, because output can be measured, in theory at least, while utility cannot. Also, in consumption theory utility is the maximand, while in the theory of the firm the production function is a constraint.

relatively trivial matter, and for many of our results it is. However, it implies that we are overlooking additional structure which can be imposed on the production function.

2.2.1. *The input distance function*

Shephard [70] first introduced the concept of a distance function for the single product firm in 1953 and he [71] and others[3] have since generalized the concept to the multiproduct firm. We consider an isoquant in n-space (represented by the curve A for $n=2$ in fig. 2.1a) and an arbitrary input point Q. The isoquant represents for some specified output vector $z=(z_1,\dots,z_m)'$ all the combinations of inputs which can be used to produce it. The point Q in fig. 2.1a is above the isoquant A; therefore it represents an input bundle which can be used to produce more than the specified output levels. The point $\bar{Q}$, where the ray OQ meets the isoquant A, represents the level of inputs, used in the same proportion as Q, which will just yield the specified output vector. We define the input distance function by

$$d_Q(\boldsymbol{q},\boldsymbol{z})=\frac{OQ}{O\bar{Q}}=\frac{q_i}{\bar{q}_i},\quad \text{for each } i. \tag{2.5}$$

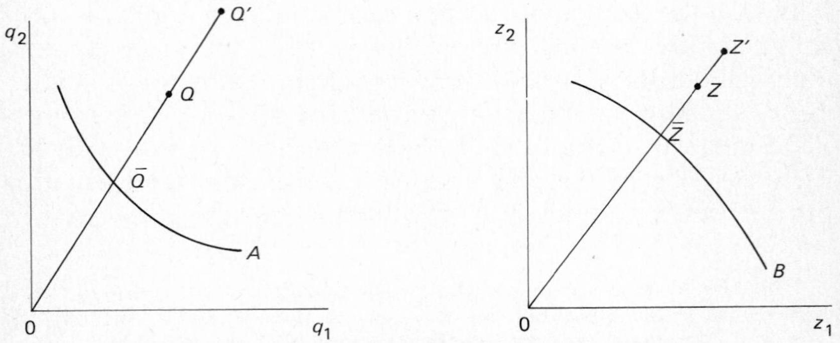

Figure 2.1. Input and output distance functions.

[3]E.g. McFadden [54].

Now note that $d_Q(\boldsymbol{q}, z) = 1$ if and only if $h_b(\boldsymbol{q}, z) = 0$, so that

$$d_Q(\boldsymbol{q}, z) = 1 \tag{2.6}$$

is another representation of the production technology.

Next, consider $Q' = \alpha Q$ for some $\alpha > 0$. Using (2.5) we have $d_Q(\alpha\boldsymbol{q}, z) = OQ'/O\bar{Q} = \alpha q_i/\bar{q}_i$ for each i, so that

$$d_Q(\alpha\boldsymbol{q}, z) = \alpha d_Q(\boldsymbol{q}, z). \tag{2.7}$$

Thus, $d_Q(\cdot)$ is homogeneous of degree one in the inputs. This property both explains why we single out $d_Q(\cdot)$ by giving it a special name and can be used to show that $d_Q(\cdot)$ is unique in the sense that it is the only representation of the production function which is positively linear homogeneous in the inputs.[4]

2.2.2. *The output distance function*

The function $h_a(\cdot)$ in (2.1) is not in general homogeneous of any degree. Note, however, that if (2.1) is divided by z, we obtain

$$h_a(\boldsymbol{q})/z = 1, \tag{2.8}$$

the left side of which, it can trivially be verified, is negatively linear homogeneous in the single output. This suggests that a representation of the multiproduct production function which is negatively linear homogeneous in the outputs may be more comparable to (2.1) than $d_Q(\cdot)$. Therefore we consider the surface B in m-space of all combinations of the outputs which can be produced using a given input vector $\boldsymbol{q} = (q_1, \ldots, q_n)'$.

[4]Actually $d_Q(\cdot)$ is unique in this respect up to multiplication by a positive constant. This uniqueness is one reason why this form of the production function is useful in duality theory; see Shephard [70] or McFadden [54]. Homogeneity is also important directly, because it permits establishment of a formal mathematical duality between distance and cost functions.

This is shown for $m=2$ in fig. 2.1b. We consider an arbitrary output point Z, which for the case illustrated is too large to be produced using the given inputs. Then we consider $\bar{Z}$, the point where the ray OZ cuts the surface B, and define the *output distance function* as[5]

$$d(\boldsymbol{q}, z) = \frac{O\bar{Z}}{OZ} = \frac{\bar{z}_r}{z_r}, \quad \text{for each } r. \tag{2.9}$$

It can then readily be verified along the same lines as in the last subsection that

$$d(\boldsymbol{q}, z) = 1 \tag{2.10}$$

is yet another representation of the firm's production technology and, using point Z' in fig. 2.1b, that $d(\cdot)$ is indeed negatively linear homogeneous in the outputs.

2.2.3. *Input and output homogeneous production functions*

Although (2.6) and (2.10) are satisfactory representations of the production function, it is notationally convenient to consider slightly different forms. Thus, we define[6]

$$h_Q(\boldsymbol{q}, z) = \log[d_Q(\boldsymbol{q}, z)] \tag{2.11}$$

and, using (2.10), verify that

$$h_Q(\boldsymbol{q}, z) = 0 \tag{2.12}$$

is another representation of the production function. The usefulness of (2.12) lies in the implications of the homogeneity of $d_Q(\cdot)$. Thus, consider the sum of the derivatives of (2.11) with

[5]Note the appearance of $\bar{z}_r$ in the numerator of (2.9) in contrast to (2.5). This is due to the opposite signs of the homogeneity.
[6]All logarithms in this volume are natural.

respect to the logarithms of the input quantities:

$$\sum_i \partial h_Q/\partial \log q_i = \sum_i q_i\, \partial h_Q/\partial q_i = \sum_i (q_i/d_Q)\, \partial d_Q/\partial q_i,$$

where the second step is based on (2.11). Using the linear homogeneity of $d_Q(\cdot)$ in the inputs and Euler's theorem, we see that the third member is simply $d_Q/d_Q = 1$ so that

$$\sum_{i=1}^{n} \frac{\partial h_Q}{\partial \log q_i} \equiv 1. \qquad (2.13)$$

This simple result is the basis for calling (2.12) the *input homogeneous* production function.[7]

In a similar way, we take the logarithm of $d(\cdot)$ to obtain

$$h(\boldsymbol{q}, \boldsymbol{z}) = \log[d(\boldsymbol{q}, \boldsymbol{z})]. \qquad (2.14)$$

It is readily verified that

$$h(\boldsymbol{q}, \boldsymbol{z}) = 0 \qquad (2.15)$$

is another representation of the technology of the firm and that the identity

$$\sum_{r=1}^{m} \frac{\partial h}{\partial \log z_r} \equiv -1 \qquad (2.16)$$

holds for $h(\cdot)$. Therefore we call $h(\cdot)$ the *output homogeneous* production function.

One difficulty which arises when we attempt to use the homogeneous production functions defined above is that in many cases one or both cannot be written in explicit form.[8] This

[7]This is a slight misnomer, since the distance functions are the ones which are homogeneous. Nevertheless, I have not been able to think of a more satisfactory terminology.

[8]A simple example is $z_1^{\alpha_1} + z_2^{\alpha_2} = h_a(\boldsymbol{q})$ which cannot be written explicitly in output homogeneous form unless $\alpha_1 = \alpha_2 = \alpha$, in which case we have $h(\boldsymbol{q}, \boldsymbol{z}) = \log(h_a(\boldsymbol{q})) - \alpha^{-1} \log(z_1^{\alpha} + z_2^{\alpha})$.

difficulty will not affect the theory developed in this volume because only the first and second derivatives of the homogeneous production functions are necessary. It is shown in Appendix A that, when $h_b(\cdot)$ in (2.2) satisfies the assumptions we made in section 2.1, the first and second derivatives of the corresponding input or output homogeneous production function can be derived from those of $h_b(\cdot)$ and are also continuous. It then follows that when we define

$$\boldsymbol{H} = \frac{\partial^2 h}{\partial \log \boldsymbol{q}\, \partial \log \boldsymbol{q}'}; \qquad \boldsymbol{H}_Q = \frac{\partial^2 h_Q}{\partial \log \boldsymbol{q}\, \partial \log \boldsymbol{q}'}, \tag{2.17}$$

$$\boldsymbol{H}^{**} = \frac{\partial^2 h}{\partial \log \boldsymbol{z}\, \partial \log \boldsymbol{z}'}; \qquad \boldsymbol{H}_Q^{**} = \frac{\partial^2 h_Q}{\partial \log \boldsymbol{z}\, \partial \log \boldsymbol{z}'}, \tag{2.18}$$

these matrices are symmetric and, moreover, that the matrices

$$\boldsymbol{H}^{*} = \frac{\partial^2 h}{\partial \log \boldsymbol{q}\, \partial \log \boldsymbol{z}'}; \qquad \boldsymbol{H}_Q^{*} = \frac{\partial^2 h_Q}{\partial \log \boldsymbol{q}\, \partial \log \boldsymbol{z}'} \tag{2.19}$$

satisfy $\boldsymbol{H}^{*\prime} = \partial^2 h/\partial \log \boldsymbol{z}\, \partial \log \boldsymbol{q}'$ and $\boldsymbol{H}_Q^{*\prime} = \partial^2 h_Q/\partial \log \boldsymbol{z}\, \partial \log \boldsymbol{q}'$. In addition, the first derivatives of the homogeneous production functions have the same signs as the corresponding derivatives of $h_b(\cdot)$.

In addition to (2.13) and (2.16), homogeneity of the input and output distance functions implies certain important restrictions on the second derivatives of the input and output homogeneous production functions. These restrictions will be necessary for certain results in Chapters 3, 4, and 5. Thus, we take the derivatives of (2.13) with respect to $\log q_j$ and $\log z_r$ to obtain, respectively,

$$\sum_{i=1}^{n} \frac{\partial^2 h_Q}{\partial \log q_i\, \partial \log q_j} \equiv 0, \qquad j = 1, \ldots, n, \tag{2.20}$$

$$\sum_{i=1}^{n} \frac{\partial^2 h_Q}{\partial \log q_i\, \partial \log z_r} \equiv 0, \qquad r = 1, \ldots, m. \tag{2.21}$$

These restrictions can be expressed more compactly in matrix notation, using (2.17) and (2.19), as

$$\boldsymbol{\iota}'\boldsymbol{H}_Q \equiv \boldsymbol{0}, \tag{2.22}$$

$$\boldsymbol{\iota}'\boldsymbol{H}_Q^* \equiv \boldsymbol{0}, \tag{2.23}$$

where $\boldsymbol{\iota}$ is an n-element vector containing unit elements.

In a similar way, we take the derivatives of (2.16) with respect to $\log z_s$ and $\log q_i$ to obtain, respectively,

$$\sum_{r=1}^{m} \frac{\partial^2 h}{\partial \log z_r\, \partial \log z_s} \equiv 0, \qquad s = 1, \ldots, m, \tag{2.24}$$

$$\sum_{r=1}^{m} \frac{\partial^2 h}{\partial \log z_r\, \partial \log q_i} \equiv 0, \qquad i = 1, \ldots, n, \tag{2.25}$$

which can be expressed in matrix notation using (2.18) and (2.19) as

$$\boldsymbol{H}^{**}\boldsymbol{\iota}^* \equiv \boldsymbol{0}, \tag{2.26}$$

$$\boldsymbol{H}^{*}\boldsymbol{\iota}^* \equiv \boldsymbol{0}, \tag{2.27}$$

where $\boldsymbol{\iota}^*$ is an m-element vector containing unit elements.[9]

2.3. Duality: Cost, revenue, and profit functions

In addition to the various forms of the production function discussed above, it has been shown by Shephard [70], McFadden [54], and others that the technology of the firm can be represented equivalently by cost, revenue, and profit functions under competitive conditions. Thus, suppose that the firm faces an input price vector $\boldsymbol{p} = (p_1, \ldots, p_n)'$ corresponding to its input

[9]The logarithm of (2.8) is $\log h_a(\boldsymbol{q}) - \log z = 0$, which was used in a slightly different form by Theil [79] to analyze the single product case. If we interpret this as $h(\boldsymbol{q}, z)$, we see that $\boldsymbol{H}^*$ is a column vector with zeros and $\boldsymbol{H}^{**}$ is a scalar zero, in agreement with (2.27) and (2.26). Also, $\partial h/\partial \log z \equiv -1$, in agreement with (2.16).

quantity vector. Also, suppose that its objective is, for given input price and output quantity vectors, to minimize the cost $C = \Sigma_i p_i q_i$ of producing the given outputs by choosing optimal input quantities. If we assume that this objective is possible,[10] the solution which results is a function of the given input prices and output quantities:

$$C = C(\boldsymbol{z}, \boldsymbol{p}). \tag{2.28}$$

This function has a number of highly interesting properties.[11] First, under the assumptions made in section 2.1 for the production function, the cost function also has continuous first and second derivatives, so that it is also neoclassical. Second, the production function and the cost function are dual in the sense that either one can be derived from the other. As a consequence, either function may be used equivalently to predict the behavior of the firm. Third, the cost function is homogeneous of degree one in the input prices.[12] Fourth, it satisfies Shephard's lemma for input quantities:[13]

$$\frac{\partial C}{\partial p_i} = q_i. \tag{2.29}$$

The cost function has other interesting properties as well, but those which are relevant to our purpose will be described in Chapters 3, 4, and 6, where their relevance is more obvious.

While the duality between cost and production functions is well known, it is not so well known that equivalent[14] duality

[10]For the condition under which cost minimization can be performed, see section 3.1.

[11]All of these are drawn from McFadden [54].

[12]This should be compared to the homogeneity of distance functions. Homogeneity of the cost function is an expression of the well-known dictum that the theory of the firm is a theory of relative prices.

[13]Strictly, this result holds wherever the relevant derivative exists, which for our purposes is everywhere.

[14]The word "equivalent" is used here in a somewhat unusual way. It is not true that any firm which can minimize cost can also maximize profit or revenue: an example is Klein's [46, 47] railroad model (1.1), under which cost can be minimized, but neither profit nor revenue can be maximized. What is meant here is that where the appropriate optimization problem can be solved, the resulting function is equivalent to the production function.

relationships can also be established for revenue and profit functions. Thus, suppose now that the firm faces an output price vector $\boldsymbol{y} = (y_1, \ldots, y_m)'$ which corresponds to its output quantity vector. Let its problem be to maximize revenue $R = \Sigma_r\, y_r z_r$ for given output prices and input quantities. The resulting value of revenue is a function of the given output prices and input quantities:

$$R = R(\boldsymbol{q}, \boldsymbol{y}). \tag{2.30}$$

This revenue function has properties similar to those of the cost function. Thus, it has continuous first and second derivatives, is dual to the production function, is homogeneous of degree one in the output prices, and satisfies a version of Shephard's lemma for output quantities:[15]

$$\frac{\partial R}{\partial y_r} = z_r. \tag{2.31}$$

In a similar way, it has been shown that if the objective of the firm is to maximize profit $\pi = \Sigma_r\, y_r z_r - \Sigma_i\, p_i q_i$ by varying both input and output quantities for given input and output prices, the resulting optimal value is a function of these prices:

$$\pi = \pi(\boldsymbol{p}, \boldsymbol{y}). \tag{2.32}$$

This function then also has continuous first- and second-order derivatives, is dual to the production function, is homogeneous of degree one in all prices, and satisfies Shephard's lemma both for inputs,

$$\frac{\partial \pi}{\partial p_i} = -q_i, \tag{2.33}$$

and for outputs,

$$\frac{\partial \pi}{\partial y_r} = z_r. \tag{2.34}$$

[15]This is sometimes called Hotelling's lemma.

There is one important difference between the profit function on one hand and the cost and revenue functions on the other, which is that the profit function can take negative values.[16]

2.4. Some specialized forms of the production function

The theory of the multiproduct firm which we shall develop in later chapters is general in the sense that it should apply to any nondynamic, competitive firm in the long run. In particular, we make no assumption that the production function takes some such specialized form as (1.1) and (1.2). Nevertheless, it is of interest to consider what the implications of such specialized forms are in the context of the more general theory.

We can now write

$$h_c(\boldsymbol{z}) = h_a(\boldsymbol{q}) \tag{2.35}$$

as a more explicit form of the production constraint (1.2) of the input–output separable firm. It is shown in Appendix A that, when input–output separability holds, the elements of the matrix $\boldsymbol{H}_Q^*$ defined in (2.19) can be written in the form

$$\frac{\partial^2 h_Q}{\partial \log q_i \, \partial \log z_r} = a_i \frac{\partial h_Q}{\partial \log z_r}, \tag{2.36}$$

where a_i does not depend on the particular output involved. Thus, in this case the matrix $\boldsymbol{H}_Q^*$ consists of a column vector postmultiplied by a row vector and has unit rank.[17] In a similar

[16]We are considering long-run profit maximization here, and it is obvious that no profit maximizing firm will be observed in the long run with negative profits. We can interpret negative values of the profit function as follows: if input and output prices are such that the profit function is negative, then the firm whose production function is dual to the profit function will not be observed in the market.

[17]If the additive separation (2.35) applies to the input homogeneous production function $h_Q(\cdot)$, both sides of (2.36) become zero. However, input–output separability is the weaker condition under which (2.35) holds for *any* function $h_b(\cdot)$ which describes the firm's technology.

way, the matrix $\boldsymbol{H}^*$ has elements of the form

$$\frac{\partial^2 h}{\partial \log q_i \, \partial \log z_r} = \frac{\partial h}{\partial \log q_i} b_r, \tag{2.37}$$

where b_r does not depend on the particular input.

In the literature on the single product firm, we frequently encounter the case where the function $h_a(\boldsymbol{q})$ in (2.1) is taken to be homogeneous, either linearly or of some degree other than one. A generalization of this homogeneous production function is the *homothetic* production function introduced by Shephard [70]. For our purposes, a function $h_a(\boldsymbol{q})$ is said to be homothetic if there is some single argument, twice continuously differentiable function $s(\cdot)$ which satisfies $s(0)=0$, $s'(x)>0$ for $x>0$, and for which $s[h_a(\boldsymbol{q})]$ is linearly homogeneous in $\boldsymbol{q}$.

The single product firm with a homothetic production function is of interest because its isoquants all have the same shape. This has the implication that if relative input prices remain the same and the firm expands output, the use of inputs by the firm will expand proportionately.

Extension of this definition to the multiproduct firm is straightforward if the production function is also input–output separable. In the general case we can distinguish several versions of homotheticity. Hanoch [36] has defined *homotheticity in inputs* in the following way. A firm with production function $h_b(\boldsymbol{q}, \boldsymbol{z})$ is said to be homothetic in inputs if there is a continuous positive function $\phi^*(\alpha, \boldsymbol{z})$ which satisfies $\phi^*(1, \boldsymbol{z}) = 1$ and $\partial\phi^*/\partial\alpha > 0$ for $\alpha > 0$ such that whenever $h_b(\boldsymbol{q}, \boldsymbol{z}) = 0$, we can also write

$$h_b[\phi^*(\alpha, \boldsymbol{z})\boldsymbol{q}, \alpha\boldsymbol{z}] = 0. \tag{2.38}$$

We can interpret this in the following way. Suppose we fix $\boldsymbol{z}$ so that $h_b(\boldsymbol{q}, \boldsymbol{z}) = 0$ then represents an isoquant in input space. Then, for a proportionate expansion of $\boldsymbol{z}$ to $\alpha\boldsymbol{z}$, eq. (2.38) implies that the input isoquant expands uniformly. The proportion of expansion of the isoquant is determined by $\phi^*(\alpha, \boldsymbol{z})$ which depends only on $\boldsymbol{z}$ and the proportion by which $\boldsymbol{z}$ was expanded.

Hanoch defined homotheticity in inputs in terms of an arbitrary implicit production function of the form (2.2). However, it should be noted that the definition is concerned only with the isoquants, so that it applies (with minor modification) to any representation of the efficient production surface. In particular, it applies without modification to both the input and output homogeneous production functions, so that $h_b(\cdot)$ in (2.38) can be interpreted as either $h_Q(\cdot)$ or $h(\cdot)$; the function $\phi^*(\cdot)$ is the same in the two cases. It is shown in Appendix A that an immediate implication of homotheticity in inputs is that when $h(\boldsymbol{q}, \boldsymbol{z}) = h_Q(\boldsymbol{q}, \boldsymbol{z}) = 0$, we can write

$$\sum_{i=1}^{n} \frac{\partial h}{\partial \log q_i} = u^*(\boldsymbol{z}); \qquad \sum_{r=1}^{m} \frac{\partial h_Q}{\partial \log z_r} = -\frac{1}{u^*(\boldsymbol{z})}, \tag{2.39}$$

where $u^*(\cdot)$ is the same function of outputs in both equations.

Hanoch defines *homotheticity in outputs* in a similar way. A firm is said to be homothetic in outputs if there is a continuous positive function $\phi(\alpha, \boldsymbol{q})$ which satisfies $\phi(1, \boldsymbol{q}) = 1$ and $\partial\phi/\partial\alpha > 0$ for $\alpha > 0$ such that whenever $h_b(\boldsymbol{q}, \boldsymbol{z}) = 0$, we can also write

$$h_b[\alpha\boldsymbol{q}, \phi(\alpha, \boldsymbol{q})\boldsymbol{z}] = 0. \tag{2.40}$$

This condition can be interpreted in a way similar to homotheticity in inputs: a proportionate expansion of inputs implies a proportionate expansion of the corresponding isoquant (or transformation surface) in output space.[18] It is shown in Appendix A that the implication of homotheticity in outputs analogous to (2.39) for inputs is that when $h(\boldsymbol{q}, \boldsymbol{z}) = h_Q(\boldsymbol{q}, \boldsymbol{z}) = 0$, we can write

$$\sum_{i=1}^{n} \frac{\partial h}{\partial \log q_i} = u(\boldsymbol{q}); \qquad \sum_{r=1}^{m} \frac{\partial h_Q}{\partial \log z_r} = -\frac{1}{u(\boldsymbol{q})}, \tag{2.41}$$

where $u(\cdot)$ is the same function of inputs in both equations.

[18]It should be apparent from this interpretation that the single product firm is trivially homothetic in outputs. In terms of the production function (2.1) we can define $\phi(\alpha, \boldsymbol{q}) = h_a(\alpha\boldsymbol{q})/h_a(\boldsymbol{q})$.

When the firm is homothetic in both inputs and outputs, (2.39) and (2.41) imply that $u(\boldsymbol{q}) = u^*(\boldsymbol{z})$. We can distinguish two important cases. The first is the case when both functions equal a constant, independent of inputs and outputs. In this case we have $\Sigma_i\ \partial h/\partial \log q_i = k$ (where k is a constant) and (2.38) can be written for the output and input homogeneous production functions as

$$h(\alpha^{1/k}\boldsymbol{q}, \alpha\boldsymbol{z}) = 0; \qquad h_Q(\alpha^{1/k}\boldsymbol{q}, \alpha\boldsymbol{z}) = 0, \tag{2.42}$$

whenever $h(\boldsymbol{q}, \boldsymbol{z}) = h_Q(\boldsymbol{q}, \boldsymbol{z}) = 0$. Equivalently, we can write (2.40) as

$$h(\alpha\boldsymbol{q}, \alpha^k\boldsymbol{z}) = 0; \qquad h_Q(\alpha\boldsymbol{q}, \alpha^k\boldsymbol{z}) = 0, \tag{2.43}$$

whenever $h(\boldsymbol{q}, \boldsymbol{z}) = h_Q(\boldsymbol{q}, \boldsymbol{z}) = 0$. The interpretation of (2.43) is that when the input vector is increased in proportion α, the output vector can also be increased proportionately in proportion α^k. This is analogous to the case when $h_a(\cdot)$ in (2.1) is homogeneous of degree k for the single product firm. Consequently, we shall call this the case of *homogeneous production.*

This should not be confused with the use of the word "homogeneity" in the context of the input or output homogeneous production function. Any production function can be written in input homogeneous and output homogeneous forms; homogeneous production is the case in which the input distance function, which by construction is homogeneous of degree one in inputs, is also homogeneous of some negative degree in outputs. Equivalently, the output distance function, which by construction is homogeneous of degree -1 in outputs, is also homogeneous of some positive degree in inputs if production is homogeneous.

An alternative situation in which production is homothetic in both inputs and outputs occurs when $u(\boldsymbol{q})$ and $u^*(\boldsymbol{z})$ depend on the levels of inputs and outputs, respectively. In this case, whenever $h(\boldsymbol{q}, \boldsymbol{z}) = 0$ we can write

$$u^*(\boldsymbol{z}) = u(\boldsymbol{q}), \tag{2.44}$$

so that the production function is input–output separable. It is shown in Appendix A that when the firm is homothetic in both inputs and outputs and is input–output separable as in (2.44), then both the functions $u^*(\cdot)$ and $u(\cdot)$ must be homothetic in the usual sense. Consequently, we shall call this the case of *input–output homotheticity*.

Any firm whose production function is homothetic in both inputs and outputs either is input–output homothetic or exhibits homogeneous production. The fact that the former case must be input–output separable is not trivially obvious; it was first proved by Hanoch [36]. It should be noted that input–output separability does not imply homotheticity in either inputs or outputs. Also, it is possible but not necessary for a firm which exhibits homogeneous production to be input–output separable as well.

As in the case of input–output separability, homotheticity implies restrictions on the matrices of second-order derivatives of the production function. These restrictions are derived in Appendix A, and apply whenever $h(\boldsymbol{q}, \boldsymbol{z}) = h_Q(\boldsymbol{q}, \boldsymbol{z}) = 0$. If the firm is homothetic in inputs (but not in outputs) we obtain

$$\boldsymbol{H\iota} = a^* \frac{\partial h}{\partial \log \boldsymbol{q}}; \qquad \boldsymbol{H}_Q^* \boldsymbol{\iota}^* = \boldsymbol{0}, \tag{2.45}$$

where a^* is a scalar. If the firm is homothetic in outputs (but not in inputs) we obtain

$$\boldsymbol{\iota}'\boldsymbol{H}^* = \boldsymbol{0}; \qquad \boldsymbol{H}_Q^{**} \boldsymbol{\iota}^* = b^* \frac{\partial h_Q}{\partial \log \boldsymbol{z}}, \tag{2.46}$$

where b^* is also a scalar. If the firm's production is homogeneous, we obtain

$$\boldsymbol{H\iota} = \boldsymbol{0}; \qquad \boldsymbol{H}_Q^* \boldsymbol{\iota}^* = \boldsymbol{0}, \tag{2.47}$$

$$\boldsymbol{\iota}'\boldsymbol{H}^* = \boldsymbol{0}; \qquad \boldsymbol{H}_Q^{**} \boldsymbol{\iota}^* = \boldsymbol{0}, \tag{2.48}$$

and finally, if the firm's production is input–output homothetic, we obtain

$$\boldsymbol{H}\boldsymbol{\iota} = a^* \frac{\partial h}{\partial \log \boldsymbol{q}}; \qquad \boldsymbol{H}_Q^* = \boldsymbol{0}, \tag{2.49}$$

$$\boldsymbol{H}^* = \boldsymbol{0}; \qquad \boldsymbol{H}_Q^{**}\boldsymbol{\iota}^* = b^* \frac{\partial h_Q}{\partial \log \boldsymbol{z}}, \tag{2.50}$$

where a^* and b^* are the same scalars which appear in (2.45) and (2.46). It should be noted that the results (2.47) and (2.48) for homogeneous production and the results (2.49) and (2.50) for input–output homothetic production are each stronger, but in different ways, than the combination of the results (2.45) for homotheticity in inputs alone, and (2.46) for homotheticity in outputs alone.

CHAPTER 3

Cost minimization

In Chapter 2 we noted that the technology of a firm can be described equally well by a production function or by the cost function which arises when the firm minimizes cost for given output quantities and input prices. In this chapter we consider more thoroughly the nature of this optimization process. Much of this material is drawn from Laitinen and Theil [50].

3.1. Conditions for a cost minimum

The firm's objective is to minimize $\Sigma_i p_i q_i$ subject to the production constraint by varying the q_i's for given positive z_r's and p_i's. We use the output homogeneous production function (2.15), which was developed in Chapter 2, to represent the production constraint and construct the Lagrangian function

$$L(\boldsymbol{q}, \rho) = \sum_{i=1}^{n} p_i q_i - \rho h(\boldsymbol{q}, \boldsymbol{z}). \tag{3.1}$$

This yields $\partial L/\partial \log q_i = p_i q_i - \rho\, \partial h/\partial \log q_i$ when differentiated with respect to $\log q_i$. By equating this to zero,

$$p_i q_i - \rho \frac{\partial h}{\partial \log q_i} = 0, \qquad i = 1, \dots, n, \tag{3.2}$$

we obtain n equations which, together with $h(\boldsymbol{q}, \boldsymbol{z}) = 0$, are assumed to yield unique positive values of the q_i's and ρ.[1]

[1]The positivity of ρ is implied by the positivity of q_i and $\partial h/\partial \log q_i$.

For the second-order condition we differentiate (3.1) with respect to $\log q_i$ and $\log q_j$ to obtain

$$\frac{\partial^2 L}{\partial \log q_i \, \partial \log q_j} = \delta_{ij} p_i q_i - \rho \frac{\partial^2 h}{\partial \log q_i \, \partial \log q_j}, \tag{3.3}$$

where δ_{ij} is the Kronecker delta, equal to one for $i = j$ and zero otherwise. To obtain a cost minimum it is sufficient that the $n \times n$ matrix with (3.3) as its (i, j)th element is symmetric positive definite. We will make this assumption.

The optimum values of the inputs can then be written as functions of the quantities taken as given by the firm, which are input prices and output quantities:

$$q_i = q_i(\boldsymbol{z}, \boldsymbol{p}), \qquad i = 1, \ldots, n. \tag{3.4}$$

In addition, since cost is $C = \Sigma_i p_i q_i$, we can write minimum cost as a function of input prices and output levels:

$$C = \sum_{i=1}^{n} p_i q_i(\boldsymbol{z}, \boldsymbol{p}) = C(\boldsymbol{z}, \boldsymbol{p}). \tag{3.5}$$

3.2. The elasticity of scale

In the single product firm the elasticity of scale is defined as the proportion by which output changes when all inputs change proportionately: $\Sigma_i \, \partial \log z / \partial \log q_i$. When the firm has more than one product, this definition is ambiguous. However, we can extend the definition unambiguously by inquiring, when all inputs change in a given proportion, by what proportion all outputs change when they are also required to change proportionately.

Consider the differential of $h(\boldsymbol{q}, \boldsymbol{z}) = 0$ in logarithmic form:

$$\sum_{i=1}^{n} \frac{\partial h}{\partial \log q_i} \, \mathrm{d}(\log q_i) + \sum_{r=1}^{m} \frac{\partial h}{\partial \log z_r} \, \mathrm{d}(\log z_r) = 0. \tag{3.6}$$

Let the inputs change proportionately and let this also be true of the outputs, so that $d(\log q_i)$ and $d(\log z_r)$ can each be put before its summation sign in (3.6). It then follows from (2.16) that each logarithmic output change equals the following multiple of each logarithmic input change:

$$\sum_{i=1}^{n} \frac{\partial h}{\partial \log q_i} = \sum_{i=1}^{n} \frac{p_i q_i}{\rho} = \frac{C}{\rho}. \tag{3.7}$$

The first equal sign in (3.7) is based on (3.2). We conclude from (3.7) that C/ρ is the elasticity of proportionate output with respect to proportionate input at the optimum or, more briefly, the *elasticity of scale* of the multiproduct firm at this point. When we define

$$\gamma = \rho / C, \tag{3.8}$$

γ then equals the reciprocal of the elasticity of scale at the optimum:

$$\sum_{i=1}^{n} \frac{\partial h}{\partial \log q_i} = \frac{1}{\gamma}. \tag{3.9}$$

Differentiation of (3.5) with respect to z_r yields the marginal cost of the rth product:

$$\frac{\partial C}{\partial z_r} = \sum_{i=1}^{n} p_i \frac{\partial q_i}{\partial z_r} = \frac{C}{z_r} \sum_{i=1}^{n} p_i q_i \frac{\partial \log q_i}{\partial \log z_r}. \tag{3.10}$$

Next we differentiate $h(\boldsymbol{q}, \boldsymbol{z}) = 0$ with respect to $\log z_r$, holding prices and other outputs constant:

$$\sum_{i=1}^{n} \frac{\partial h}{\partial \log q_i} \frac{\partial \log q_i}{\partial \log z_r} + \frac{\partial h}{\partial \log z_r} = 0.$$

It follows from (3.2) and (3.10) that this is equivalent to

$$\frac{z_r}{\rho}\frac{\partial C}{\partial z_r}+\frac{\partial h}{\partial \log z_r}=0. \tag{3.11}$$

Recall from (2.16) that the output homogeneous production function has the property $\Sigma_r\, \partial h/\partial \log z_r \equiv -1$. We conclude from this that summation of (3.11) over r yields

$$\rho=\sum_{r=1}^{m} z_r \frac{\partial C}{\partial z_r}=\sum_{r=1}^{m}\frac{\partial C}{\partial \log z_r}. \tag{3.12}$$

Now, division of (3.12) by C yields

$$\sum_{r=1}^{m}\frac{\partial \log C}{\partial \log z_r}=\gamma, \tag{3.13}$$

so that γ, besides being the reciprocal of the elasticity of scale, is also the elasticity of cost with respect to a proportionate output increase.[2]

Equation (3.12) implies that ρ is the marginal cost of a proportionate increase in outputs or, equivalently, ρ equals *total marginal cost*, each product being evaluated at a shadow price equal to its marginal cost. Thus, (3.8) indicates that γ has a third interpretation as the ratio of total marginal cost to total cost.

3.3. Factor and product shares

We define the share of the ith factor in C (or the ith *factor share*) as the proportion of total cost which is attributed to the ith input:

$$f_i=\frac{p_i q_i}{C}. \tag{3.14}$$

[2]This double interpretation of γ is the multiproduct extension of Theil's interpretation for the single product firm [79, p. 1303].

It follows from (3.5) that these factor shares have unit sum; also, since p_i, q_i, and C are each positive, so is the ith factor share. At the optimum (3.2) and (3.8) then imply that

$$f_i = \gamma \frac{\partial h}{\partial \log q_i}. \tag{3.15}$$

These factor shares figure prominently in the Divisia [30] decomposition of cost. Consider the total differential of (3.14), which is $\mathrm{d}f_i = (q_i/C)\,\mathrm{d}p_i + (p_i/C)\,\mathrm{d}q_i - (p_iq_i/C^2)\,\mathrm{d}C$, and can be written

$$\mathrm{d}f_i = f_i\,\mathrm{d}(\log p_i) + f_i\,\mathrm{d}(\log q_i) - f_i\,\mathrm{d}(\log C). \tag{3.16}$$

Thus, the differential change in a factor share consists of a price component, a quantity component, and a cost component. Since the sum of the factor shares is unity, the sum of these differential changes must be zero. Consequently, when we sum (3.16) over i, we obtain

$$\mathrm{d}(\log C) = \sum_{i=1}^{n} f_i\,\mathrm{d}(\log p_i) + \sum_{i=1}^{n} f_i\,\mathrm{d}(\log q_i), \tag{3.17}$$

which is the Divisia decomposition of the logarithmic change in cost into an index which measures the change in prices,

$$\mathrm{d}(\log P) = \sum_{i=1}^{n} f_i\,\mathrm{d}(\log p_i), \tag{3.18}$$

and an index which measures the change in quantities,

$$\mathrm{d}(\log Q) = \sum_{i=1}^{n} f_i\,\mathrm{d}(\log q_i). \tag{3.19}$$

Because these indexes are associated with the decomposition (3.17), we will refer to (3.18) as the *Divisia input price index* and to (3.19) as the *Divisia input volume index*.

By considering expression (3.12) for ρ we can similarly define

$$g_r = \frac{z_r}{\rho}\frac{\partial C}{\partial z_r} \tag{3.20}$$

as the share of the rth product in total marginal cost. Like the factor shares, these product shares are necessarily positive and have unit sum. Now, (3.11) and (3.20) imply the following result at the point of the firm's optimum:

$$g_r = -\frac{\partial h}{\partial \log z_r}. \tag{3.21}$$

The differential of (3.20) can be written

$$\mathrm{d}g_r = g_r\,\mathrm{d}(\log z_r) + g_r\,\mathrm{d}\left(\log\frac{\partial C}{\partial z_r}\right) - g_r\,\mathrm{d}(\log\rho). \tag{3.22}$$

Summation of this over r then yields the Divisia decomposition

$$\mathrm{d}(\log\rho) = \sum_{r=1}^{m} g_r\,\mathrm{d}(\log z_r) + \sum_{r=1}^{m} g_r\,\mathrm{d}\left(\log\frac{\partial C}{\partial z_r}\right), \tag{3.23}$$

with an implied Divisia volume index of the outputs equal to

$$\mathrm{d}(\log Z) = \sum_{r=1}^{m} g_r\,\mathrm{d}(\log z_r). \tag{3.24}$$

3.4. Marginal shares of the inputs

In the previous section we defined the shares of the inputs in total cost and the shares of the outputs in total marginal cost. It is not in general possible to define the shares of the outputs in cost,[3] but it is possible to consider the shares of the inputs in

[3]This is the problem encountered in accounting contexts of allocating costs among different outputs. We shall have more to say about this problem in the context of output independence in Chapter 4.

marginal cost. Thus, let us define

$$\theta_i^r = \frac{\partial(p_i q_i)/\partial z_r}{\partial C/\partial z_r}, \tag{3.25}$$

which is the share of the ith input in the marginal cost of the rth product.[4]

When we multiply θ_i^r by g_r and sum over r we obtain (see (3.20))

$$\theta_i = \sum_{r=1}^{m} g_r \theta_i^r = \frac{1}{\rho} \sum_{r=1}^{m} \frac{\partial(p_i q_i)}{\partial \log z_r}. \tag{3.26}$$

Consulting the first and third members of (3.12) we see that θ_i, defined in (3.26), can be interpreted as the share of the ith input in total marginal cost. An alternative interpretation is provided by the second member of (3.26), which indicates that θ_i is the weighted sum, with the product shares as weights, of the shares of the ith input in the marginal costs of the different products. Thus, θ_i can be regarded as the mean share of the ith input in the marginal cost of the firm. Since the weights g_r also appear in the Divisia index (3.24), which can thus also be regarded as a weighted mean of the logarithmic changes in the outputs, we shall refer to θ_i as the *Divisia mean* of the shares θ_i^r.

3.5. Input demand equations

Both $h(\boldsymbol{q}, \boldsymbol{z}) = 0$ and the n equilibrium conditions (3.2) hold for any positive values of the outputs and the input prices. Consequently, we can differentiate these $n+1$ equations with respect to $\log z_r$ and $\log p_i$ to determine how the optimum changes in response to changes in these given variables. This matter is pursued in Appendix B, where it is shown that the derivatives of

[4]The word "share" is used in a generalized sense. Both θ_i^r of (3.25) and θ_i of (3.26) add up to 1 when summed over i, but they need not be non-negative. Becker [12, pp. 139–143] has commented qualitatively on the role of marginal shares in the single product firm.

the production constraint and (3.2) with respect to $\log z_r$ for $r=1,\ldots,m$ and $\log p_i$ for $i=1,\ldots,n$ can be written in the form of a partitioned matrix equation which may be viewed as an extension to the multiproduct firm of Barten's [9] fundamental matrix equation of the consumer.

When this equation is solved, we obtain solutions in matrix form for the derivatives of input quantities with respect to input prices,

$$\boldsymbol{F}\frac{\partial \log \boldsymbol{q}}{\partial \log \boldsymbol{p}'} = -\psi(\boldsymbol{\Theta} - \boldsymbol{\theta\theta}'), \tag{3.27}$$

and output quantities,

$$\boldsymbol{F}\frac{\partial \log \boldsymbol{q}}{\partial \log \boldsymbol{z}'} = \gamma\boldsymbol{\theta g}' + \gamma\psi(\boldsymbol{\Theta} - \boldsymbol{\theta\theta}')\boldsymbol{F}^{-1}\boldsymbol{H}^*. \tag{3.28}$$

Here $\boldsymbol{F}$ is the $n\times n$ diagonal matrix which contains the factor shares (3.14) on the diagonal, $\boldsymbol{g}'$ is an m-element row vector whose rth element is the product share (3.20), and $\boldsymbol{H}^*$ is defined in (2.19).

The $n\times n$ matrix $\boldsymbol{\Theta}=[\theta_{ij}]$ is defined by

$$\boldsymbol{\Theta} = \frac{1}{\psi}\boldsymbol{F}(\boldsymbol{F}-\gamma\boldsymbol{H})^{-1}\boldsymbol{F} \tag{3.29}$$

and is hence symmetric positive definite.[5] The positive scalar coefficient ψ is defined by

$$\psi = \boldsymbol{\iota}'\boldsymbol{F}(\boldsymbol{F}-\gamma\boldsymbol{H})^{-1}\boldsymbol{F\iota}, \tag{3.30}$$

which implies that $\boldsymbol{\Theta}$ is also normalized so that its elements add up to one:

[5]This follows from the assumption in section 3.1 that the matrix whose (i,j)th element is (3.3), is symmetric positive definite. The latter matrix is a multiple C of $\boldsymbol{F}-\gamma\boldsymbol{H}$. It then follows that ψ in (3.30) is positive. For further interpretation of ψ see the end of section 3.6.

$$\boldsymbol{\iota}'\boldsymbol{\Theta}\boldsymbol{\iota} = \sum_{i=1}^{n}\sum_{j=1}^{n} \theta_{ij} = 1. \tag{3.31}$$

The n-element vector $\boldsymbol{\theta}$ has the marginal share θ_i defined in (3.26) as its ith element and can also be obtained from the row sums of $\boldsymbol{\Theta}$:

$$\boldsymbol{\theta} = \boldsymbol{\Theta}\boldsymbol{\iota}; \qquad \theta_i = \sum_{j=1}^{n} \theta_{ij}. \tag{3.32}$$

If we define $\boldsymbol{K}$ as the $n \times m$ matrix which has θ_i^r as its (i, r)th element, we can then write (3.28) in the simpler form

$$\boldsymbol{F}\frac{\partial \log \boldsymbol{q}}{\partial \log \boldsymbol{z}'} = \gamma \boldsymbol{K}\boldsymbol{G}, \tag{3.33}$$

where $\boldsymbol{G}$ is the $m \times m$ diagonal matrix with the product shares on the diagonal. The relation among the marginal shares shown by the first two members of (3.26) can then be written in matrix form,

$$\boldsymbol{\theta} = \boldsymbol{K}\boldsymbol{g}, \tag{3.34}$$

while the property that the marginal shares of all inputs in any output add up to one can be expressed by

$$\boldsymbol{\iota}'\boldsymbol{K} = \boldsymbol{\iota}^{*\prime}. \tag{3.35}$$

In order to express changes in the inputs in terms of changes in the outputs and the input prices, we take the differential of the matrix version of (3.4):

$$\mathrm{d}(\log \boldsymbol{q}) = \frac{\partial \log \boldsymbol{q}}{\partial \log \boldsymbol{z}'}\,\mathrm{d}(\log \boldsymbol{z}) + \frac{\partial \log \boldsymbol{q}}{\partial \log \boldsymbol{p}'}\,\mathrm{d}(\log \boldsymbol{p}).$$

We premultiply this by $\boldsymbol{F}$ and use (3.33) and (3.27):

$$\boldsymbol{F}\,\mathrm{d}(\log \boldsymbol{q}) = \gamma \boldsymbol{K}\boldsymbol{G}\,\mathrm{d}(\log \boldsymbol{z}) - \psi(\boldsymbol{\Theta} - \boldsymbol{\theta}\boldsymbol{\theta}')\,\mathrm{d}(\log \boldsymbol{p}). \tag{3.36}$$

The ith element of the vector on the left is $f_i\, d(\log q_i)$. This is the quantity component of the change in the ith factor share, whose decomposition is shown in (3.16). It is also the contribution of the ith factor to the Divisia index of inputs (3.19). The ith element of the price term in (3.36) can be written $-\psi \sum_j (\theta_{ij} - \theta_i\theta_j)\, d(\log p_j)$. Now, using the definition of $\boldsymbol{K}$, we see that (3.36) for the ith input takes the form

$$f_i\, d(\log q_i) = \gamma \sum_{r=1}^{m} \theta_i^r g_r\, d(\log z_r) - \psi \sum_{j=1}^{n} (\theta_{ij} - \theta_i\theta_j)\, d(\log p_j). \tag{3.37}$$

This equation describes the change in the demand for the ith input, measured by the quantity component of the change in the ith factor share, in terms of output changes and input price changes. Consequently, we call this the ith *differential demand equation* of the firm or, for short, the ith *demand equation.*

3.6. Comparative statics: Price changes

An alternative view of the demand equation (3.37) follows from the fact that it describes the *change* in the firm's demand for the ith factor in response to *changes* in input prices and output quantities. The study of such changes is the domain of comparative statics; consequently, interpretation of (3.37) for $i = 1, \ldots, n$ amounts to a statement of the properties of the comparative statics of the firm under cost minimization.

It follows from (3.32) that when all input price changes are proportionate in (3.37) the price term vanishes. Thus, if output remains unchanged and all input prices change proportionately the demand for each input is unchanged. This property, known generally as homogeneity because it implies that the factor demand functions (3.4) are homogeneous of degree zero in input prices, indicates clearly that only relative prices affect the cost minimizing firm. When input prices do not change proportionately, the price term in (3.37) defines a pure substitution effect among the inputs, since the effects of changes in output are captured by the other term.

An alternative view of this follows when we define

$$d(\log P') = \sum_{i=1}^{n} \theta_i \, d(\log p_i) \tag{3.38}$$

as the *Frisch price index* of the inputs.[6] Since $\boldsymbol{\Theta} - \boldsymbol{\theta\theta}' = \boldsymbol{\Theta}(\boldsymbol{I} - \boldsymbol{\iota\theta}')$ holds in view of (3.32), the ith element of $-\psi(\boldsymbol{\Theta} - \boldsymbol{\theta\theta}') \, d(\log \boldsymbol{p})$ equals

$$-\psi \sum_{j=1}^{n} \theta_{ij}[d(\log p_j) - d(\log P')].$$

We substitute this for the price term in (3.27), with the expression in brackets abbreviated as $d[\log(p_j/P')]$, which gives

$$f_i \, d(\log q_i) = \gamma \sum_{r=1}^{m} \theta_i^r g_r \, d(\log z_r) - \psi \sum_{i=1}^{n} \theta_{ij} \, d\left(\log \frac{p_j}{P'}\right). \tag{3.39}$$

This equation, like (3.37), describes the change in the firm's demand for the ith input, but now the relative prices enter directly. Note that if absolute price changes are proportionate, the relative price changes $d[\log(p_j/P')]$ in (3.39) are each zero in view of (3.32) and (3.38).

The coefficients θ_{ij} in (3.39) will be referred to as the *normalized price coefficients* since they add up to one (see (3.31)). Since θ_{ii} is positive, (3.39) implies that for constant output an increase in the ith relative price will cause a decrease in the firm's use of the corresponding input. Thus, the firm's demand curves, properly compensated, are downward sloping, which is completely analogous to the theory of the consumer and the single product firm.

[6] This terminology is motivated by Frisch's introduction of the analogous marginally weighted price index in consumption theory [32, pp. 74–82]. The prime attached to P in (3.38) emphasizes the marginal weighting. This index should be contrasted to the Divisia index (3.18), whose weights are factor shares instead of marginal shares.

When θ_{ij} for $i \neq j$ is negative, (3.39) implies for constant output that the firm will increase use of the ith factor when the relative price of the jth factor increases. We express this by calling the ith and jth inputs *specific substitutes* (*complements*) when θ_{ij} is negative (positive). This terminology is an extension of Houthakker's [43] definition of specific substitutes and complements in consumption theory.

An alternative analysis is obtained when we consider the absolute price coefficient $\theta_{ij} - \theta_i\theta_j$ in (3.37). Evidently when this coefficient is negative the firm will increase use of the ith factor when the *absolute* price of the jth factor increases (with output held constant). This coefficient is closely related to Allen's [1] *partial elasticity of substitution.*[7] It is shown in Appendix B that this is equal to

$$\sigma_{ij}^{A} = -\psi \frac{\theta_{ij} - \theta_i\theta_j}{f_i f_j}, \qquad i \neq j. \tag{3.40}$$

It should be noted that knowledge of ψ and θ_{ij} for each i and j together with the factor shares permits evaluation of both specific substitution and complementarity and the Allen partial elasticities of substitution. Knowledge of the latter, however, does not permit evaluation of specific substitution and complementarity, since the matrix $\psi(\boldsymbol{\Theta} - \boldsymbol{\theta\theta}')$ is semidefinite.[8] As a consequence, it appears that specific substitution and complementarity is a more basic aspect of the firm than the Allen partial elasticities of substitution.

It is shown in Appendix B that

$$\frac{1}{\psi} = 1 + \frac{1}{\gamma^2} \sum_{r=1}^{m} \sum_{s=1}^{m} \frac{\partial^2 \log C}{\partial \log z_r \, \partial \log z_s}, \tag{3.41}$$

which shows that ψ may be regarded as a measure of the

[7]These are sometimes called the Allen–Uzawa elasticities of substitution as a result of Uzawa's [83] discussion of them.

[8]The relation between $\boldsymbol{\Theta}$ and $\psi(\boldsymbol{\Theta} - \boldsymbol{\theta\theta}')$ will be discussed in more detail in section 5.4 and Appendix D; the related question of the identifiability of ψ will be discussed at the end of section 8.1.

curvature of the logarithmic cost function. Recall from (3.13) that γ is the elasticity of cost with respect to a proportionate change in outputs. It follows that we can write (3.41) as

$$\frac{1}{\psi} = 1 + \frac{1}{\gamma} \sum_{r=1}^{n} \frac{\partial \log \gamma}{\partial \log z_r}. \tag{3.42}$$

Thus, ψ also measures the change in this elasticity with respect to a proportionate change in outputs. If γ does not change, it follows that ψ is 1. If γ decreases (increases) when the outputs increase proportionately, then ψ is larger (smaller) than one.

Since the magnitude of ψ affects the magnitude of the price term in (3.39) for a given matrix $\boldsymbol{\Theta}$ of normalized price coefficients, we can also interpret ψ as describing the sensitivity of the firm to changes in relative prices. It follows that these relative price effects are larger if γ decreases when the outputs increase proportionately than they are if γ increases.

3.7. Comparative statics: Volume changes

If relative price changes are zero in (3.39), the only changes in factor use will be caused by changes in the levels of outputs. It is readily verified that the sum over i of the substitution term in (3.39) vanishes. So, using $\Sigma_i \theta_i^r = 1$, (3.19), and (3.24), we obtain the following result by summing (3.39) over i:

$$\mathrm{d}(\log Q) = \gamma\, \mathrm{d}(\log Z). \tag{3.43}$$

This is the *total-input decision* of the multiproduct firm, expressing the Divisia volume index of the inputs as proportional to the corresponding index of the outputs. Changes in input prices play no role in the total-input decision. In fact, it may be verified by substituting (3.15) and (3.21) into (3.6) that the total-input decision is simply a differential version of the production constraint $h(\boldsymbol{q}, \boldsymbol{z}) = 0$, which holds at the firm's optimum both before and after the output change.

If outputs change proportionately so that $\mathrm{d}(\log z_r) = \mathrm{d}(\log Z)$ for each r, the output effect in (3.39) is simplified to $\gamma\theta_i \,\mathrm{d}(\log Z) = \theta_i \,\mathrm{d}(\log Q)$. Then, if relative input prices do not change, we have $\mathrm{d}(\log q_i) = (\theta_i/f_i)\,\mathrm{d}(\log Q)$, so that the elasticity of the ith input with respect to the Divisia index of aggregate input is θ_i/f_i. This elasticity is called the *Divisia elasticity* of the ith input and plays a role in the input side of the firm which is closely analogous to the role of the income elasticity in consumption theory. When θ_i/f_i is greater than one, the firm's use of the ith input increases more rapidly than the firm's "average" input. Similarly, when θ_i/f_i is between zero and one, the firm's use of the ith input increases when average input does, but not so quickly. It is also possible for the Divisia elasticity of the ith input to be negative. This is the case of an *inferior* input, where use of the ith input actually decreases when output increases. An additional similarity to income elasticities is that the cost-share-weighted sum of the Divisia elasticities is unity.

When output changes are not proportionate, the reactions of the firm are more complex. If the ith input is particularly important for production of the rth output, θ_i^r is greater than θ_i, and vice versa. This implies that the contributions of the outputs to the Divisia index of the change in aggregate output, $g_r\,\mathrm{d}(\log z_r)$, are weighted by the importance of the ith input in producing them in order to obtain the change in the ith input.

This can also be viewed in another way. We multiply (3.43) by θ_i and substitute the result in (3.39):

$$f_i \,\mathrm{d}(\log q_i) = \theta_i \,\mathrm{d}(\log Q) + \gamma \sum_{r=1}^{m} g_r(\theta_i^r - \theta_i)\,\mathrm{d}(\log z_r) - \psi \sum_{j=1}^{n} \theta_{ij}\,\mathrm{d}\left(\log \frac{p_j}{P'}\right). \tag{3.44}$$

A more elegant form emerges when we recall from section 3.4 that $\mathrm{d}(\log Z)$ and θ_i in (3.24) and (3.26) are weighted means, with the product shares as weights, of the $\mathrm{d}(\log z_r)$'s and the θ_i^r's respectively. The associated covariance is

$$\Gamma_i = \sum_{r=1}^{m} g_r(\theta_i^r - \theta_i)\,[\mathrm{d}(\log z_r) - \mathrm{d}(\log Z)]. \tag{3.45}$$

Since $\Sigma_r\, g_r(\theta_i^r - \theta_i)\,\mathrm{d}(\log Z) = 0$ (see (3.26)) this covariance is equal to a multiple $(1/\gamma)$ of the output term in (3.44). Substitution yields

$$f_i\,\mathrm{d}(\log q_i) = \theta_i\,\mathrm{d}(\log Q) + \gamma\Gamma_i - \psi \sum_{j=1}^{n} \theta_{ij}\,\mathrm{d}\!\left(\log \frac{p_j}{P'}\right), \tag{3.46}$$

which is the *input allocation decision* of the multiproduct firm for the ith input. This decision describes the change in the demand for the ith input in terms of the Divisia volume index $\mathrm{d}(\log Q)$ which is obtained from the total-input decision (3.43), the covariance (3.45), and the changes in the relative prices.

The covariance term $\gamma\Gamma_i$ in (3.46) implies that a change in outputs raises the demand for the ith input in excess of the Divisia value $\theta_i\,\mathrm{d}(\log Q)$ when the output changes are positively correlated with the marginal shares of this input. But note that such a correlation cannot occur when outputs increase proportionately, which was the result we obtained above.

3.8. Specialized forms

3.8.1. The input–output separable firm

Equations (3.28) and (3.33) are the same because the matrix $\boldsymbol{K}$ of the individual marginal shares θ_i^r can be written

$$\boldsymbol{K} = \boldsymbol{\theta}\boldsymbol{\iota}^{*\prime} + \psi(\boldsymbol{\Theta} - \boldsymbol{\theta}\boldsymbol{\theta}')\boldsymbol{F}^{-1}\boldsymbol{H}^{*}\boldsymbol{G}^{-1}. \tag{3.47}$$

The constraint (3.35) follows from this because $\boldsymbol{\iota}'\boldsymbol{\theta} = 1$ and $\boldsymbol{\iota}'(\boldsymbol{\Theta} - \boldsymbol{\theta}\boldsymbol{\theta}') = \boldsymbol{0}$; the constraint (3.34) follows because $\boldsymbol{G}^{-1}\boldsymbol{g} = \boldsymbol{\iota}^{*}$

and the property (2.27) of the output homogeneous production function.

When the firm is input–output separable the elements of the matrix $\boldsymbol{H}^*$ also satisfy (2.37). Since the factor shares satisfy (3.15) under cost minimization, we can write (2.37) for all i and r as

$$\boldsymbol{H}^* = \frac{1}{\gamma}\boldsymbol{f}\boldsymbol{b}', \tag{3.48}$$

where $\boldsymbol{f} = \boldsymbol{F}\boldsymbol{\iota}$ is the n-element vector with the factor shares as elements, and $\boldsymbol{b}'$ is the m-element row vector with rth element b_r. It then follows that $\boldsymbol{F}^{-1}\boldsymbol{H}^* = (1/\gamma)\boldsymbol{\iota}\boldsymbol{b}'$; substitution of this result into (3.47) yields

$$\boldsymbol{K} = \boldsymbol{\theta}\boldsymbol{\iota}^{*\prime} \tag{3.49}$$

under input–output separability. In scalar notation this is $\theta_i^r = \theta_i$ for each i and r.

This means that if the firm is input–output separable, any input has the same share of each marginal cost. This result establishes in more precise terms the lack of individual interaction between inputs and outputs of the input–output separable firm which was remarked in the paragraph below (1.2).

Further implications of input–output separability can be established by consulting (3.45), where it is evident that the covariance Γ_i is then necessarily zero. This means that (3.46) can be written in the simpler form

$$f_i \,\mathrm{d}(\log q_i) = \theta_i \,\mathrm{d}(\log Q) - \psi \sum_{j=1}^{n} \theta_{ij} \,\mathrm{d}\left(\log \frac{p_j}{P'}\right). \tag{3.50}$$

When the firm is input–output separable the input allocation decision involves only the Divisia volume index of inputs and the changes in relative input prices; it is independent of the changes in individual outputs.[9]

[9]Note that the single product firm, whose production constraint is shown in (2.1), is necessarily input–output separable. Hence, its input allocation decision is of the form (3.50), which was shown by Theil [79].

3.8.2. Homotheticity in inputs

When the firm is homothetic in inputs, the equation on the left in (2.45) in conjunction with (3.15) implies that

$$\boldsymbol{H\iota} = \frac{a^*}{\gamma} f. \tag{3.51}$$

We next consider the inverse of (3.29), namely $\boldsymbol{\Theta}^{-1} = \psi \boldsymbol{F}^{-1}(\boldsymbol{F} - \gamma \boldsymbol{H})\boldsymbol{F}^{-1}$, which we postmultiply by $\boldsymbol{f} = \boldsymbol{F\iota}$ to obtain $\boldsymbol{\Theta}^{-1}\boldsymbol{f} = \psi \boldsymbol{F}^{-1}(\boldsymbol{f} - \gamma \boldsymbol{H\iota})$. Now the application of (3.51) and premultiplication by $\boldsymbol{\Theta}$ yields $\boldsymbol{f} = \psi(1 - a^*)\boldsymbol{\theta}$. Since $\boldsymbol{\iota}'\boldsymbol{f} = \boldsymbol{\iota}'\boldsymbol{\theta} = 1$, this evidently implies that

$$1/\psi = 1 - a^*, \tag{3.52}$$

$$\boldsymbol{\theta} = \boldsymbol{f}, \tag{3.53}$$

when the firm is homothetic in inputs. Eq. (3.52) should be compared to (3.41) and (3.42) in the general case; in conjunction with (3.51) we have $\boldsymbol{\iota}'\boldsymbol{H\iota} = \Sigma_r\, \partial \log \gamma / \partial \log z_r$.

Equation (3.53) is an extension of Theil's [79] result for the homothetic single product firm. The effect of homotheticity in inputs is that the marginal shares θ_i are identical to the factor shares f_i. This has two effects on the input allocation decision (3.46). First, the Divisia elasticities of the inputs are all unity. Second, the Frisch price index of the inputs (3.38) is identical to the Divisia price index (3.18). Thus, the input allocation decision can be written

$$\mathrm{d}(\log q_i) = \mathrm{d}(\log Q) + \frac{\gamma}{f_i}\Gamma_i - \frac{\psi}{f_i}\sum_{j=1}^{n} \theta_{ij}\, \mathrm{d}\left(\log \frac{p_j}{P}\right) \tag{3.54}$$

when the firm is homothetic in inputs. When prices change proportionately so that the substitution term is zero, and outputs also change proportionately so that the covariance term is also zero, then the use of each input also changes proportionately. In the more general case when the firm is not homothetic in inputs, these input changes will be made disproportionate by differing Divisia elasticities.

When the firm is also homothetic in outputs, so that it is either homogeneous in production or is input–output homothetic, these results can be made stronger. When the firm is homogeneous in production, the first equation in (2.47) applies; this can be interpreted as a special case of (3.51) with $a^* = 0$. Thus, from (3.52) we obtain $\psi = 1$. This corresponds to the case where γ is constant and equal to the reciprocal of k in (2.42) and (2.43). In this case the input allocation decision takes the form (3.54) with $\psi = 1$ and γ equal to a constant.

When the firm is input–output homothetic it is also input–output separable, so that (3.54) can be further simplified by deleting the covariance term. Evidently in this case only relative price changes can cause disproportionate changes in inputs; if prices change proportionately, then any change in outputs will lead to a proportionate change in inputs.[10]

3.8.3. *Input independence*

If the output homogeneous production function can be decomposed additively in the inputs,[11] i.e.

$$h(\boldsymbol{q}, \boldsymbol{z}) = \sum_{i=1}^{n} h_i(q_i, \boldsymbol{z}) \tag{3.55}$$

then the matrix $\boldsymbol{H}$ of second derivatives of $h(\cdot)$ with respect to

[10] Note that the production functions estimated by Klein [46, 47] and Hasenkamp [37, 38] are homogeneous in production *and* input–output separable. When this is the case, (3.54) is even further simplified, with $\psi = 1$ and the covariance term deleted.

[11] The most obvious example is a production function studied by Hasenkamp [37], which is input–output separable, as in (2.35), with $h_a(\cdot)$ a Cobb–Douglas function of inputs and $h_c(\cdot)$ a constant elasticity of transformation function of outputs $(z_1^\alpha + z_2^\alpha)^{\gamma/\alpha}$ with $\alpha, \gamma > 1$ (see Powell and Gruen [63]). This yields an output homogeneous production function $h(\boldsymbol{q}, \boldsymbol{z}) = (1/\gamma)\Sigma_i \beta_i \log q_i - (1/\alpha)\log(z_1^\alpha + z_2^\alpha)$. In this case $\boldsymbol{H} = \boldsymbol{0}$, which is certainly diagonal.

inputs is diagonal:

$$\frac{\partial^2 h}{\partial \log q_i \, \partial \log q_j} = 0, \quad \text{for } i \neq j. \tag{3.56}$$

A glance at the definition (3.29) of $\boldsymbol{\Theta}$ indicates, since $\boldsymbol{F}$ is always diagonal, that when $\boldsymbol{H}$ is also diagonal, then so is $\boldsymbol{\Theta}$:

$$\theta_{ij} = 0, \quad \text{for } i \neq j. \tag{3.57}$$

The constraint (3.32) and the positive definiteness of $\boldsymbol{\Theta}$ then imply that

$$\theta_{ii} = \theta_i > 0, \tag{3.58}$$

and hence that the input allocation decision (3.46) can be written

$$f_i \, \mathrm{d}(\log q_i) = \theta_i \, \mathrm{d}(\log Q) + \gamma \Gamma_i - \psi \theta_i \, \mathrm{d}\left(\log \frac{p_i}{P'}\right). \tag{3.59}$$

When (3.57) holds, no input is a specific substitute or complement (see section 3.6) of any other; we express this by saying that a firm whose production function satisfies (3.56) is *input independent*.[12] The form (3.59) of the input allocation decision indicates that when the firm is input independent only the ith relative input price change is relevant to the change in the use of the ith input. The inequality in (3.58) implies that the firm which is input independent cannot have inferior inputs.

[12]This terminology was used by Theil [79] in the context of the single product firm. Input independence is analogous to the case in the theory of the consumer which arises when the utility function can be written in an additively decomposable manner. Theil [78] refers to this case as "preference independence".

CHAPTER 4

Profit maximization

The advantage of considering cost minimization by itself, as we did in Chapter 3, is that any of a broad range of assumptions about the way the firm chooses its output levels implies cost minimizing behavior. Thus, if the firm is a classical monopolist in the market for one or more of its products, profit maximizing behavior implies cost minimizing behavior as well.[1]

Here we consider the simplest case: the competitive multiproduct firm. It is assumed that the firm faces exogenously given input and output prices and desires to maximize profit by choosing an optimal level of operations. The result of the analysis, which is drawn mainly from Laitinen and Theil [50], is a system of supply equations in the same general form as the system of demand equations derived in Chapter 3.

4.1. Conditions for a profit maximum

We now assume that the firm's objective is to maximize profit for given input and output prices. Since $\boldsymbol{y} = (y_1, \ldots, y_m)'$ is the vector of output prices, the firm's revenue is $R = \Sigma_r y_r z_r = \boldsymbol{y}'\boldsymbol{z}$. The objective is to maximize profit, $R - C$, by varying $\boldsymbol{q}$ and $\boldsymbol{z}$

[1]Note, however, that this does not apply to all possible behavioral assumptions about the firm. Dayan [27] has shown that a single product firm which is a profit maximizing monopolist operating under rate-of-return regulation may well not minimize cost; this undoubtedly extends to the multiproduct firm. The case of the multiproduct monopolist is in many respects more complex than that of the single product monopolist, and consequently will not be considered here.

subject to the production constraint $h(\boldsymbol{q}, \boldsymbol{z}) = 0$ for given $\boldsymbol{p}$ and $\boldsymbol{y}$. Suppose that we know the solution for $\boldsymbol{z}$, so that $R = \boldsymbol{y}'\boldsymbol{z}$ is also known (since $\boldsymbol{y}$ is given). Maximizing $R - C$ is then equivalent to minimizing $C = \boldsymbol{p}'\boldsymbol{q}$ by varying $\boldsymbol{q}$ subject to the production constraint with $\boldsymbol{z}$ specified as the known solution. This problem was considered in Chapter 3 and yielded the input demand equations (3.36). Evidently it is sufficient to find the values $\mathrm{d}(\log \boldsymbol{z})$ in (3.36) which maximize profit.

For this purpose we consider profit as a function of $\boldsymbol{z}$, which means that the first-order condition is $\partial(R - C)/\partial \boldsymbol{z} = \boldsymbol{0}$. This yields

$$\frac{\partial C}{\partial z_r} = y_r, \qquad r = 1, \ldots, m, \tag{4.1}$$

because $\partial R/\partial z_r = y_r$ follows from the assumption that $\boldsymbol{y}$ is given. Using (3.20) we can write (4.1) as $\rho g_r = y_r z_r$, which we sum over r:

$$\rho = \sum_{r=1}^{m} y_r z_r = R. \tag{4.2}$$

Hence, ρ now equals the firm's revenue and $\rho g_r = y_r z_r$ can be written as

$$g_r = \frac{y_r z_r}{R}, \tag{4.3}$$

so that g_r is now the share of the rth product in revenue. Also, (4.1) implies that (3.25) can be simplified to

$$\theta_i^r = \frac{\partial(p_i q_i)}{\partial(y_r z_r)}. \tag{4.4}$$

Thus, under profit maximization θ_i^r is the additional expense on the ith input incurred for the production of an additional dollar's worth of the rth output. The condition $\Sigma_i \theta_i^r = 1$ is then equivalent to the proposition that a dollar's worth of the rth output requires an additional dollar's worth of inputs, obviously a necessary condition for profit maximization. Finally, (3.8) and (4.2) show that γ is now the revenue–cost ratio:

$$\gamma = R/C. \tag{4.5}$$

The second-order condition requires $\partial^2(R-C)/\partial z\,\partial z'$ to be negative definite, for which it is sufficient that

$$\frac{\partial^2 C}{\partial z\,\partial z'} \quad \text{is symmetric positive definite,} \tag{4.6}$$

because $\partial^2 R/\partial z\,\partial z' = \mathbf{0}$ follows from the assumption that $\boldsymbol{y}$ is given. We shall assume that (4.6) is true.

4.2. The supply of the products

The following results are proved in Appendix C. First, the supply equations for the products of the firm which are implied by profit maximization can be written in matrix form as

$$\boldsymbol{G}\,\mathrm{d}(\log \boldsymbol{z}) = \psi^* \boldsymbol{\Theta}^*[\mathrm{d}(\log \boldsymbol{y}) - \boldsymbol{K}'\,\mathrm{d}(\log \boldsymbol{p})], \tag{4.7}$$

where $\boldsymbol{\Theta}^* = [\theta_{rs}^*]$ is an $m \times m$ symmetric positive definite matrix which is normalized so that its elements add up to one:

$$\sum_{r=1}^{m} \sum_{s=1}^{m} \theta_{rs}^* = 1. \tag{4.8}$$

Second, the coefficient ψ^* in (4.7) satisfies

$$\psi^* \geq \frac{\psi}{\gamma - \psi} > 0. \tag{4.9}$$

The left-hand variable of the rth equation in (4.7) is $g_r\, d(\log z_r)$, which is the contribution of the rth product to the Divisia volume index (3.24) of the outputs. It is also the quantity component of the change in the rth revenue share, which can be verified by taking the differential of (4.3):

$$dg_r = g_r\, d(\log z_r) + g_r\, d(\log y_r) - g_r\, d(\log R). \tag{4.10}$$

This should be compared to (3.16) and (3.22). The sth element of $\boldsymbol{K}'\, d(\log \boldsymbol{p})$ can be written as $\Sigma_i\, \theta_i^s\, d(\log p_i)$, which we write as the Frisch price index

$$d(\log P'^s) = \sum_{i=1}^{n} \theta_i^s\, d(\log p_i). \tag{4.11}$$

Thus, the rth equation of (4.7) can be written, using $d(\log y_s) - d(\log P'^s) = d[\log(y_s/P'^s)]$, as

$$g_r\, d(\log z_r) = \psi^* \sum_{s=1}^{m} \theta_{rs}^*\, d\left(\log \frac{y_s}{P'^s}\right). \tag{4.12}$$

This *supply equation* describes the change in the firm's supply of the rth product, measured by the quantity component of dg_r, as a linear combination of all output price changes, each deflated by its own Frisch input price index.

4.3. Comparative statics: Input price changes

As was the case with the input demand equations of Chapter 3, interpretation of the output supply equations (4.12) amounts to a statement of the properties of the comparative statics of the firm's supply of outputs to the market when it is competitive and maximizes profit.

First, note that $d(\log P'^s)$ in (4.12) is an input price index. This means that the role of deflation in the supply equations is not to define a pure substitution effect as is the case in the input demand equations. If all input prices are unchanged so that each $d(\log P'^s)$ is zero, (4.12) becomes

$$g_r \, d(\log z_r) = \psi^* \sum_{s=1}^{m} \theta^*_{rs} \, d(\log y_s), \tag{4.13}$$

which can be regarded as describing the *expansion path* of the firm's output in response to output price changes. The role of the deflators in (4.12) is to correct the output price changes so that the expansion path is optimal. We shall express this by calling the price change $d[\log(y_s/P'^s)]$ the *input-deflated* output price change.

The deflators $d(\log P'^s)$ in (4.12) are specific for the output prices which they deflate, and are different in general from the deflator $d(\log P')$ which deflates all input price changes in the input demand equations (3.39) and (3.46). There is a simple relationship among them which is implied by (3.38) and the first two members of (3.26):

$$d(\log P') = \sum_{r=1}^{m} g_r \, d(\log P'^r). \tag{4.14}$$

This means that the input price deflator in the input demand system is the Divisia mean of the output price deflators in the output supply system of the multiproduct firm.

It should be noted that if all input and output prices increase proportionately, each $d(\log P'^s)$ is the same as each $d(\log y_s)$ in (4.12) so that $g_r \, d(\log z_r) = 0$ for each r. This is another form of the proposition that only relative prices are important to the firm. Also, if all input prices increase proportionately, all of the deflators $d(\log P')$ and $d(\log P'^s)$ are the same.

The condition (4.9) must be satisfied if the firm's production function is consistent with a competitive profit maximum. Note, however, that this is a long-run profit maximum, so that the firm will go out of business if profit, $R - C$, is negative. From (4.5) we see that this additional requirement is

$$\gamma > 1, \tag{4.15}$$

which should be compared to $\gamma > \psi$, implied by (4.9). Recall from (3.42) that ψ is related to the elasticity of γ with respect to a proportionate change in outputs. If $\psi \geq 1$, then (4.15) is a weaker condition than $\gamma > \psi$. If ψ is less than 1, then the firm can evidently attain a profit maximum which is negative. From (3.42) we see that a necessary condition for this to occur is that γ increases when outputs increase proportionately, for then it is possible to have $\psi < \gamma < 1$.

Note that this is not the case of declining marginal cost often associated with natural monopoly for the single product firm. Declining marginal cost in the multiproduct firm can be associated with a negative value of the double sum in (3.41), which implies $\psi > 1$ and γ decreasing as output increases – an entirely different situation. The situation described above is comparable to the case in the theory of the single product firm where output price is below minimum average cost, so that the firm has a profit maximum (at the output level associated with minimum average cost) which yields negative profit. In the case of the multiproduct firm, the given levels of output prices are not high enough to yield positive profit, so the firm will manufacture nothing. At some higher levels of output prices the firm would enter the market.

4.4. Comparative statics: Output price changes

We define

$$\theta_r^* = \sum_{s=1}^{m} \theta_{rs}^*, \tag{4.16}$$

and note that $\Sigma_r \theta_r^* = 1$ is implied by (4.8). The following are weighted means of the logarithmic price changes which occur in (4.12):

$$\mathrm{d}(\log Y') = \sum_{r=1}^{m} \theta_r^* \,\mathrm{d}(\log y_r), \tag{4.17}$$

$$\mathrm{d}(\log P'') = \sum_{r=1}^{m} \theta_r^* \, \mathrm{d}(\log P''). \tag{4.18}$$

When we sum (4.12) over r and use the symmetry of $\boldsymbol{\Theta}^*$ we obtain

$$\mathrm{d}(\log Z) = \psi^* \, \mathrm{d}\left(\log \frac{Y'}{P''}\right). \tag{4.19}$$

This is the *total-output decision* of the firm, which shows that ψ^* is the price elasticity of the supply of the firm's output as a whole.

Next, we multiply (4.19) by θ_r^* and subtract the result from (4.12):

$$g_r \, \mathrm{d}(\log z_r) = \theta_r^* \, \mathrm{d}(\log Z) + \psi^* \sum_{s=1}^{m} \theta_{rs}^* \, \mathrm{d}\left(\log \frac{y_s/P'^s}{Y'/P''}\right). \tag{4.20}$$

This is the *output allocation decision* for the rth product. The deflator in its price term is

$$\mathrm{d}\left(\log \frac{Y'}{P''}\right) = \sum_{r=1}^{m} \theta_r^* [\mathrm{d}(\log y_r) - \mathrm{d}(\log P'')], \tag{4.21}$$

which is the same for each input-deflated output price change in (4.20). If these corrected output price changes are proportionate, then the sum in (4.20) is zero, which shows that in the formulation (4.20) the relative input-deflated output price changes have only a substitution effect. This is in agreement with the role of prices in (3.39) and (3.46).

We therefore proceed as we did for input price substitution (see below (3.39)) and describe the rth and sth products as *specific substitutes* (*complements*) when θ_{rs}^* is negative (positive), since $\theta_{rs}^* < 0$ implies that an increase in the sth relative input-deflated output price leads to a decrease in the production of the rth product. Note in addition that θ_{ss}^* is necessarily positive so that the same relative price increase leads to an increase in the production of the sth product. It is also possible to define a *partial elasticity of substitution*[2] among outputs similar to (3.40):

$$\sigma^*_{rs} = \psi^* \frac{\theta^*_{rs} - \theta^*_r\theta^*_s}{g_r g_s}, \tag{4.22}$$

but as with (3.40) it does not appear that this is as fundamental as the concept of specific substitution and complementarity.

Division of (4.20) by g_r shows that θ^*_r/g_r is the Divisia elasticity of the rth product (the elasticity of its supply with respect to the Divisia volume index of all outputs) in the same way that θ_i/f_i is the Divisia elasticity of the ith input (see below (3.43)).[3] Since the numerator θ_i of θ_i/f_i is the marginal share of this input, it is natural to call θ^*_r the marginal share of the rth product,[4] so that the weighted means in (4.17) and (4.18) become Frisch indexes.

If all input prices remain unchanged the price changes in (4.20) become $d[\log(y_s/Y')]$. If in addition all output prices increase proportionately, the substitution term in (4.20) is zero and output changes are determined by the Divisia elasticities.

[2]This is a generalization of the elasticity of transformation considered by Powell and Gruen [63] in the same sense that there are several alternative generalizations of the two-input elasticity of substitution. I prefer the term "elasticity of substitution" for outputs as well, because the alternative appears to imply that outputs are transformed into each other, while the firm actually transforms inputs into outputs.

[3]It is shown in Appendix C that the $\geq$ sign in (4.9) becomes equal if and only if all products have unitary Divisia elasticities. Hence, the price elasticity in (4.19) becomes $\psi/(\gamma-\psi)$ in that case. Since $\theta^*_1 = g_1 = 1$ necessarily for a single product firm, this result always holds then, as was shown by Theil [79]. The excess of ψ^* over $\psi/(\gamma-\psi)$ when the Divisia elasticities are not one represents additional gains to the firm from "substitution" among outputs as it expands.

[4]This definition may be justified more directly as follows. Suppose that output prices do not change so that $d(\log Z) = d(\log R)$. Since the left-hand side of (4.20) equals $(y_r/R)\,dz_r$ and the first term on the right becomes $(\theta^*_r/R)\,dR$, θ^*_r is then the proportion of an additional revenue dollar accounted for the rth product. We shall have more to say about this when we consider revenue maximization in Chapter 5. Note that the deflator (4.21) is also a Frisch index of the input-deflated output price changes. Also, note that θ^*_r is not necessarily positive for each r. This is analogous to the input case where $\theta_i \leq 0$ is also possible.

Outputs whose Divisia elasticities are greater than one increase more rapidly than output as a whole, measured by the Divisia volume index of the outputs. Outputs whose Divisia elasticities are between zero and one increase when total output increases, but not so rapidly. It is possible for some outputs to have negative Divisia elasticities, in which case they actually decrease when the firm increases output as a whole. As was the case with inputs, we shall call such outputs *inferior.*

The substitution term in (4.20) induces additional changes in output whenever the input-deflated output price changes are not proportionate. The output changes which are determined by growth in the firm (that is, by a positive value of the Divisia volume index of output) and by price substitution can then be substituted into the input demand equations (3.39), which hold for any cost minimizing firm. Any disproportionality in output changes is then reflected in input changes as determined by the input demand system.

4.5. Properties of the cost function

The duality between cost and production functions implies that it should be possible to derive the systems (4.7) of supply equations and (3.36) of demand equations equally well from either function. This is obvious for the cost shares, which can be obtained directly from Shephard's lemma (2.29). This can be written, after multiplication by p_i/C, as

$$f_i = \frac{\partial \log C}{\partial \log p_i}. \tag{4.23}$$

In a similar way, γ can be obtained from (3.13), after which substitution of $\rho = \gamma C$ in (3.20) yields

$$g_r = \frac{1}{\gamma}\frac{\partial \log C}{\partial \log z_r}. \tag{4.24}$$

In Appendix C it is shown that the matrices of second derivatives of the cost function satisfy

$$-\psi(\boldsymbol{\Theta}-\boldsymbol{\theta}\boldsymbol{\theta}')=\frac{1}{C}\boldsymbol{P}\frac{\partial^2 C}{\partial \boldsymbol{p}\,\partial \boldsymbol{p}'}\boldsymbol{P}, \tag{4.25}$$

$$\boldsymbol{K}=\boldsymbol{P}\frac{\partial^2 C}{\partial \boldsymbol{p}\,\partial \boldsymbol{z}'}\boldsymbol{Y}^{-1}, \tag{4.26}$$

$$\psi^*\boldsymbol{\Theta}^*=\frac{1}{R}\boldsymbol{Y}\left[\frac{\partial^2 C}{\partial \boldsymbol{z}\,\partial \boldsymbol{z}'}\right]^{-1}\boldsymbol{Y}, \tag{4.27}$$

where $\boldsymbol{P}$ is the $n \times n$ diagonal matrix of input prices and $\boldsymbol{Y}$ is the $m \times m$ diagonal matrix of output prices.[5]

From (4.27) and (4.8) the coefficients θ^*_{rs} and ψ^* can be derived, while (4.26) yields the coefficients θ^r_i directly. The coefficients θ_i can then be obtained from (3.34) and ψ from (3.41), after which the coefficients θ_{ij} can be found using (4.25).

An alternative way to obtain the coefficient ψ is suggested by (3.41), which relates ψ to the matrix of the second derivatives of the logarithm of cost with respect to the logarithms of output, and by (4.27), which relates $\psi^*\boldsymbol{\Theta}^*$ to the inverse of the matrix of second derivatives of cost with respect to outputs. It is shown in Appendix C that these relationships imply

$$\frac{1}{\psi^*}\sum_{r=1}^{m}\sum_{s=1}^{m} g_r g_s \theta^{*rs}=\frac{\gamma}{\psi}-1, \tag{4.28}$$

where θ^{*rs} is the (r, s)th element of the inverse of $\boldsymbol{\Theta}^*$.

4.6. Specialized forms

4.6.1. The input–output separable firm

It will be recalled from section 3.8 that when the firm is input–output separable, eq. (3.49) holds, so that the marginal

[5]When output prices are not defined, as for cost minimization, $\boldsymbol{Y}$ can be interpreted as the diagonal matrix of marginal costs, $\partial C/\partial z_r$.

coefficients θ_i^r are the same for each output. This implies that the individual input price indexes defined in (4.11) are the same for each output and equal to the Frisch input price index (3.38):

$$\mathrm{d}(\log P'') = \mathrm{d}(\log P'). \tag{4.29}$$

It then follows that the rth supply equation (4.12) takes the form

$$g_r\,\mathrm{d}(\log z_r) = \psi^* \sum_{s=1}^{m} \theta_{rs}^*\,\mathrm{d}\left(\log \frac{y_s}{P'}\right), \tag{4.30}$$

and that the input-deflated output price changes are each deflated by the same input price index.

The price index (4.18) is also equal to (3.38),

$$\mathrm{d}(\log P'') = \mathrm{d}(\log P'), \tag{4.31}$$

when the firm is input–output separable. Thus, the total-output decision (4.19) and the output allocation decision (4.20) can be simplified to

$$\mathrm{d}(\log Z) = \psi^*\,\mathrm{d}\left(\log \frac{Y'}{P'}\right), \tag{4.32}$$

$$g_r\,\mathrm{d}(\log z_r) = \theta_r^*\,\mathrm{d}(\log Z) + \psi^* \sum_{s=1}^{m} \theta_{rs}^*\,\mathrm{d}\left(\log \frac{y_s}{Y'}\right). \tag{4.33}$$

Note that, in contrast to (4.20), eq. (4.33) contains no input price changes. Therefore, under input–output separability the output allocation decision is independent of the changes in input prices in the same way that the input allocation decision is then independent of changes in the output quantities.

Input–output separability is also reflected in the form of the cost function. McFadden [54] and various others have shown that the firm is input–output separable if and only if its cost function can be written as

$$C(z, p) = C(h_f(z), p). \tag{4.34}$$

Thus, the cost of producing an output vector z depends only on the value of the function of output $h_f(z)$, so there can be no interactions in the cost function between individual output levels and input prices. It can readily be verified, using (4.26), that (3.49) holds when (4.34) does.

4.6.2. *Output independence*

Recall from section 3.8 that when no input is a specific substitute or complement of any other input (the case of input independence), a drastic simplification of the input demand equations of the firm is achieved. A similar simplification of the output supply equations of the firm occurs if no output is a specific substitute or complement of any other output, a condition we will call *output independence*. In this case we have

$$\theta^*_{rs} = 0, \quad \text{for } r \neq s, \tag{4.35}$$

$$\theta^*_{rr} = \theta^*_r > 0, \tag{4.36}$$

and the rth supply equation (4.5) becomes

$$g_r \, \mathrm{d}(\log z_r) = \psi^* \theta^*_r \, \mathrm{d}\left(\log \frac{y_r}{P'^r}\right). \tag{4.37}$$

Thus, only the rth input-deflated output price change appears in the equation which describes the firm's supply of the rth product. The inequality in (4.36) implies that when the firm is output independent no output can be inferior.

Equations (4.35) and (4.36) imply that the matrix of normalized output price coefficients $\boldsymbol{\Theta}^*$ is diagonal; eq. (4.27) then implies that $\partial^2 C/\partial z \, \partial z'$ and its inverse are both diagonal. If this condition holds for any output vector z with positive components, the cost function must take the additive form

$$C(z, p) = \sum_{r=1}^{m} C_r(z_r, p). \tag{4.38}$$

We take output independence to be the case where $\boldsymbol{\Theta}^*$ is diagonal for all feasible output vectors; thus, if the firm is output independent, the cost function must be the sum of m cost functions, each of which describes the cost of one output.

Hall [35] has shown that (4.38) is necessary and sufficient for the firm's technology to be *nonjoint* in the following sense.[6] Consider m single product production functions

$$z_r = h_{ar}(q_1^r, \ldots, q_n^r), \qquad r = 1, \ldots, m. \tag{4.39}$$

Output independence of the multiproduct firm means that functions $h_{a1}(\cdot), \ldots, h_{am}(\cdot)$ exist so that, first, if (2.15) holds, there is a factor allocation

$$q_i^1 + \cdots + q_i^m = q_i, \qquad i = 1, \ldots, n, \tag{4.40}$$

such that (4.39) holds for each of $h_{a1}(\cdot), \ldots, h_{am}(\cdot)$ and, second, if (4.39) holds, then (2.15) holds for the values of z_r in (4.39) and of q_i in (4.40).

In other words, output independence means that the multiproduct firm with technology (2.15) could be broken up into m single product firms, each with one of the production functions (4.39), and that the latter firms, independently adjusting inputs and outputs so as to maximize profit, would use the same

[6] Hall's use of the term "nonjoint" follows Hirota and Kuga [41] and Samuelson [68], who originally considered the two-output case: the meaning is that there are no economies or diseconomies of jointness in producing the outputs. When three or more outputs are produced, this term becomes ambiguous because it is possible for two or more groups of outputs to be produced with no economies or diseconomies of jointness among the groups. Thus, production can be simultaneously nonjoint among the groups and joint within the groups. Use of the term "output independence" when all goods are produced nonjointly permits the term "block independence" to be used for the case of nonjoint groups. This case was considered by Burmeister and Turnovsky [19] who extended the approach of Samuelson [68] and Hirota and Kuga [41]. All of these results describe complex restrictions on the derivatives of the production function which must hold under independence or block independence. Hall's result cited above is intuitively appealing and much easier to apply.

aggregate level of each input and produce the same aggregate level of each output as the multiproduct firm.

The relationship of the additive form (4.38) of the cost function to the equivalence in this sense of the multiproduct production function (2.15) and the single product production functions (4.39) is clear if the duality of cost and production is considered. If m single product firms with the production functions (4.39) exist, each by duality has a cost function $C_r(z_r, \boldsymbol{p})$. Merging these firms into one multiproduct firm when there are no economies or diseconomies of jointness implies that (4.38) is the cost function of the multiproduct firm; duality then yields the corresponding multiproduct production constraint. If there are economies of jointness, we will have $C(z, \boldsymbol{p}) < \Sigma_r C_r(z_r, \boldsymbol{p})$, which means that the multiproduct production function dual to $C(z, \boldsymbol{p})$ is not equivalent to (4.39) in the sense described above. If there are diseconomies of jointness, a similar argument applies.

The simple form of the supply equation (4.37) when the firm is output independent follows from the fact that the marginal cost of the rth output depends only on input prices and the level of the rth output; this follows from (4.38). It should be noted that (4.38) implies that it is possible when production is nonjoint to measure the cost of each output in the multiproduct firm. The converse is obviously also true from Hall's theorem: when production of the rth product is joint with other products, it is impossible to measure its cost because this cost is also jointly attributable to other outputs.

4.6.3. Homotheticity

The simple results which we obtained in section 3.8 when the firm is homothetic in inputs have no simple extension to the case when the firm is homothetic in outputs. In fact, it will be convenient to defer discussion of this case until we consider the revenue maximizing firm in Chapter 5.

It is well known that homotheticity in the single product firm implies that the cost function can be decomposed multiplicatively into a unit cost function and a function of output alone,

$$C(z, \boldsymbol{p}) = h_c(z)C(1, \boldsymbol{p}), \tag{4.41}$$

where $h_c(\cdot)$ is the same function which appears in (2.35), if we reinterpret z as a scalar and $h_a(\cdot)$ in (2.35) as a linearly homogeneous function of $\boldsymbol{q}$.[7] When the multiproduct firm is both homothetic in inputs and input–output separable, a similar decomposition is possible:

$$C(\boldsymbol{z}, \boldsymbol{p}) = h_c(\boldsymbol{z})\lambda(\boldsymbol{p}). \tag{4.42}$$

Here $\lambda(\boldsymbol{p})$ can be interpreted as $C(h_f(\boldsymbol{z}), \boldsymbol{p})$ in (4.34) with $h_f(\boldsymbol{z})$ equal to some constant, and $h_c(\cdot)$ is the same function as in (2.35) with $h_a(\cdot)$ linearly homogeneous. In the more general case when the firm is homothetic in inputs, but not input–output separable, a more complex result proved by McFadden [54] is that the cost function is multiplicatively separable into a "unit cost function" which depends only on input prices and the relative proportions of the outputs (i.e., the direction of the output ray), and a function of the outputs.

The forms of the cost function under output independence and input–output separability imply a rather surprising result when the firm is both input–output separable and output independent.[8] When the firm is input–output separable, its cost function must have the form (4.34); when it is output independent its cost function must be additively separable, as in (4.38). When both apply, the implication is that the cost function must take the form

$$C(\boldsymbol{z}, \boldsymbol{p}) = \lambda(\boldsymbol{p}) \sum_{r=1}^{m} h_{cr}(z_r). \tag{4.43}$$

[7]When (2.1) is homothetic, there is an increasing function $s(\cdot)$ such that $s[h_a(\boldsymbol{q})]$ in (2.1) is linearly homogeneous (see section 2.4). We interpret $h_c(z)$ and $h_a(\boldsymbol{q})$ in (2.35) as $s(z)$ and $s[h_a(\boldsymbol{q})]$ in (2.1). Duality of cost and production functions for this case and that of (4.42) becomes duality of the unit cost function and $h_a(\boldsymbol{q})$.

[8]Hall [35] has proved this result for a special case. A rigorous proot appears in Appendix C of this volume.

Comparison of (4.42) and (4.43) indicates that a firm which is both input–output separable and output independent must also be homothetic in inputs. Moreover, it is possible to write the production technology of this firm as

$$\sum_{r=1}^{m} h_{cr}(z_r) = h_a(\boldsymbol{q}), \tag{4.44}$$

where $h_a(\cdot)$ is linearly homogeneous.

In addition, (4.38) and (4.33) imply that $C_r(z_r, \boldsymbol{p}) = h_{cr}(z_r)\lambda(\boldsymbol{p})$. Comparison of this result to (4.41) with z interpreted as z_r then implies that each of the m single product firms into which the output independent, input–output separable firm can be decomposed is itself homothetic, and that the production constraint of the rth can be written

$$h_{cr}(z_r) = h_a(q_1^r, \ldots, q_n^r), \tag{4.45}$$

where $h_a(\cdot)$ is the same function as in (4.44).

This result does not imply that each component single product firm has the same production technology, since $h_{cr}(\cdot)$ may be different for each r. It does, however, imply that each component firm combines inputs in the same way and, considering (4.25), that each component firm has the same substitution reactions to input price changes.

CHAPTER 5

The revenue maximizing firm

Cost minimization is of interest to economists because it applies to any firm which faces competitive markets for its inputs, as long as the firm's objective (e.g. profit maximization) is consistent with minimizing cost.[1] It may be the case, however, that input markets are not competitive: this is the case of the monopsonistic firm. Revenue maximization for given input levels and output prices will be a goal of any profit maximizing firm which faces competitive output markets, as long as its input markets are sufficiently uncomplicated. If inputs are rationed or, more generally, if the firm faces an upward sloping supply curve for one or more inputs, the firm will practice revenue maximization if its output prices are given.

In the single product firm, maximizing revenue for a given output price amounts to maximizing output. Since the input quantities are also given, maximum output can be determined trivially by consulting the production function. In the multiproduct firm there is a genuine problem of choice because of the opportunity of substitution among outputs; hence, revenue maximization is intrinsically a "multiproduct" problem.

The duality between cost and production functions permitted us in Chapter 4 to consider competitive profit maximization by using cost minimization as an intermediate step. The similar duality between revenue and production functions permits us to

[1]This excludes the case mentioned at the beginning of Chapter 4 (see fn. 1), in which output markets are subject to rate-of-return regulation. Similar exclusions no doubt exist for revenue maximization if input markets are regulated in suitably complex ways.

take a different route in this chapter: first we consider revenue maximization and then we use the revenue function to study competitive profit maximization. The result describes changes in the firm's supply of outputs and demand for inputs in an alternative system of equations in which the roles of inputs and outputs have been interchanged.

5.1. Conditions for a revenue maximum

We return to the firm whose technology is represented by the output homogeneous production function (2.15). Its objective is now to maximize revenue, $R = \Sigma_r y_r z_r$, by varying $z = (z_1, \ldots, z_m)'$ for given $\boldsymbol{y}$ and $\boldsymbol{q}$. We construct the Lagrangian $\bar{L}(z, \bar{\rho}) = \Sigma_r y_r z_r + \bar{\rho} h(\boldsymbol{q}, z)$ and differentiate with respect to $\log z_r$:

$$\frac{\partial \bar{L}}{\partial \log z_r} = y_r z_r + \bar{\rho} \frac{\partial h}{\partial \log z_r}. \tag{5.1}$$

By setting each such derivative equal to zero,

$$y_r z_r + \bar{\rho} \frac{\partial h}{\partial \log z_r} = 0, \tag{5.2}$$

we obtain m equations which, together with $h(\boldsymbol{q}, z) = 0$, are assumed to yield unique positive values of the z_r's and $\bar{\rho}$.

Summation of (5.2) over r yields, using $\Sigma_r \partial h / \partial \log z_r = -1$ (see (2.16)),

$$\bar{\rho} = \sum_{r=1}^{m} y_r z_r = R, \tag{5.3}$$

so that the multiplier $\bar{\rho}$ can be interpreted directly as revenue. This should be compared to the multiplier ρ in (3.1), which can be interpreted as revenue when profit is maximized (see (4.2)). We let $g_r = y_r z_r / R$ be the revenue share of the rth product and use (5.2) and (5.3) to confirm that (3.21) holds at the optimum for the revenue maximizing as well as the cost minimizing firm.

The derivative of (5.1) with respect to $\log z_s$ is

$$\frac{\partial^2 \bar{L}}{\partial \log z_r \, \partial \log z_s} = \delta_{rs} y_r z_r + \bar{\rho} \frac{\partial^2 h}{\partial \log z_r \, \partial \log z_s}. \tag{5.4}$$

Conversion to matrix notation after use of (5.3) then yields

$$\frac{\partial^2 \bar{L}}{\partial \log \boldsymbol{z} \, \partial \log \boldsymbol{z}'} = R(\boldsymbol{G} + \boldsymbol{H}^{**}), \tag{5.5}$$

where $\boldsymbol{G}$ is interpreted as in Chapter 3 (see below (3.33)) and $\boldsymbol{H}^{**}$ is defined in (2.18). It is not possible to assume that (5.5) is negative definite (the usual sufficient second-order condition for a maximum) because $\boldsymbol{\iota}^{*\prime}(\boldsymbol{G} + \boldsymbol{H}^{**})\boldsymbol{\iota}^* = 1$ follows from $\Sigma_r g_r = 1$ and $\boldsymbol{H}^{**}\boldsymbol{\iota}^* = \boldsymbol{0}$ (see (2.26)).[2] Therefore we assume the weaker necessary second-order condition for a maximum: that the Hessian matrix (5.5) of the Lagrangian be negative definite with respect to vectors $\mathrm{d}(\log \boldsymbol{z})$ of output changes which obey the constraint implied by the production function (see, for example, Takayama [75, p. 125]). This is pursued in Appendix D, where it is shown that this assumption implies that $\boldsymbol{G} + \boldsymbol{H}^{**}$ is nonsingular with one positive and $m-1$ negative characteristic roots.[3]

The optimum output quantities of the revenue maximizing firm can now be written as a function of the quantities of inputs available to it and the prices it receives for its outputs:

$$z_r = z_r(\boldsymbol{q}, \boldsymbol{y}), \qquad r = 1, \ldots, m. \tag{5.6}$$

[2]Note that this result and others in Appendix D concerning $\boldsymbol{G} + \boldsymbol{H}^{**}$ follow from the output homogeneity of (2.15). The problem is not an artifact of that particular representation of the production technology, but a fundamental characteristic of revenue maximization. Use of the output homogeneous production function makes the problem obvious and also simplifies its solution.

[3]These characteristic roots are taken with respect to the matrix $\boldsymbol{G}$ rather than the identity matrix. For further details see Appendix D.

In addition, since revenue is $R = \Sigma_r y_r z_r$, we can write the amount of revenue received by the firm as a function of the same variables:

$$R = \sum_{r=1}^{m} y_r z_r(\boldsymbol{q}, \boldsymbol{y}) = R(\boldsymbol{q}, \boldsymbol{y}). \tag{5.7}$$

5.2. Shadow cost and input shares

Recall that in section 3.2 we considered the effect on the outputs, when they are constrained to change proportionately, of a proportionate change in inputs. This effect, the elasticity of scale, was found to be equal to $\Sigma_i \partial h/\partial \log q_i$ (see (3.7)) and also to the reciprocal of $\gamma = \rho/C$. Here neither ρ nor C is defined, but we can take (3.9) as defining γ strictly in terms of the production function.

We consider the derivative of (5.7) with respect to the ith input:

$$\frac{\partial R}{\partial q_i} = \sum_{r=1}^{m} y_r \frac{\partial z_r}{\partial q_i} = \frac{R}{q_i} \sum_{r=1}^{m} g_r \frac{\partial \log z_r}{\partial \log q_i}. \tag{5.8}$$

Since the production constraint should hold both before and after a change in inputs (which are arbitrarily specified for the revenue maximizing firm), we can take the derivative of $h(\boldsymbol{q}, \boldsymbol{z}) = 0$ with respect to $\log q_i$, holding the other inputs constant and allowing the outputs to vary:

$$\frac{\partial h}{\partial \log q_i} + \sum_{r=1}^{m} \frac{\partial h}{\partial \log z_r} \frac{\partial \log z_r}{\partial \log q_i} = 0.$$

It follows from (3.21) that this is equivalent to

$$\frac{\partial h}{\partial \log q_i} = \sum_{r=1}^{m} g_r \frac{\partial \log z_r}{\partial \log q_i}. \tag{5.9}$$

Substitution of (5.9) into (5.8) then yields

$$q_i \frac{\partial R}{\partial q_i} = R \frac{\partial h}{\partial \log q_i}. \tag{5.10}$$

Summation of (5.10) over i yields, using (3.9),

$$\frac{R}{\gamma} = \sum_{i=1}^{n} q_i \frac{\partial R}{\partial q_i}. \tag{5.11}$$

This indicates that R/γ can be interpreted as the marginal revenue[4] of a proportionate increase in inputs. It can also be interpreted as the *shadow cost*, with each input evaluated at a shadow price equal to its marginal revenue. We use $\bar{C}$ as a symbol for this shadow cost,

$$\bar{C} = \sum_{i=1}^{n} q_i \frac{\partial R}{\partial q_i}, \tag{5.12}$$

and define f_i as the share of the ith input in shadow cost

$$f_i = \frac{q_i}{\bar{C}} \frac{\partial R}{\partial q_i}. \tag{5.13}$$

Now, (5.10), (5.12), and (5.13) can be used to show that (3.15) holds at the point of the firm's optimum for revenue maximization.

We divide (5.11) by R to obtain

$$\sum_{i=1}^{n} \frac{\partial \log R}{\partial \log q_i} = \frac{1}{\gamma}, \tag{5.14}$$

[4]Here "marginal revenue" is marginal with respect to inputs and not, as is the case when monopoly is discussed, with respect to outputs. Note that the marginal revenue of an individual input can be interpreted as the value of its marginal product, as shown by the first two members of (5.8). Thus, shadow cost can also be interpreted as the value of the marginal product of the input bundle, i.e., the value of an additional dose of inputs used in the same proportion as the original inputs.

which shows that γ can also be interpreted as the reciprocal of the elasticity of revenue with respect to a proportionate change in inputs.[5] Also, (5.11) and (5.12) together imply

$$\gamma = R/\bar{C}, \tag{5.15}$$

which should be compared to (3.8) and (4.5).

5.3. Revenue maximizing supply equations

As was the case for the cost minimizing firm, it is possible to differentiate the first-order conditions with respect to the uncontrolled variables (in this case input quantities and output prices) to obtain a partitioned matrix equation which can be solved for the derivatives of the controlled variables (now the output quantities). A result similar to those of section 3.5 is that the inverse of the Hessian matrix (5.5) of the Lagrangian figures prominently in this solution. Since $\boldsymbol{G} + \boldsymbol{H}^{**}$ is nonsingular, we can define

$$\bar{\boldsymbol{\Theta}}^* = [\bar{\theta}^*_{rs}] = \boldsymbol{G}(\boldsymbol{G} + \boldsymbol{H}^{**})^{-1}\boldsymbol{G}. \tag{5.16}$$

The following result is proved in Appendix D:

$$\bar{\boldsymbol{\Theta}}^* \boldsymbol{\iota}^* = \boldsymbol{g}. \tag{5.17}$$

It follows immediately that

$$\boldsymbol{\iota}^{*\prime} \bar{\boldsymbol{\Theta}}^* \boldsymbol{\iota}^* = \sum_{r=1}^{m} \sum_{s=1}^{m} \bar{\theta}^*_{rs} = 1. \tag{5.18}$$

In addition, $\bar{\boldsymbol{\Theta}}^*$ has one positive and $m-1$ negative characteristic roots,[6] and the matrix $\bar{\boldsymbol{\Theta}}^* - \boldsymbol{g}\boldsymbol{g}'$ is negative semidefinite.

[5] For other interpretations see section 3.2.

[6] These roots are also taken with respect to $\boldsymbol{G}$ (see fn. 3 in this chapter). The positive root is necessarily unity.

In Appendix D it is shown that the solution for the derivatives of outputs with respect to input quantities and output prices can be written in the following form:

$$G\frac{\partial \log z}{\partial \log \boldsymbol{y}'} = -(\bar{\boldsymbol{\Theta}}^* - \boldsymbol{g}\boldsymbol{g}'), \tag{5.19}$$

$$G\frac{\partial \log z}{\partial \log \boldsymbol{q}'} = \frac{1}{\gamma}\boldsymbol{g}\boldsymbol{f}' - \bar{\boldsymbol{\Theta}}^*\boldsymbol{G}^{-1}\boldsymbol{H}^{*\prime}, \tag{5.20}$$

which should be compared to (3.27) and (3.28).

We define

$$\bar{\theta}_r^i = \frac{\partial(y_r z_r)/\partial q_i}{\partial R/\partial q_i} \tag{5.21}$$

as the share of the rth output in the marginal revenue of the ith input. This should be compared to (3.25) for the cost minimizing firm. It is shown in Appendix D that the $m \times n$ matrix of these coefficients, which we shall call $\bar{\boldsymbol{K}}$, can be written

$$\bar{\boldsymbol{K}} = [\bar{\theta}_r^i] = \boldsymbol{g}\boldsymbol{\iota}' - \gamma\bar{\boldsymbol{\Theta}}^*\boldsymbol{G}^{-1}\boldsymbol{H}^{*\prime}\boldsymbol{F}^{-1}. \tag{5.22}$$

Substitution into (5.20) yields

$$G\frac{\partial \log z}{\partial \log \boldsymbol{q}'} = \frac{1}{\gamma}\bar{\boldsymbol{K}}\boldsymbol{F}. \tag{5.23}$$

Note that (5.17) together with (2.27) implies that premultiplication of (5.22) by $\boldsymbol{\iota}^{*\prime}$ yields

$$\boldsymbol{\iota}^{*\prime}\bar{\boldsymbol{K}} = \boldsymbol{\iota}', \tag{5.24}$$

so that the sum of the marginal output shares is one for each input, in agreement with (5.21).

As in section 3.5, we can now take the differential in logarithmic form of the matrix version of (5.6) in order to express changes in the outputs in terms of changes in the input quantities and the output prices:

$$\mathrm{d}(\log \boldsymbol{z}) = \frac{\partial \log \boldsymbol{z}}{\partial \log \boldsymbol{q}'}\,\mathrm{d}(\log \boldsymbol{q}) + \frac{\partial \log \boldsymbol{z}}{\partial \log \boldsymbol{y}'}\,\mathrm{d}(\log \boldsymbol{y}).$$

We premultiply this by $\boldsymbol{G}$ and substitute from (5.23) and (5.19):

$$\boldsymbol{G}\,\mathrm{d}(\log \boldsymbol{z}) = \frac{1}{\gamma}\bar{\boldsymbol{K}}\boldsymbol{F}\,\mathrm{d}(\log \boldsymbol{q}) - (\bar{\boldsymbol{\Theta}}^* - \boldsymbol{g}\boldsymbol{g}')\,\mathrm{d}(\log \boldsymbol{y}). \tag{5.25}$$

The rth element of the vector on the left is $g_r\,\mathrm{d}(\log z_r)$, which is the quantity component of the change in the rth revenue share (see (4.10)). The rth element of the price term in (5.25) may be written $-\Sigma_s\,(\bar{\theta}^*_{rs} - g_r g_s)\,\mathrm{d}(\log y_s)$. Now, using (5.22), we can write the supply equation for the rth product as

$$g_r\,\mathrm{d}(\log z_r) = \frac{1}{\gamma}\sum_{i=1}^{n} \bar{\theta}^i_r f_i\,\mathrm{d}(\log q_i) - \sum_{s=1}^{m} (\bar{\theta}^*_{rs} - g_r g_s)\,\mathrm{d}(\log y_s). \tag{5.26}$$

This equation should be compared to (3.37) for the ith input of the cost minimizing firm. It describes the change in the supply of the rth product, measured by the quantity component of $\mathrm{d}g_r$, in terms of input changes and output price changes. We shall call this the rth *supply equation* of the revenue maximizing firm or, when it is important to distinguish, the rth equation of the *revenue based supply system*.

5.4. Comparative statics: Price changes

Interpretation of the supply equations (5.26) for all r can be regarded, in a way similar to that explained in Chapters 3 and 4, as a discussion of the comparative statics of the revenue maximizing firm. Much of the interpretation of the revenue maximizing firm is closely parallel to the corresponding interpretation of the cost minimizing firm in Chapter 3. There are some differences, however, and we shall focus most closely on these.

Equation (5.17) can be written in scalar form as

$$\sum_{s=1}^{m} \bar{\theta}^*_{rs} = g_r, \tag{5.27}$$

which implies that, when inputs are held constant, proportionate output price changes in (5.26) have no effect on output. This is the revenue maximizing firm's version of homogeneity in prices. The fact that the matrix $\bar{\boldsymbol{\Theta}}^* - \boldsymbol{gg}'$ is negative semidefinite implies that the coefficient $-(\bar{\theta}^*_{rr} - g_r^2)$ of the rth price change in (5.26) is positive: the effect of an increase in the rth price is increased production of the rth product if all other prices and the input quantities remain unchanged. The symmetry of the same matrix implies that cross-price effects are symmetric: this is the revenue maximizing firm's version of Slutsky symmetry.

We take the sum of (4.10) over r, using $\Sigma_r g_r = 1$, to obtain

$$\mathrm{d}(\log R) = \sum_{r=1}^{m} g_r \,\mathrm{d}(\log z_r) + \sum_{r=1}^{m} g_r \,\mathrm{d}(\log y_r). \tag{5.28}$$

This is the Divisia decomposition of the change in revenue which implies not only that $\mathrm{d}(\log Z)$ in (3.24) is the Divisia volume index of the outputs, but also that

$$\mathrm{d}(\log Y) = \sum_{r=1}^{m} g_r \,\mathrm{d}(\log y_r) \tag{5.29}$$

is the Divisia price index of the outputs. Since $\bar{\boldsymbol{\Theta}}^* - \boldsymbol{gg}' = \bar{\boldsymbol{\Theta}}^*(\boldsymbol{I} - \boldsymbol{\iota}^*\boldsymbol{g}')$ holds in view of (5.17) the rth element of $-(\bar{\boldsymbol{\Theta}}^* - \boldsymbol{gg}')\,\mathrm{d}(\log \boldsymbol{y})$ equals

$$-\sum_{s=1}^{m} \bar{\theta}^*_{rs}[\mathrm{d}(\log y_s) - \mathrm{d}(\log Y)].$$

We substitute this for the price term in (5.26) to obtain

$$g_r \, d(\log z_r) = \frac{1}{\gamma} \sum_{i=1}^{n} \bar{\theta}^i_r f_i \, d(\log q_i) - \sum_{s=1}^{m} \bar{\theta}^*_{rs} \, d\left(\log \frac{y_s}{Y}\right). \tag{5.30}$$

This equation, to be compared to (3.39) for the ith input, describes the firm's supply of the rth output in terms of changes in the inputs and changes in relative output prices.

As in (3.39), the relative price changes in (5.30) each vanish when absolute prices change proportionately. This indicates that the price term in (5.30) is a pure substitution effect. Note, however, that there are three significant differences between the substitution terms in (3.39) and (5.30). First, there is no normalizing coefficient in (5.30). Second, the deflator in (5.30) is a Divisia rather than a Frisch index. Third, the matrix of substitution coefficients $[\bar{\theta}^*_{rs}]$ in (5.30) is not definite.

The first and second of these differences are artifacts caused by the use of the output homogeneous production constraint (2.15). In Appendix D it is shown that use of the input homogeneous production constraint (2.12) instead leads to another representation of the matrix $\bar{\boldsymbol{\Theta}}^* - \boldsymbol{gg}'$ which involves a normalizing coefficient similar to ψ in (3.39) and leads to deflation by a marginally weighted index of price changes. However, the square matrix which corresponds to $\boldsymbol{\Theta}$ in (3.27) and $\bar{\boldsymbol{\Theta}}^*$ in (5.19) is not in general definite, but instead has one characteristic root of different sign from the others.

In a similar way, use of the input homogeneous production constraint (2.12) in the Lagrangian for cost minimization leads to an alternative representation of the matrix $\psi(\boldsymbol{\Theta} - \boldsymbol{\theta\theta}')$ which implies Divisia deflation of input price changes and does not involve a normalizing coefficient. In this case, however, the square matrix can be assumed to be positive definite.[7]

The conclusion we have to draw is that the question of

[7]This matrix can be written as $\psi(\boldsymbol{\Theta} - \boldsymbol{\theta\theta}') + \boldsymbol{ff}'$ which is the sum of two positive semidefinite matrices. Summation of its elements yields 1 because the sum of the elements of $\psi(\boldsymbol{\Theta} - \boldsymbol{\theta\theta}')$ is zero. Also, postmultiplication by $\boldsymbol{\iota}$ yields $\boldsymbol{f}$, which is similar to (5.17).

whether Frisch or Divisia deflation is required, with its correlate of whether a normalizing coefficient is necessary, is a matter of convenience. Either is a satisfactory representation of the firm's substitution behavior. The "maverick" root of $\bar{\boldsymbol{\Theta}}^*$, on the other hand, is an intrinsic part of revenue maximization, and requires interpretation.

The chief implication of this maverick root is that it is not necessary that the diagonal elements of $-\bar{\boldsymbol{\Theta}}^*$ be positive. Thus, when the substitution effect of relative price changes is studied, as in (5.30), it is not necessarily the case that an increase in the rth relative price leads to an increase in production of the rth good when all other relative prices are kept constant.

To understand why this can be the case, we have to consider more carefully what price deflation accomplishes in the firm. Suppose that the firm has optimized its output by maximizing revenue for given inputs and output prices, so that its revenue is $R = \Sigma_r y_r z_r$. Next, suppose that one of the prices, say y_1, increases to $y_1(1+\delta)$, so that $\mathrm{d}y_1 = \delta y_1$ and $\mathrm{d}(\log y_1) = \delta$. The effect of this, if the firm continues to produce the same output quantities, is to raise revenue by a quantity $\delta y_1 z_1$; revenue will be raised even more when price substitution is taken into account.

Since only y_1 has changed, the Divisia output price index is $g_1\,\mathrm{d}(\log y_1) = g_1\delta$. Deflation of the output prices by their Divisia index then implies $\mathrm{d}[\log(y_1/Y)] = (1-g_1)\delta$ and $\mathrm{d}[\log(y_r/Y)] = -g_1\delta$ for $r \neq 1$. The corresponding absolute price levels are then $y_1' = [1+(1-g_1)\delta]y_1$ and $y_r' = (1-g_1\delta)y_r$ for $r \neq 1$.[8] The original levels of production when evaluated at these new prices yield a revenue equal to the sum of $y_1'z_1 = y_1z_1 + (1-g_1)\delta y_1 z_1$ and $y_r'z_r = y_r z_r - g_1\delta y_r z_r$ for all $r \neq 1$. When this sum is evaluated, it is readily seen that $\Sigma_r y_r' z_r = \Sigma_r y_r z_r = R$.

Thus, the effect of Divisia deflation in the revenue maximizing firm is to provide a set of compensated prices which yield the same revenue at the original output levels as it enjoyed before

[8]These levels are, of course, approximate for finite δ. If we regard δ as infinitesimal, the result is exact. Note that an implication of this line of reasoning is that it is impossible to have only one relative price change.

the price change took place. In a similar way, the effect of Divisia deflation in the cost minimizing firm is to yield a set of compensated input prices which will make the firm's inputs cost the same as they did before the price change took place.

Now it is possible to understand why the effect of a relative price increase may be to lower output of the particular good if other associated relative price changes are disregarded. To do this we consult fig. 5.1, which applies to the two-output case. The firm has inputs which enable it to produce any combination of outputs which lies on the transformation surface T. Originally, prices are such that it chooses to produce the combination represented by the point Z_0; i.e. the line AE has slope $-y_1/y_2$ and corresponds to all combinations of outputs which would produce the same revenue at those prices. Next, we suppose that the price of z_1 increases, so that the new family of constant revenue lines has the same slope as BD. This implies that the new optimum combination of outputs is represented by the point Z_1; this point corresponds to greater production of z_1 and less of z_2, as we would expect, and as is implied by the

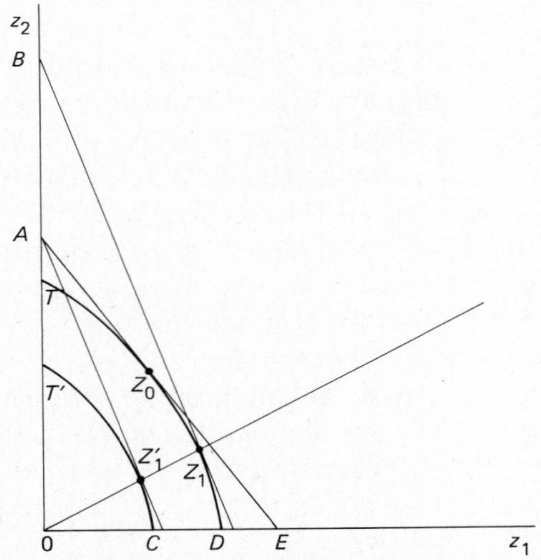

Figure 5.1. The effect of a relative price change on output.

semidefiniteness of $-(\bar{\boldsymbol{\Theta}}^* - \boldsymbol{gg}')$, the matrix of coefficients of the absolute price changes.

In the relative price version (5.30), however, we are interested in the effect of the change in relative prices, and in particular we are interested in the effect of the first relative price change on production of the first output. Since the effect of introducing relative prices is to keep revenue constant, it appears that the appropriate constant revenue line to consider is AC, which has the same slope as BD so that relative prices are the same as for the undeflated new prices, and z_2 intercept A so that it represents the same level of revenue as AE.

This revenue line, of course, is not tangent to T. If we reduce the scale of T, keeping the same shape, until the scaled down version T' is tangent to AC, we obtain the point Z_1', which also lies on the ray OZ_1. Note that reducing the scale of T can be thought of conceptually as reducing the available inputs to such a level that only the same revenue as before the price change is possible.

The point Z_1' represents the amounts of z_1 and z_2 which the firm would produce if only the first relative price had changed. However, the second relative price has also changed, and the effect of this second change is to expand production out to Z_1. Alternatively, we can regard this procedure as splitting the overall change from Z_0 to Z_1 into two parts, somewhat similar to the income and substitution effects in consumption theory. The first part is the change from Z_0 to Z_1', which represents the effect of a price change when production is "scaled down" to keep revenue constant; the second part is the expansion from Z_1' to Z_1 which represents the revenue effect.

The z_1 coordinate of Z_1' is smaller than that of Z_0, which indicates that this diagram is an example of the case which occurs when a diagonal element of $-\bar{\boldsymbol{\Theta}}^*$ is negative. This is possible because of the curvature of the transformation surface T which is concave to the origin. When we consider a similar analysis for cost minimization using fig. 5.2, we begin with an isoquant S, which represents all combinations of inputs which can be used to produce the given quantities of outputs. Prices

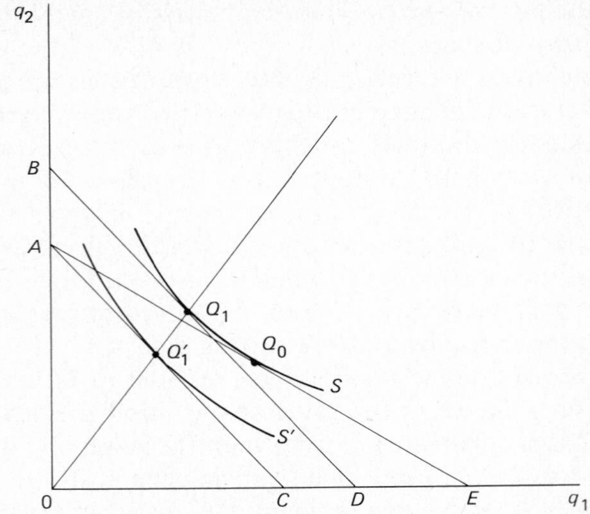

Figure 5.2. The effect of a relative price change on input.

are originally such that input demand is represented by the point Q_0; the constant cost line through this point is AE. When the price of q_1 is raised so that the new family of constant cost lines is parallel to BD, production shifts so that the new levels of input demand are represented by Q_1, which indicates increased use of q_2 and decreased use of q_1, as we would expect. Now when we draw a line parallel to BD through point A to represent the effect of the first relative price and scale down the isoquant to S', we obtain the new point Q_1' which represents input demand if production is reduced to permit cost to remain the same as before.

It is evident that the convexity of the isoquant S to the origin in fig. 5.2 implies that Q_1' necessarily has a q_1 coordinate which is less than that of Q_0. Thus, for cost minimization, relative and absolute price effects must have the same sign. In fact, the way fig. 5.2 is drawn implies that the q_1 coordinate of Q_1' must also be less than that of Q_1. This is a result of the fact that we were analyzing the effects of Divisia deflation of prices. If instead we considered Frisch deflation, the effect on fig. 5.2 would be that S' would be another isoquant, not necessarily of the same shape as S, and that the ray OQ_1 would be converted to a not necessarily linear expansion path of the firm's use of inputs as outputs expand proportionately. Essentially the same remarks apply to fig. 5.1.

5.5. Comparative statics: Volume changes

In contrast to the behavior of the revenue maximizing firm in response to nonproportional price changes, the behavior of the revenue maximizing firm in response to volume changes is essentially the same as that of the cost minimizing firm, if we take into account the interchange of the roles of inputs and outputs.

It is readily verified that the substitution term in (5.30) vanishes when summed over r. Using $\Sigma_r \bar{\theta}^i_r = 1$, (3.24) and (3.19),[9] we find that the sum of (5.30) over r is

$$\mathrm{d}(\log Z) = \frac{1}{\gamma}\,\mathrm{d}(\log Q), \tag{5.31}$$

which is equivalent to the total-input decision (3.43) of the cost minimizing firm.

We define $\bar{\theta}^*_r$ as the weighted sum of the marginal shares $\bar{\theta}^i_r$ using the factor shares f_i as weights:

$$\bar{\theta}^*_r = \sum_{i=1}^{n} f_i \bar{\theta}^i_r = \frac{1}{\bar{C}} \sum_{i=1}^{n} \frac{\partial (y_r z_r)}{\partial \log q_i}, \tag{5.32}$$

where the third member follows from (5.21) and (5.13). This should be compared to (3.26) for inputs, and indicates that $\bar{\theta}^*_r$ can be regarded as the share of the rth output in shadow cost or

[9]Note that from (5.13) we obtain $\mathrm{d}f_i = f_i\,\mathrm{d}(\log q_i) + f_i\,\mathrm{d}(\log \partial R/\partial q_i) - f_i\,\mathrm{d}(\log \bar{C})$. This yields $\mathrm{d}(\log \bar{C}) = \Sigma_i f_i\,\mathrm{d}(\log q_i) + \Sigma_i f_i\,\mathrm{d}(\log \partial R/\partial q_i)$, which shows that (3.19) is the implied Divisia volume index of the inputs here also.

equivalently as the share of the rth product in the marginal revenue of a proportionate increase in inputs, or the rth *marginal share.*[10] We let $\bar{\boldsymbol{\theta}}^* = (\bar{\theta}_1^*, \ldots, \bar{\theta}_m^*)'$, so that the first two members of (5.32) can be written for all r as

$$\bar{\boldsymbol{K}}\boldsymbol{f} = \bar{\boldsymbol{\theta}}^*. \tag{5.33}$$

We multiply (5.31) by $\bar{\theta}_r^*$ and substitute the result into (5.30):

$$g_r \, \mathrm{d}(\log z_r) = \bar{\theta}_r^* \, \mathrm{d}(\log Z) + \frac{1}{\gamma} \sum_{i=1}^{n} f_i(\bar{\theta}_r^i - \bar{\theta}_r^*) \, \mathrm{d}(\log q_i) - \sum_{s=1}^{m} \bar{\theta}_{rs}^* \, \mathrm{d}\left(\log \frac{y_s}{Y}\right). \tag{5.34}$$

As in section 3.7, we note that $\mathrm{d}(\log Q)$ in (3.19) and $\bar{\theta}_r^*$ in (5.32) are weighted means, with the f_i's as weights, of the $\mathrm{d}(\log q_i)$'s and $\bar{\theta}_r^i$'s respectively. The associated covariance is

$$\bar{\Gamma}_r = \sum_{i=1}^{n} f_i(\bar{\theta}_r^i - \bar{\theta}_r^*) \, [\mathrm{d}(\log q_i) - \mathrm{d}(\log Q)], \tag{5.35}$$

which we substitute in (5.34):

$$g_r \, \mathrm{d}(\log z_r) = \bar{\theta}_r^* \, \mathrm{d}(\log Z) + \frac{1}{\gamma} \bar{\Gamma}_r - \sum_{s=1}^{m} \bar{\theta}_{rs}^* \, \mathrm{d}\left(\log \frac{y_s}{Y}\right). \tag{5.36}$$

This equation should be compared to (3.46) for inputs.

The supply equation (5.36) implies an alternative definition $\bar{\theta}_r^*/g_r$ of the Divisia elasticity of the rth product. This definition does not in general coincide with the one given in section 4.4. In (5.35) we have $\bar{\Gamma}_r = 0$ when the input changes are proportionate, so that the term $\bar{\theta}_r^* \, \mathrm{d}(\log Z)$ in (5.36) is the effect of a propor-

[10]In section 4.4 we defined another "marginal" output share, θ_r^*. It is evident from (5.32) that $\bar{\theta}_r^*$ is a true marginal output share, but in (shadow) cost rather than in revenue. The relationship between these shares will be clarified below and in Chapter 6.

tionate change in *inputs* on g_r d(log z_r) when output prices also change proportionately. In (4.20) the term θ_r^* d(log Z) is the effect of a proportionate change in *input prices* on g_r d(log z_r) when output prices also change proportionately (but in a different proportion from the input prices).

5.6. Profit maximization

Now we follow a line of argument parallel to that of Chapter 4 to provide an alternative analysis of profit maximization. The results are closely similar to those of Chapter 4, so we shall present them rather briefly.

5.6.1. Conditions for a profit maximum

We suppose that the vector $\boldsymbol{p}$ of input prices is given so that $C = \Sigma_i p_i q_i = \boldsymbol{p}'\boldsymbol{q}$ is the firm's cost. The firm's objective is to maximize profit, $R - C$, by varying $\boldsymbol{q}$ and $\boldsymbol{z}$ subject to $h(\boldsymbol{q}, \boldsymbol{z}) = 0$ for given $\boldsymbol{p}$ and $\boldsymbol{y}$. As in section 4.1 we argue that if $\boldsymbol{q}$ is known, the solution (5.25) applies for $\boldsymbol{z}$ so that it is sufficient to find the values d(log $\boldsymbol{q}$) in (5.25) which maximize profit.

For this purpose we consider profit as a function of $\boldsymbol{q}$, so that the first-order condition is $\partial(R - C)/\partial \boldsymbol{q} = \boldsymbol{0}$. This yields

$$\partial R/\partial q_i = p_i, \qquad i = 1, \ldots, n, \tag{5.37}$$

because $\partial C/\partial q_i = p_i$ follows from the assumption that $\boldsymbol{p}$ is given. Using (5.13) we can write (5.37) as $\bar{C} f_i = p_i q_i$, which we sum over i:

$$\bar{C} = \sum_{i=1}^{n} p_i q_i = C. \tag{5.38}$$

Hence, shadow cost $\bar{C}$ now equals actual cost C and $f_i = p_i q_i / C$ applies here as well. In addition, (5.38) and (5.15) imply that

(4.5) applies here also, and (5.37) implies that (5.21) can be simplified to

$$\bar{\theta}_r^i = \frac{\partial(y_r z_r)}{\partial(p_i q_i)}. \tag{5.39}$$

Thus, under profit maximization $\bar{\theta}_r^i$ is the revenue which the firm gains from additional production of the rth product for an additional dollar's worth of the ith input.

The second-order condition requires $\partial^2(R-C)/\partial \boldsymbol{q}\,\partial \boldsymbol{q}'$ to be negative definite, for which it is sufficient that

$$\frac{\partial^2 R}{\partial \boldsymbol{q}\,\partial \boldsymbol{q}'} \quad \text{is symmetric negative definite,} \tag{5.40}$$

because $\partial^2 C/\partial \boldsymbol{q}\,\partial \boldsymbol{q}' = \boldsymbol{0}$ follows from the assumption that $\boldsymbol{p}$ is given. We shall assume that (5.40) is true.

5.6.2. *The demand for factors*

In Appendix D it is shown that the demand equations for the inputs of the firm which are implied by profit maximization can be written in matrix form as

$$\boldsymbol{F}\,\mathrm{d}(\log \boldsymbol{q}) = -\bar{\psi}\bar{\boldsymbol{\Theta}}[\mathrm{d}(\log \boldsymbol{p}) - \bar{\boldsymbol{K}}'\,\mathrm{d}(\log \boldsymbol{y})], \tag{5.41}$$

where $\bar{\boldsymbol{\Theta}} = [\bar{\theta}_{ij}]$ is an $n \times n$ symmetric positive definite matrix which is normalized so that its coefficients add up to one:

$$\sum_{i=1}^{n} \sum_{j=1}^{n} \bar{\theta}_{ij} = 1. \tag{5.42}$$

It is shown in Chapter 6 that the coefficient $\bar{\psi}$ is equal to $\gamma\psi^*$, where ψ^* is the same coefficient which appears in (4.7) and hence satisfies (4.9).

The left-hand variable of the ith equation in (5.41) is $f_i\,\mathrm{d}(\log q_i)$, which is the same as the left-hand variable of (3.37).

The jth element of $\bar{\boldsymbol{K}}' \,\mathrm{d}(\log \boldsymbol{y})$ can be written (see (5.22)) as $\Sigma_r \bar{\theta}^j_r \,\mathrm{d}(\log y_r)$, which we write as the Frisch price index

$$\mathrm{d}(\log Y'^j) = \sum_{r=1}^{m} \bar{\theta}^j_r \,\mathrm{d}(\log y_r). \tag{5.43}$$

Thus, the ith equation of (5.41) can be written as

$$f_i \,\mathrm{d}(\log q_i) = -\bar{\psi} \sum_{j=1}^{n} \bar{\theta}_{ij} \,\mathrm{d}\left(\log \frac{p_j}{Y'^j}\right). \tag{5.44}$$

This demand equation describes the change in the firm's demand for the ith factor, measured by the quantity component of the change in the ith factor share (see (3.16)), as a linear combination of all input price changes, each deflated by its own Frisch index of output price changes.

The interpretation of (5.44) is entirely analogous to that of (4.12) for outputs. We can regard $\mathrm{d}[\log (p_j/Y'^j)]$ as an *output-deflated* input price change, and then interpret (5.44) as describing the expansion path of the firm's inputs in response to output-deflated input price changes. Note that the caveat in the last paragraph of section 4.3 applies here as well.

5.6.3. *The total-input and input allocation decisions of the revenue maximizing firm*

We define

$$\bar{\theta}_i = \sum_{j=1}^{n} \bar{\theta}_{ij}. \tag{5.45}$$

It will be shown in Chapter 6 that the following results hold:

$$\bar{\theta}_i = \sum_{r=1}^{m} \theta^*_r \theta'^r_i, \tag{5.46}$$

$$\theta^*_r = \sum_{i=1}^{n} \bar{\theta}_i \bar{\theta}^i_r. \tag{5.47}$$

Comparison of (5.46) with (3.26) shows that θ_i and $\bar{\theta}_i$ are each weighted means of the marginal shares θ_i^r. The weights for θ_i are the revenue shares g_r, while for $\bar{\theta}_i$ they are the marginal shares θ_r^* defined in (4.16). Eqs. (5.46) and (4.11) imply that (4.18) can also be written

$$\mathrm{d}(\log P'') = \sum_{i=1}^{n} \bar{\theta}_i \, \mathrm{d}(\log p_i). \tag{5.48}$$

Similarly, comparison of (5.47) to (5.32) shows that θ_r^* and $\bar{\theta}_r^*$ are each weighted means of the marginal shares $\bar{\theta}_r^i$. Here the weights for $\bar{\theta}_r^*$ are the cost shares f_i, while for θ_r^* they are the coefficients $\bar{\theta}_i$. Eqs. (5.47) and (5.43) imply that (4.17) can also be written

$$\mathrm{d}(\log Y') = \sum_{i=1}^{n} \bar{\theta}_i \, \mathrm{d}(\log Y''^i). \tag{5.49}$$

Now we sum (5.44) over i, using (5.48), (5.49), and the symmetry of $\bar{\boldsymbol{\Theta}}$ to obtain

$$\mathrm{d}(\log Q) = -\bar{\psi} \, \mathrm{d}\left(\log \frac{P''}{Y'}\right), \tag{5.50}$$

which is the total-input decision of the revenue maximizing firm. This is equivalent, in view of (5.31) and $\bar{\psi} = \gamma\psi^*$, to the total-output decision (4.19) of the cost minimizing firm. Note that $-\bar{\psi}$ can be interpreted as the price elasticity of the firm's demand for inputs as a whole.

We multiply (5.50) by $\bar{\theta}_i$ and substitute the result in (5.44):

$$f_i \, \mathrm{d}(\log q_i) = \bar{\theta}_i \, \mathrm{d}(\log Q) - \bar{\psi} \sum_{j=1}^{n} \bar{\theta}_{ij} \, \mathrm{d}\left(\log \frac{p_j/Y''^j}{P''/Y'}\right). \tag{5.51}$$

This is the input allocation decision of the revenue maximizing firm, and should be compared to (4.20) for outputs and (3.46) for inputs of the cost minimizing firm. The interpretation of (5.51) is entirely analogous to (4.20). In particular, the price term in (5.51) is a pure substitution effect defined in terms of relative output-deflated input price changes.

Division of (5.51) by f_i shows that $\bar{\theta}_i/f_i$ can be regarded as an alternative definition of the Divisia elasticity of the ith input. Comparison of (5.51) and (3.46) indicates that the term $\theta_i\, \mathrm{d}(\log Q)$ in (3.46) is the effect of a proportionate change in *outputs* on $f_i\, \mathrm{d}(\log q_i)$ when input price changes are also proportionate, while $\bar{\theta}_i\, \mathrm{d}(\log Q)$ in (5.51) is the effect of a proportionate change in *output prices* on $f_i\, \mathrm{d}(\log q_i)$ when input prices also change proportionately. This indicates that the relationship of $\bar{\theta}_i/f_i$ to θ_i/f_i is completely analogous to the relationship of θ_r^*/g_r to $\bar{\theta}_r^*/g_r$. We can call $\bar{\theta}_i$ a marginal share in the same sense that we called θ_r^* a marginal share in section 4.4, which means that θ_r^* in (5.47) is a marginally weighted mean of the $\bar{\theta}_r^i$.

CHAPTER 6

Relationships among cost minimization, revenue maximization, and profit maximization

We have now developed two systems of equations which describe the firm's behavior when it maximizes profit in competitive markets. This might be thought an embarrassment of riches, but in fact the two systems considered each as a whole are equivalent. This equivalence permits us to consider the relationships which exist among cost minimizing, revenue maximizing, and profit maximizing behaviors of the firm. These relationships can generally be stated in terms of the coefficients which were defined in Chapters 3, 4, and 5, but they can also be expressed in terms of the derivatives of the cost, revenue, and profit functions.

We also further consider the implications of specialized forms of the production technology in terms of their implications for revenue and profit maximization; it is convenient to do so here because these specialized forms also imply simplified relationships among the various optimizing behaviors of the firm. In addition, simultaneous consideration of the cost minimizing and revenue maximizing firm permits us to define a scalar measure of the degree of departure of the firm from input–output separability. We also introduce measures of the degree of departure of the firm from other simplified behaviors.

6.1. Cost, revenue, and profit based systems

Thus far, we have concentrated our attention primarily on the individual demand and supply equations implied by different assumptions about the optimizing behavior of the firm. Now, however, it is convenient to consider the *systems* of equations more closely. In Chapter 3 we found that the system of input demand equations implied by cost minimization was (3.36), reproduced below:

$$\boldsymbol{F}\,\mathrm{d}(\log \boldsymbol{q}) = \gamma \boldsymbol{K}\boldsymbol{G}\,\mathrm{d}(\log \boldsymbol{z}) - \psi(\boldsymbol{\Theta} - \boldsymbol{\theta}\boldsymbol{\theta}')\,\mathrm{d}(\log \boldsymbol{p}). \tag{6.1}$$

In Chapter 4 we considered profit maximization and obtained the system of output supply equations (4.7), also reproduced here:

$$\boldsymbol{G}\,\mathrm{d}(\log \boldsymbol{z}) = \psi^{*}\boldsymbol{\Theta}^{*}[\mathrm{d}(\log \boldsymbol{y}) - \boldsymbol{K}'\,\mathrm{d}(\log \boldsymbol{p})]. \tag{6.2}$$

The system (6.2) expresses the change in supply of the m products of the profit maximizing multiproduct firm when input and output prices change. The system (6.1) was derived for the cost minimizing firm, but can be interpreted conditionally for the profit maximizing firm. Thus, the profit maximizing firm chooses its output levels in accordance with (6.2) and then, conditional upon this decision, chooses its input levels to minimize cost in accordance with (6.1). In effect, then, by substituting (6.2) into (6.1) we obtain the input decision of the firm in terms of changes in prices alone:

$$\begin{aligned}\boldsymbol{F}\,\mathrm{d}(\log \boldsymbol{q}) = {} & \gamma\psi^{*}\boldsymbol{K}\boldsymbol{\Theta}^{*}\,\mathrm{d}(\log \boldsymbol{y}) \\ & - [\gamma\psi^{*}\boldsymbol{K}\boldsymbol{\Theta}^{*}\boldsymbol{K}' + \psi(\boldsymbol{\Theta} - \boldsymbol{\theta}\boldsymbol{\theta}')]\,\mathrm{d}(\log \boldsymbol{p}).\end{aligned} \tag{6.3}$$

The system consisting of (6.2) and (6.3) can be interpreted as the unconditional supply and demand system of the profit maximizing firm, describing its changes in the supply of outputs and demand for inputs in terms of all price changes.

In Chapter 5 we studied revenue maximization and found that the implied system of supply equations was (5.25), which we reproduce here:

$$\boldsymbol{G}\,\mathrm{d}(\log \boldsymbol{z}) = \frac{1}{\gamma}\bar{\boldsymbol{K}}\boldsymbol{F}\,\mathrm{d}(\log \boldsymbol{q}) - (\bar{\boldsymbol{\Theta}}^* - \boldsymbol{g}\boldsymbol{g}')\,\mathrm{d}(\log \boldsymbol{y}). \tag{6.4}$$

Consideration of profit maximization then led to the system of demand equations (5.41), also reproduced:

$$\boldsymbol{F}\,\mathrm{d}(\log \boldsymbol{q}) = -\bar{\psi}\bar{\boldsymbol{\Theta}}[\mathrm{d}(\log \boldsymbol{p}) - \bar{\boldsymbol{K}}'\,\mathrm{d}(\log \boldsymbol{y})]. \tag{6.5}$$

This system expresses the change in demand for the n factors of the profit maximizing multiproduct firm when input and output prices change. The supply system (6.4) can be interpreted conditionally in a manner entirely analogous to the above conditional interpretation of (6.1). As a consequence, when we substitute (6.5) into (6.4) to obtain

$$\boldsymbol{G}\,\mathrm{d}(\log \boldsymbol{z}) = \left[\frac{\bar{\psi}}{\gamma}\bar{\boldsymbol{K}}\bar{\boldsymbol{\Theta}}\bar{\boldsymbol{K}}' - (\bar{\boldsymbol{\Theta}}^* - \boldsymbol{g}\boldsymbol{g}')\right]\mathrm{d}(\log \boldsymbol{y}) - \frac{\bar{\psi}}{\gamma}\bar{\boldsymbol{K}}\bar{\boldsymbol{\Theta}}\,\mathrm{d}(\log \boldsymbol{p}), \tag{6.6}$$

the resulting system consisting of (6.5) and (6.6) can be interpreted unconditionally as the demand and supply system of the profit maximizing firm.

We conclude that the two systems consisting of (6.2) and (6.3), which we shall call the *cost based system*, since the cost function was used to obtain them, and (6.5) and (6.6), which we shall call the *revenue based system*, each describe the behavior of the profit maximizing firm. Hence, they must describe the same behavior.

We can infer immediately from comparison of (6.2) and (6.6)

that[1]

$$\bar{\psi} = \gamma\psi^*, \tag{6.7}$$

as was asserted in Chapter 5. Also, we have[2]

$$\bar{\boldsymbol{\Theta}}\bar{\boldsymbol{K}}' = \boldsymbol{K}\boldsymbol{\Theta}^*, \tag{6.8}$$

which is one relation among the coefficients of the revenue maximizing firm on the left and the cost minimizing firm on the right. Premultiplication of this result by $\boldsymbol{\iota}'$ leads to the matrix version of (5.47), using (5.45) and (3.35); postmultiplication by $\boldsymbol{\iota}^*$ similarly leads to (5.46).

Comparison of the coefficient matrices of $d(\log \boldsymbol{y})$ in (6.6) and (6.2) yields, after substitution from (6.7),

$$\psi^*\boldsymbol{\Theta}^* = \psi^*\bar{\boldsymbol{K}}\bar{\boldsymbol{\Theta}}\bar{\boldsymbol{K}}' - (\bar{\boldsymbol{\Theta}}^* - \boldsymbol{g}\boldsymbol{g}'), \tag{6.9}$$

which shows how the matrix $\boldsymbol{\Theta}^*$ of the cost based system can be obtained from the coefficients of the revenue based system. A similar comparison of the coefficient matrices of $d(\log \boldsymbol{p})$ in (6.5) and (6.3) yields

$$\gamma\psi^*\bar{\boldsymbol{\Theta}} = \gamma\psi^*\boldsymbol{K}\boldsymbol{\Theta}^*\boldsymbol{K}' + \psi(\boldsymbol{\Theta} - \boldsymbol{\theta}\boldsymbol{\theta}'), \tag{6.10}$$

which shows how the matrix $\bar{\boldsymbol{\Theta}}$ of the revenue based system can be obtained from the coefficients of the cost based system.

In fact, these relationships are sufficient to obtain the coefficients of either the cost based system or the revenue based system from the other. Suppose first that we know the coefficients of the revenue based system. From (6.7) we can

[1]This follows from the coefficients of $d(\log \boldsymbol{p})$, which are $-\psi^*\boldsymbol{\Theta}^*\boldsymbol{K}'$ in (6.2) and $-(\bar{\psi}/\gamma)\bar{\boldsymbol{K}}\bar{\boldsymbol{\Theta}}$ in (6.6). Summation of the elements of $\boldsymbol{\Theta}^*\boldsymbol{K}'$ and $\bar{\boldsymbol{K}}\bar{\boldsymbol{\Theta}}$ amounts to premultiplication by $\boldsymbol{\iota}^{*\prime}$ and postmultiplication by $\boldsymbol{\iota}$; from (3.35) and (4.8) the first sum is one, while (5.24) and (5.42) imply the same for the second. Hence, the scalars are equal.

[2]This follows directly from the considerations of fn. 1, above.

obtain ψ^* and then from (6.9) $\boldsymbol{\Theta}^*$. Since $\boldsymbol{\Theta}^*$ is positive definite, we can then use (6.8) to obtain $\boldsymbol{K}$. This is sufficient to permit us to find $\psi(\boldsymbol{\Theta} - \boldsymbol{\theta\theta}')$ from (6.10). Eq. (4.28) permits us to obtain ψ, while (3.34) can be used to obtain $\boldsymbol{\theta}$, after which $\boldsymbol{\Theta}$ can be obtained from $\psi(\boldsymbol{\Theta} - \boldsymbol{\theta\theta}')$. Now suppose that we know the coefficients of the cost based system. Then we can obtain $\bar{\boldsymbol{\Theta}}$ from (6.10), $\bar{\psi}$ from (6.7), $\bar{\boldsymbol{K}}$ from (6.8), and $\bar{\boldsymbol{\Theta}}^*$ from (6.9) in that order.

The equivalence of the cost based and revenue based systems follows from the fact that both systems represent profit maximizing behavior. In one case we considered cost minimization first, followed by profit maximization; in the other we considered revenue maximization first, also followed by profit maximization. These procedures are represented in fig. 6.1 by the pairs of arrows on the left and the right. Obviously it is also possible to proceed directly to profit maximization as represented by the arrow in the center: this was the procedure followed by Hicks [40]. This leads to a third *profit based system* which consists in essence of the subsystems (6.2) for supply and (6.5) for demand. The major difference from the other systems is that the coefficients in the supply system of input prices, $-\psi^*\boldsymbol{\Theta}^*\boldsymbol{K}'$, and in the demand system of output prices, $\gamma\psi^*\bar{\boldsymbol{\Theta}}\bar{\boldsymbol{K}}'$, cannot be interpreted as meaningfully as their constituent matrices $\boldsymbol{\Theta}^*$, $\bar{\boldsymbol{\Theta}}$, $\boldsymbol{K}$, and $\bar{\boldsymbol{K}}$. This advantage of relatively strong interpretation is a result of the two-step procedures which we employed in Chapters 3, 4, and 5.

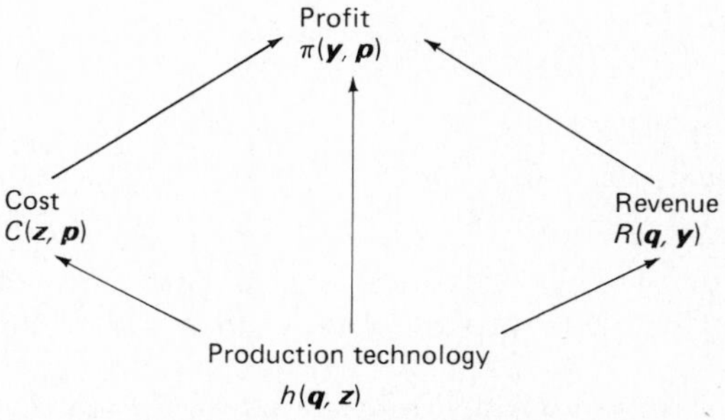

Figure 6.1. Paths of profit maximization.

6.2. Properties of the revenue and profit functions

In section 4.5 we noted that the coefficients which appear in the cost based system are all closely related to derivatives of the cost function. In a similar way, the coefficients of the revenue and profit based systems are all closely related to derivatives of the revenue and profit functions, respectively.

Thus, we can use (5.13) to obtain γ from the revenue function, while (5.13) and (5.15) imply

$$f_i = \gamma \frac{\partial \log R}{\partial \log q_i}. \tag{6.11}$$

Shephard's lemma (2.31) for the revenue function immediately implies

$$g_r = \frac{\partial \log R}{\partial \log y_r}. \tag{6.12}$$

In Appendix D it is shown that the following relationships also hold:

$$-(\bar{\boldsymbol{\Theta}}^* - \boldsymbol{g}\boldsymbol{g}') = \frac{1}{R} \boldsymbol{Y} \frac{\partial^2 R}{\partial \boldsymbol{y}\, \partial \boldsymbol{y}'} \boldsymbol{Y}, \tag{6.13}$$

$$\bar{\boldsymbol{K}} = \boldsymbol{Y} \frac{\partial^2 R}{\partial \boldsymbol{y}\, \partial \boldsymbol{q}'} \boldsymbol{P}^{-1}, \tag{6.14}$$

$$-\gamma\psi^* \bar{\boldsymbol{\Theta}} = \frac{1}{C} \boldsymbol{P} \left[\frac{\partial^2 R}{\partial \boldsymbol{q}\, \partial \boldsymbol{q}'} \right]^{-1} \boldsymbol{P}, \tag{6.15}$$

where $\boldsymbol{Y}$ and $\boldsymbol{P}$ are the diagonal matrices of output and input prices, respectively.[3] Now (6.15) and (5.42) permit evaluation of the coefficients ψ^* and $\bar{\theta}_{ij}$, while (6.14) gives the coefficients $\bar{\theta}_r^i$ directly. Eq. (5.33) permits evaluation of the marginal coefficients $\bar{\theta}_r^*$, and from (6.13) we obtain the coefficients $\bar{\theta}_{rs}^*$.

[3]When the input prices are not defined, we take $\boldsymbol{P}$ to be the diagonal matrix of shadow input prices $\partial R/\partial q_i$.

If we consider direct profit maximization we obtain similar results. Using Shephard's lemma (2.33) and (2.34) for the profit function, we can define cost and revenue in terms of the input and output prices as

$$C(\boldsymbol{p}, \boldsymbol{y}) = -\sum_{i=1}^{n} p_i \frac{\partial \pi}{\partial p_i}, \tag{6.16}$$

$$R(\boldsymbol{p}, \boldsymbol{y}) = \sum_{r=1}^{m} y_r \frac{\partial \pi}{\partial y_r}. \tag{6.17}$$

Using these definitions we can obtain $\gamma = R/C$, $f_i = p_i q_i/C$, and $g_r = y_r z_r/R$, where q_i and z_r are obtained from (2.33) and (2.34). This is pursued in Appendix E, where it is shown that the following relationships hold for the second derivatives of the profit function:

$$\psi^* \boldsymbol{\Theta}^* = \frac{1}{R} \boldsymbol{Y} \frac{\partial^2 \pi}{\partial \boldsymbol{y}\, \partial \boldsymbol{y}'} \boldsymbol{Y}, \tag{6.18}$$

$$\psi^* \boldsymbol{\Theta}^* \boldsymbol{K}' = \frac{1}{R} \boldsymbol{Y} \frac{\partial^2 \pi}{\partial \boldsymbol{y}\, \partial \boldsymbol{p}'} \boldsymbol{P}, \tag{6.19}$$

$$\gamma \psi^* \bar{\boldsymbol{\Theta}} = -\frac{1}{C} \boldsymbol{P} \frac{\partial^2 \pi}{\partial \boldsymbol{p}\, \partial \boldsymbol{p}'} \boldsymbol{P}, \tag{6.20}$$

$$\gamma \psi^* \bar{\boldsymbol{\Theta}} \bar{\boldsymbol{K}}' = -\frac{1}{C} \boldsymbol{P} \frac{\partial^2 \pi}{\partial \boldsymbol{p}\, \partial \boldsymbol{y}'} \boldsymbol{Y}. \tag{6.21}$$

Here ψ^*, $\boldsymbol{\Theta}$, and $\bar{\boldsymbol{\Theta}}$ can be obtained directly from (6.18) and (6.20). Since the inverses of the two matrices exist, it is then possible to obtain $\boldsymbol{K}$ and $\bar{\boldsymbol{K}}$ from (6.19) and (6.21). It is then possible, in the same way as in the last section, to obtain the other coefficients of both the cost based and the revenue based systems.

The fact that each of these systems can be obtained from the others is an expression of the duality results described in section 2.3. The duality among production, cost, revenue, and profit functions is also illustrated in fig. 6.1; the interpretation is that each of the four functions describes the same technology, but in terms of different variables.

6.3. Specialized forms

6.3.1. The input–output separable firm

When the firm is input–output separable, (3.48) holds for the revenue maximizing as well as the cost minimizing firm. When we substitute this into the third member of (5.22) we obtain

$$\bar{\boldsymbol{K}} = (\boldsymbol{g} - \bar{\boldsymbol{\Theta}}^* \boldsymbol{G}^{-1} \boldsymbol{b})\boldsymbol{\iota}'.$$

Postmultiplication of this by $\boldsymbol{f}$ then leads to $\bar{\boldsymbol{\theta}}^* = \boldsymbol{g} - \bar{\boldsymbol{\Theta}}^* \boldsymbol{G}^{-1} \boldsymbol{b}$. We conclude that when the firm is input–output separable the marginal shares of each output are the same across inputs: $\bar{\theta}_r^i = \bar{\theta}_r^*$ for each r and i, or

$$\bar{\boldsymbol{K}} = \bar{\boldsymbol{\theta}}^* \boldsymbol{\iota}'. \tag{6.22}$$

This result is the revenue maximizing firm's version of (3.49).

The immediate implications of this are similar to the implications of input–output separability for the cost minimizing firm. Thus, in (5.35) we see that the covariance $\bar{\Gamma}_r$ vanishes when the firm is input–output separable and moreover from (5.43) that each $\mathrm{d}(\log Y'^j)$ must be the same in this case. Somewhat stronger results can be obtained from (5.46) and (5.47), where we observe that

$$\bar{\theta}_i = \theta_i, \qquad \theta_r^* = \bar{\theta}_r^*; \tag{6.23}$$

both hold when $\theta_i^r = \theta_i$ and $\bar{\theta}_r^i = \bar{\theta}_r^*$. Thus, when the firm is input–output separable the alternative definitions of the marginal coefficients coincide for both inputs and outputs.

A consequence is that the output allocation decision (5.36) of the revenue maximizing firm is simplified to

$$g_r \, d(\log z_r) = \theta_r^* \, d(\log Z) - \sum_{s=1}^{m} \bar{\theta}_{rs}^* \, d\left(\log \frac{y_s}{Y}\right). \tag{6.24}$$

In addition, (5.48) and (3.38) imply that $d(\log P') = d(\log P'')$, and (5.43) and (4.17) that $d(\log Y') = d(\log Y''^j)$ for each j. Consequently, the demand equation (5.44) of the revenue maximizing firm is

$$f_i \, d(\log q_i) = -\gamma\psi^* \sum_{j=1}^{n} \bar{\theta}_{ij} \, d\left(\log \frac{p_j}{Y'}\right) \tag{6.25}$$

and the input allocation decision (5.51) is

$$f_i \, d(\log q_i) = \theta_i \, d(\log Q) - \gamma\psi^* \sum_{j=1}^{n} \bar{\theta}_{ij} \, d\left(\log \frac{p_j}{P'}\right) \tag{6.26}$$

when the firm is input–output separable.[4]

6.3.2. *Homotheticity*

When the firm is homothetic in outputs, one of (2.46), (2.48), or (2.50) holds, so that in any case we have $\boldsymbol{\iota}'\boldsymbol{H}^* = \boldsymbol{0}$. Substitution of (5.22) into (5.33) gives $\bar{\boldsymbol{\theta}}^* = \boldsymbol{g}\boldsymbol{\iota}'\boldsymbol{f} - \gamma\bar{\boldsymbol{\Theta}}^*\boldsymbol{G}^{-1}\boldsymbol{H}^{*\prime}\boldsymbol{F}^{-1}\boldsymbol{f}$. Since $\boldsymbol{F}^{-1}\boldsymbol{f} = \boldsymbol{\iota}$, we then have

$$\bar{\boldsymbol{\theta}}^* = \boldsymbol{g}, \tag{6.27}$$

which should be compared to (3.53).

[4]A comparison of (6.26) and (3.50), both of which hold when the firm is input–output separable, might seem to indicate that $\gamma\psi^*\bar{\theta}_{ij}$ and $\psi\theta_{ij}$ are the same. To see that this is not true, note that the price term can be written $-\psi\Sigma_j\,(\theta_{ij} - \theta_i\theta_j)\,d(\log p_j)$ in (3.50) and $-\gamma\psi^*\,\Sigma_j\,(\bar{\theta}_{ij} - \theta_i\theta_j)\,d(\log p_j)$ in (6.26). This implies that $\psi(\theta_{ij} - \theta_i\theta_j) = \gamma\psi^*(\bar{\theta}_{ij} - \theta_i\theta_j)$, so $\theta_{ij} \neq \bar{\theta}_{ij}$ if $\psi \neq \gamma\psi^*$. In turn, (4.9) implies $\gamma\psi^* \geq \psi(\psi^* + 1) > \psi$, and thus θ_{ij} cannot equal $\bar{\theta}_{ij}$.

The implications of homotheticity are now clear. When the firm is homothetic in inputs, the true marginal input shares are equal to the factor shares. Similarly, when the firm is homothetic in outputs, the true marginal output shares are equal to the revenue shares.

The quasimarginal output shares θ_r^* defined in Chapter 4 and the quasimarginal input shares $\bar{\theta}_i$ defined in Chapter 5 do not in general share this property. However, when the firm is input–output separable, the true and quasimarginal shares are the same for both inputs and outputs; consequently, when the firm is also homothetic in either inputs or outputs, the corresponding true and quasimarginal shares are both equal to the factor shares or the revenue shares, respectively.

The cases of input–output homotheticity and the input–output separable firm whose production is homogeneous as well are particularly strong. In these cases all input shares (true marginal, quasimarginal, and factor shares) coincide, and the same is true for all output shares.

6.3.3. Independence

In Chapters 3 and 4 input independence and output independence were each defined in terms of a square symmetric positive definite matrix of price coefficients which takes a diagonal form. In the case of output independence in particular, interpretation of this diagonality is very strong, since this condition is equivalent to the situation where there is no jointness of production.

It is natural but, as it turns out, not very fruitful to consider other independence conditions based on the price coefficients of the revenue maximizing firm. To see why this does not lead to any acceptable simplification, we consider first the matrix $\bar{\boldsymbol{\Theta}}^*$ whose single positive characteristic root has already been remarked at length. If this matrix were diagonal, condition (5.17) would then imply that only one g_r can be positive, and that the others would be strictly negative.[5]

This, of course, is nonsensical: we should interpret the result to mean that it is not possible for the multiproduct firm to have a diagonal $\bar{\boldsymbol{\Theta}}^*$. Nor can this matrix be block diagonal, since the positive root would then have to be associated with one of the blocks. This in turn means that at least one of the g_r values associated with every other block would have to be negative. We can take (5.17) to mean that the positive root must be "distributed" over the entire matrix.

No such impossibility occurs if the matrix $\bar{\boldsymbol{\Theta}}$ of input price coefficients is diagonal, but the implications of such a condition are extremely implausible.[6] The main implication is that the revenue function is then additive in the inputs: $R(\boldsymbol{q}, \boldsymbol{y}) = \Sigma_i R_i(q_i, \boldsymbol{y})$. This condition, similar to the case of an additive cost function, occurs when the inputs are not used jointly. In words, this means that the firm could be broken up into n single input firms, the ith of which has the revenue function $R_i(q_i, \boldsymbol{y})$ and produces all outputs using its single input. This is another extremely implausible result, and consequently we shall not consider this a useful restriction.

6.4. Measures of interaction

Theil [78, ch. 12] has defined a measure of the degree of interaction of preferences for the consumer which can be ap-

[5]Nothing is gained by considering the matrix associated with marginal price deflation (see section 5.4), because diagonality of this matrix means that all but one marginal share must be negative. This is not an impossible condition, but an extremely unlikely one; it is comparable to the situation in consumption theory where it is possible for all but one income elasticity to be negative. There is certainly no reason to consider imposing this.

[6]For a more explicit treatment of these implications see Lau [51] who discusses them in terms of the profit instead of the revenue function. The relationships (6.15) and (6.20) indicate that the two are equivalent.

plied directly to the multiproduct firm. Thus, consider

$$\sum_{i=1}^{n} \log \theta_{ii} - \log |\boldsymbol{\Theta}|, \tag{6.28}$$

where $|\boldsymbol{\Theta}|$ is the determinant of $\boldsymbol{\Theta}$, and the logarithms are permissible because $\boldsymbol{\Theta}$, defined in (3.29), is positive definite. If $\boldsymbol{\Theta}$ is diagonal, its determinant is the product of its diagonal elements and hence (6.28) is zero. When the off-diagonal elements of $\boldsymbol{\Theta}$ are nonzero, the determinant of $\boldsymbol{\Theta}$ is less than the product of its diagonal elements,[7] and hence (6.28) is positive. When the off-diagonal elements are large enough in absolute value to make $\boldsymbol{\Theta}$ nearly semidefinite, the determinant is close to zero, and hence (6.28) is large. Consequently, we can regard (6.28) as a measure of the degree to which $\boldsymbol{\Theta}$ is not diagonal or, in terms of our previous definition of input independence, as a measure of the degree of *input interaction* in the firm.

In a similar way we can define

$$\sum_{r=1}^{m} \log \theta^*_{rr} - \log |\boldsymbol{\Theta}^*| \tag{6.29}$$

as a measure of the degree to which $\boldsymbol{\Theta}^*$ is not diagonal or, in terms of our previous definition of output independence, as a measure of the degree of *output interaction* in the multiproduct firm. This measure is zero if the firm is output independent or has only one product and positive otherwise, moving to infinity as the determinant of $\boldsymbol{\Theta}^*$ approaches zero. An alternative designation for (6.29), which is more in keeping with the usual

[7]If we multiply each element θ_{ij} of $\boldsymbol{\Theta}$ by $(\theta_{ii}\theta_{jj})^{-1/2}$, we obtain a correlation matrix, i.e., a positive definite matrix with ones on the diagonal. Such a matrix always has a positive determinant no greater than one. The measure (6.28) is minus the logarithm of this determinant. An important reason why Theil [78] chose this measure for the consumer is that when $\boldsymbol{\Theta}$ is block diagonal (6.28) can be decomposed additively into similar measures for each block considered separately.

terminology, is as a measure of the degree of jointness in production of the multiproduct firm.[8]

Now consider the quantity

$$\operatorname{tr}(\boldsymbol{K}\bar{\boldsymbol{K}})=\sum_{r=1}^{m}\sum_{i=1}^{n}\theta_i^r\bar{\theta}_r^i=1+\sum_{r=1}^{m}\sum_{i=1}^{n}(\theta_i^r-\theta_i)(\bar{\theta}_r^i-\bar{\theta}_r^*), \tag{6.30}$$

where $\operatorname{tr}(\boldsymbol{K}\bar{\boldsymbol{K}})$ is the trace of $\boldsymbol{K}\bar{\boldsymbol{K}}$. Since $\theta_i^r=\theta_i$ and $\bar{\theta}_r^i=\bar{\theta}_r^*$ both hold when the firm is input–output separable, (6.30) must equal one under this condition. More generally, it is proven in Appendix E that (6.30) satisfies

$$1\le\operatorname{tr}(\boldsymbol{K}\bar{\boldsymbol{K}})\le\operatorname{r}(\boldsymbol{K}\bar{\boldsymbol{K}})\le\min(m,n), \tag{6.31}$$

where $\operatorname{r}(\boldsymbol{K}\bar{\boldsymbol{K}})$ is the rank of $\boldsymbol{K}\bar{\boldsymbol{K}}$. Equality holds for the first two $\le$ signs if and only if the firm is input–output separable. This relationship has prompted Laitinen and Theil [50] to call (6.30) a measure of the *input–output specificity* of the multiproduct firm. To clarify this, we suppose that the ith input is of little use in producing the rth output. This means for the cost minimizing firm that an increase in the quantity of the rth output will require little more of the ith input, or that θ_i^r is less than θ_i. For the revenue maximizing firm, an increase in the availability of the ith input will have little effect on the firm's decision to produce the rth output, so that $\bar{\theta}_r^i$ is less than $\bar{\theta}_r^*$. In turn, this means that the (i,r)th contribution to the sum in the third member of (6.30) is the product of two negative numbers and is therefore positive. A similar analysis indicates that when the ith input is of great use in producing the rth output, the (i,r)th contribution to this sum is the product of two positive numbers and is therefore also positive. Thus, the specific interaction of the inputs and outputs leads to positive increments in (6.30),

[8]This should not be confused with the "degree of joint production" as used by Burmeister and Turnovsky [19], which refers to block diagonal structures of $\boldsymbol{\Theta}^*$ corresponding to block independence (see section 4.6).

which we can regard as a measure of the degree to which inputs and outputs have such interaction.

In a manner similar to Laitinen [48] for the consumer, we can also measure the degree to which the firm fails to be homothetic by considering the measure[9]

$$(\boldsymbol{\theta}-\boldsymbol{f})'\boldsymbol{\Theta}^{-1}(\boldsymbol{\theta}-\boldsymbol{f})=\boldsymbol{f}'\boldsymbol{\Theta}^{-1}\boldsymbol{f}-1. \tag{6.32}$$

The quantity on the left in (6.32) is zero when $\theta_i = f_i$ for each i, which is the condition which holds when the firm is homothetic in inputs. When the vectors $\boldsymbol{\theta}$ and $\boldsymbol{f}$ are different, then (6.32) is positive because $\boldsymbol{\Theta}$ is positive definite; in general, the more divergent $\boldsymbol{\theta}$ is from $\boldsymbol{f}$, the larger we can expect this quantity to be. As a consequence, we can regard (6.32) as a measure of the degree to which the firm is *heterothetic in inputs.*

Finally, it is shown in Appendix E that the quantity

$$-(\bar{\boldsymbol{\theta}}^*-\boldsymbol{g})'\bar{\boldsymbol{\Theta}}^{*-1}(\bar{\boldsymbol{\theta}}^*-\boldsymbol{g})=1-\bar{\boldsymbol{\theta}}^{*\prime}\bar{\boldsymbol{\Theta}}^{*-1}\bar{\boldsymbol{\theta}}^* \tag{6.33}$$

has properties similar to (6.32): that is to say, (6.33) is zero when $g_r = \bar{\theta}_r^*$ for each r, which is the condition which holds when the firm is homothetic in outputs; and when $\bar{\boldsymbol{\theta}}^*$ is different from $\boldsymbol{g}$, (6.33) is strictly positive, taking larger values the more divergent $\bar{\boldsymbol{\theta}}^*$ is from $\boldsymbol{g}$. Thus, we regard (6.33) as a measure of the degree to which the firm is *heterothetic in outputs.*

[9]Laitinen's [48] measure τ of the degree of heterotheticity for the consumer involves the income flexibility, which is analogous to ψ; the effect is to identify τ even though $\boldsymbol{\Theta}$ is not identified. No such necessity arises for the firm, where $\boldsymbol{\Theta}$ and ψ are identified (see section 8.1).

CHAPTER 7

Rational random behavior

The system of demand and supply equations which was derived for the profit maximizing firm in Chapter 6 is optimal in the sense that, for particular changes of input and output prices which appear on the right, the left-hand variable of each equation describes the reaction of the firm which will keep profit at a maximum. In practice, this requires us to assume that the firm has perfect knowledge of all price changes; such an assumption seems too strong. A similar problem exists for the purely cost minimizing or revenue maximizing firm.

This is the subject of the theory of rational random behavior, which postulates that economic agents actively acquire information about uncontrolled variables, i.e., prices of inputs and outputs in the case of the profit maximizing firm. It is assumed that information is costly, so that it is not in general optimal to acquire full information about such variables when the cost of information is taken into account. The effect of this nonoptimality is to add a random component to the decisions of the firm.[1]

One of the fundamental results of this theory is that if the marginal cost of information is small, the optimal distribution of the decision variables is multinormal with a mean equal to the full information optimum and a covariance matrix which is proportional to the inverse of the Hessian matrix of the criterion function. The assumption of a small marginal cost of information

[1]This, of course, is closely related to the cost of search described by Stigler [72, 73], and numerous similar economic analyses involving costly information. The difference is that this approach describes the effect of costly information in terms of an explicit random component of behavior.

is not necessarily valid, but it is weaker than the implicit previous assumption that the cost of information is zero. Accordingly, it yields results which can be taken as a closer approximation to the actual behavior of the firm.

Details about the theory of rational random behavior can be found in Theil [77, 80] and Barbosa [7]. We apply the theory to the multiproduct firm in Appendix F. Results for the cost based system of supply and demand equations are reported in section 7.1, which is followed by results for the revenue and profit based systems in section 7.2.

7.1. The cost based system

The theory of rational random behavior implies that a disturbance ε_i must be added to the input demand equation (3.39),

$$f_i \, \mathrm{d}(\log q_i) = \gamma \sum_{r=1}^{m} \theta_i^r g_r \, \mathrm{d}(\log z_r) - \psi \sum_{j=1}^{n} \theta_{ij} \, \mathrm{d}\left(\log \frac{p_j}{P'}\right) + \varepsilon_i, \tag{7.1}$$

and that $\varepsilon_1, \ldots, \varepsilon_n$ have an n-variate normal distribution with zero means, and variances and covariances of the form

$$\operatorname{cov}(\varepsilon_i, \varepsilon_j) = \sigma^2 \psi(\theta_{ij} - \theta_i \theta_j), \qquad i, j = 1, \ldots, n, \tag{7.2}$$

where σ^2 is proportional to the marginal cost of information. This result holds for both cost minimization and profit maximization.

When profit is maximized and supply equations of the form (4.12) emerge, the theory implies that a disturbance ε_r^* must be added,

$$g_r \, \mathrm{d}(\log z_r) = \psi^* \sum_{s=1}^{m} \theta_{rs}^* \, \mathrm{d}\left(\log \frac{y_s}{P'^s}\right) + \varepsilon_r^*, \tag{7.3}$$

and that $\varepsilon_1^*, \ldots, \varepsilon_m^*$ have an m-variate normal distribution with zero means, and variances and covariances of the form

$$\operatorname{cov}(\varepsilon_r^*, \varepsilon_s^*) = \frac{\sigma^2 \psi^*}{\gamma} \theta_{rs}^*, \qquad r, s = 1, \ldots, m, \tag{7.4}$$

where σ^2 is the same coefficient as in (7.2).

The vectors $\boldsymbol{\varepsilon} = (\varepsilon_1, \ldots, \varepsilon_n)'$ and $\boldsymbol{\varepsilon}^* = (\varepsilon_1^*, \ldots, \varepsilon_m^*)'$ are independently distributed. Hence, the input demand equations for cost minimization and the output supply equations for profit maximization constitute a two-stage block-recursive system.[2] The first stage consists of (7.3), which yields the m output changes, and the second consists of (7.1), which yields the n input changes when the output changes are given. This can be interpreted as meaning that the firm's decision on output supply changes is separate from and takes precedence over the firm's decision on input demand changes.[3] Note that this is a general result which does not require the assumption of input–output separability.

The sum of $\varepsilon_1, \ldots, \varepsilon_n$ has zero variance in view of (7.2) and (3.32). Consequently the total-input decision continues to take the nonstochastic form (3.43) when the theory of rational random behavior is applied to the firm. It follows that the input allocation decision (3.46) must be modified by adding ε_i,

$$f_i \,\mathrm{d}(\log q_i) = \theta_i \,\mathrm{d}(\log Q) + \gamma \Gamma_i - \psi \sum_{j=1}^{n} \theta_{ij} \,\mathrm{d}\left(\log \frac{p_j}{P'}\right) + \varepsilon_i, \tag{7.5}$$

and that this decision is (trivially) stochastically independent of the total-input decision. The nonstochastic nature of (3.43) follows from the fact that this equation is equivalent to the

[2]See Theil [76, section 9.6] for a description of this. The crucial point is that $g_r \,\mathrm{d}(\log z_r)$ in (7.1) has to be regarded as random under profit maximization. However, since its random component, ε_r^*, is independent of ε_i, (7.1) can be regarded as describing $f_i \,\mathrm{d}(\log q_i)$ conditional upon the value of $g_r \,\mathrm{d}(\log z_r)$ for $r = 1, \ldots, m$.

[3]More succinctly, this means that the output manager is the boss of the input manager. But note that in the next section the opposite interpretation is possible.

production function in differential form (see below (3.43)). The theory of rational random behavior is concerned with random errors in optimization, not with random variations of the firm's technology.

This explains why (7.2) is the same for cost minimization and profit maximization. Since production is in any case efficient, only incomplete information about input prices affects the firm's decisions for cost minimization. When output prices are also relevant, the firm's lack of knowledge about these shows up in the output disturbances $\varepsilon_1^*, \ldots, \varepsilon_m^*$. The independence of the input and output disturbances can be interpreted as meaning that the firm gathers information about the two sets of prices independently.

Another independence result holds for the firm's supply side. Summation of (7.3) over r yields the stochastic version of the total-output decision,

$$\mathrm{d}(\log Z) = \psi^* \,\mathrm{d}\left(\log \frac{Y'}{P''}\right) + E^*, \tag{7.6}$$

where $E^* = \Sigma_r \varepsilon_r^*$. It follows from (4.8) and (7.4) that

$$\operatorname{var} E^* = \frac{\sigma^2 \psi^*}{\gamma}. \tag{7.7}$$

The stochastic version of the output allocation decision (4.20) is

$$g_r \,\mathrm{d}(\log z_r) = \theta_r^* \,\mathrm{d}(\log Z) + \psi^* \sum_{s=1}^{m} \theta_{rs}^* \,\mathrm{d}\left(\log \frac{y_s/P'^s}{Y'/P''}\right) + \varepsilon_r^{**}, \tag{7.8}$$

where $\varepsilon_r^{**} = \varepsilon_r^* - \theta_r^* E^*$. It is readily verified using (4.16), (7.4), and (7.7) that ε_r^{**} and E^* are uncorrelated. Given the normality of these random variables, uncorrelated means independent; hence the total-output decision is stochastically independent of the output allociation decision. In addition we have

$$\operatorname{cov}(\varepsilon_r^{**}, \varepsilon_s^{**}) = \frac{\sigma^2\psi^*}{\gamma}(\theta_{rs}^* - \theta_r^*\theta_s^*). \tag{7.9}$$

These covariances form a singular $m \times m$ matrix, just as the covariances in (7.2) form a singular $n \times n$ matrix. This results from the fact that (7.5) and (7.8) are allocation decisions.

When the firm is output independent, we have $\theta_{rs}^* = 0$ for $r \neq s$, so that (7.4) then implies that $\operatorname{cov}(\varepsilon_r^*, \varepsilon_s^*) = 0$ for $r \neq s$. Given the fact that these disturbances are normal, they are also stochastically independent. We conclude that when production is nonjoint, the disturbances in the supply equations are independent. This can be interpreted as meaning that the possibility of breaking the output independent firm into m single product firms which are equivalent is also confirmed in the stochastic model implied by rational random behavior.

Also, note that the covariance structure (7.2) implies that the covariance of $d(\log q_i)$ and $d(\log q_j)$ is proportional to the Allen partial elasticity of substitution defined in (3.40). In a similar way, the covariance of $d(\log z_r)$ and $d(\log z_s)$ in the output allocation decision (7.8) is proportional to the partial elasticity of substitution between these outputs as defined in (4.22). Since an elasticity of substitution measures the degree to which one input or output will be substituted for another, these proportionalities imply that the firm's mistakes in optimization under rational random behavior are, on average, consistent mistakes.[4]

[4]For example, if (3.40) is negative, we can speak of the ith and jth inputs as being complements in Hicks's sense; that is, an increase in the jth input price leads to a decrease in use of the ith input. In that case (7.2) is positive, which means that on average positive values of ε_i will be accompanied by positive values of ε_j; in words, too much use of q_i is on average accompanied by too much use of q_j. But this is consistent with what would happen if the price of q_j were slightly lower. The analysis of other cases and of outputs is analogous.

7.2. The revenue and profit based systems

The implications of the theory of rational random behavior for the revenue maximizing firm are very similar to those for the cost minimizing firm, with correspondingly analogous interpretations. We add a disturbance $\bar{\varepsilon}_r^*$ to the output supply equation (5.30):

$$g_r \, \mathrm{d}(\log z_r) = \frac{1}{\gamma} \sum_{i=1}^{n} \bar{\theta}_r^i f_i \, \mathrm{d}(\log q_i) - \sum_{s=1}^{m} \bar{\theta}_{rs}^* \, \mathrm{d}\left(\log \frac{y_s}{Y}\right) + \bar{\varepsilon}_r^*. \tag{7.10}$$

Then $\bar{\varepsilon}_1^*, \ldots, \bar{\varepsilon}_m^*$ have an m-variate normal distribution with zero means, and variances and covariances of the form

$$\operatorname{cov}(\bar{\varepsilon}_r^*, \bar{\varepsilon}_s^*) = -\frac{\sigma^2}{\gamma} (\bar{\theta}_{rs}^* - g_r g_s), \qquad r, s = 1, \ldots, m, \tag{7.11}$$

where σ^2 is the same coefficient as in section 7.1. This result holds for both revenue maximization and profit maximization.

When profit is maximized, we add a disturbance $\bar{\varepsilon}_i$ to the demand equation (5.44), after substitution from (6.7),

$$f_i \, \mathrm{d}(\log q_i) = -\gamma\psi^* \sum_{j=1}^{n} \bar{\theta}_{ij} \, \mathrm{d}\left(\log \frac{p_j}{Y'^j}\right) + \bar{\varepsilon}_i, \tag{7.12}$$

where $\bar{\varepsilon}_1, \ldots, \bar{\varepsilon}_n$ have an n-variate normal distribution with zero means, and variances and covariances of the form

$$\operatorname{cov}(\bar{\varepsilon}_i, \bar{\varepsilon}_j) = \sigma^2 \gamma \psi^* \bar{\theta}_{ij}, \qquad i, j = 1, \ldots, n. \tag{7.13}$$

As in the cost minimizing case, the vectors $\bar{\boldsymbol{\varepsilon}} = (\bar{\varepsilon}_1, \ldots, \bar{\varepsilon}_n)'$ and $\bar{\boldsymbol{\varepsilon}}^* = (\bar{\varepsilon}_1^*, \ldots, \bar{\varepsilon}_m^*)$ are independently distributed, so that the output supply equations for revenue maximization and the input demand equations for profit maximization also form a two-stage block-recursive system. In this case, however, the first stage is (7.12), which yields the n input changes, and the second stage consists of (7.10), which yields the m output changes when the input changes are given.

In contrast to the situation in section 7.1, this can be interpreted as meaning that the firm's input decision takes precedence over the firm's output decision. Evidently, then, by choosing whether to operate on a cost minimizing or a revenue maximizing basis, the profit maximizing firm decides whether the output manager or the input manager is to take precedence over the other.

Implications analogous to the other independence results of section 7.1 also hold for revenue maximization. It is not difficult to verify that the total-output decision and the total-input decision are stochastically independent of the output allocation and input allocation decisions, respectively, where each of these decisions is interpreted as in Chapter 5.

For the firm which maximizes profit directly, rational random behavior implies that the output supply equations are (7.3) and the input demand equations are (7.12). The variance–covariance results given in (7.4) and (7.13) continue to hold. The stochastic independence of input and output decisions characteristic of the other equation systems does not hold here, however, since

$$\operatorname{cov}(\varepsilon_r^*, \bar{\varepsilon}_i) = \sigma^2\psi^* \sum_{s=1}^{m} \theta_{rs}^*\theta_i^s = \sigma^2\psi^* \sum_{j=1}^{n} \bar{\theta}_{ij}\bar{\theta}_r^j. \tag{7.14}$$

This result can be interpreted as meaning that both the cost based and the revenue based systems are simpler than the profit based system in the sense that the firm's decisions are displayed by the former systems in a less interconnected way.

CHAPTER 8

Econometric specification and estimation

The model of the multiproduct firm which we have developed in earlier chapters is entirely theoretical. It is also entirely general with respect to the assumptions we have maintained throughout: exogenously determined prices and long-run optimization. Now, however, we turn to econometric specification and estimation of a model which is based on the theoretical model of the multiproduct firm. Additional assumptions are required to do this; these assumptions are similar to those made by Theil [78] for the Rotterdam model of consumption behavior. In fact, the Rotterdam model has a relationship to the differential version of the theory of the consumer which is very similar to the relationship of the econometric model described below to the differential version of the theory of the multiproduct firm.

In section 8.1 we describe the specification of this model, which is mostly based on Theil and Laitinen [81]. In section 8.2 we consider a set of hypotheses which it is natural to test in this model; these are based on various general and specialized results of earlier chapters. In section 8.3 we consider the problems of estimation and testing. This leads to a family of related models, more or less constrained, which can conveniently be estimated using maximum likelihood techniques.

8.1. Specification of an econometric model

In Chapter 6 we established that the cost based system is somewhat more attractive than either the revenue or profit based systems. The reasons for this superiority, in the case of the revenue based system, have to do with the interesting implications of input and output independence. In effect, we shall be interested in testing whether the firm is output independent, which amounts to a diagonal $\boldsymbol{\Theta}^*$, while we have no such reason to be interested in whether $\bar{\boldsymbol{\Theta}}$ in the revenue based system is diagonal.

The profit based system has the disadvantage that its coefficients are not so directly interpretable as those of the cost based system. In particular, the marginal coefficients θ_i^r which appear in the cost based system do not appear directly in the profit based system. In addition, we found in Chapter 7 that the theory of rational random behavior implies that the disturbances in the supply equations (7.3) are independent of those in the cost based demand equations (7.1). No such independence result applies for the profit based system. This result for the cost based system, we shall see, can also be tested. If true, it should lead to more precise estimates.

As a consequence of these considerations, we shall base our econometric model on the cost based system in its conditional form consisting of input demand equations and output supply equations of the form (7.1) and (7.3), respectively. These demand and supply equations describe the behavior of the firm in terms of infinitesimal changes in the logarithms of prices and quantities. Observation of a firm will not, of course, yield infinitesimal changes; consequently, we shall need to reformulate the model in terms of finite changes. The natural way to do this is by using the log change operator, $\mathrm{D}x_t = \log x_t - \log x_{t-1}$, as a finite change version of the logarithmic differential $\mathrm{d}(\log x)$. Here x stands for any of the prices or quantities which are relevant to the firm, and x_t stands for the value of x in period t. Note that this immediately implies that the model will be suited for time series data.

The factor and product shares $f_i = p_i q_i / C$ and $g_r = y_r z_r / R$ are also observable, and can be calculated for any period from price and quantity data. As in the Rotterdam model, these shares are used to weight logarithmic quantity changes, and consequently either f_{it} or $f_{i,t-1}$ is a plausible candidate to weight $\mathrm{D}q_{it} = \log q_{it} - \log q_{i,t-1}$. We follow the Rotterdam model by using the arithmetic means

$$\bar{f}_{it} = \tfrac{1}{2}(f_{it} + f_{i,t-1}); \qquad \bar{g}_{rt} = \tfrac{1}{2}(g_{rt} + g_{r,t-1}). \tag{8.1}$$

This has the effect of stressing that we are interested in the transition from the equilibrium at time $t-1$ to the equilibrium at time t rather than directly in the equilibria themselves. In effect, we evaluate the change in the factor or product share with respect to the midpoint of that change.

It will be recalled from Chapter 7 that according to the theory of rational random behavior the total input decision (3.43) holds without disturbance. Since finite change versions of the Divisia indexes $\mathrm{d}(\log Q)$ and $\mathrm{d}(\log Z)$ can readily be calculated from observed data as

$$\mathrm{D}Q_t = \sum_{i=1}^{n} \bar{f}_{it}\, \mathrm{D}q_{it}; \qquad \mathrm{D}Z_t = \sum_{r=1}^{m} \bar{g}_{rt}\, \mathrm{D}z_{rt}, \tag{8.2}$$

it follows that in principle γ is observable. The possibility that $\mathrm{D}Z_t$ may be zero makes it unattractive to use the finite change version of the total-input decision to calculate γ; instead we use $\gamma = R/C$ from eq. (4.5) to define

$$\bar{\gamma}_t = \sqrt{\left(\frac{R_t R_{t-1}}{C_t C_{t-1}}\right)}, \tag{8.3}$$

which is the geometric mean of γ in period t and period $t-1$.

There is no reason to expect the finite change version of the total-input decision to hold exactly, although we expect it in general to hold approximately. We therefore compute the residual quantity

$$E_t = \mathrm{D}Q_t - \bar{\gamma}_t\, \mathrm{D}Z_t \tag{8.4}$$

and "correct" the input changes by computing

$$x_{it} = \bar{f}_{it}(\mathrm{D}q_{it} - E_t). \tag{8.5}$$

This correction amounts to enforcing the finite change version of the total-input decision, since summation of the corrected input changes yields

$$\sum_{i=1}^{n} x_{it} = \mathrm{D}Q_t - E_t = \bar{\gamma}_t \,\mathrm{D}Z_t. \tag{8.6}$$

The interpretation of (8.5) as correcting for inexactness induced by finite changes is similar to the interpretation of use of the Divisia volume index in place of the difference between the logarithmic change in expenditure and the Divisia price index in the Rotterdam model. If the residuals E_t are large, it may be difficult to attribute them only to this kind of inexactness. In this case it may be necessary to attribute them instead to changes in productivity. Eq. (8.5) can then be interpreted as correcting for these changes, if it is assumed that they obey a form of neutrality which is a generalization of Hicks-neutral technical change.[1]

Given these modifications in the data, we can now rewrite (7.1) for finite changes as

$$x_{it} = \sum_{r=1}^{m} \theta_i^r w_{rt} + \sum_{j=1}^{n} \pi_{ij} \,\mathrm{D}p_{jt} + \varepsilon_{it}, \tag{8.7}$$

where $w_{rt} = \bar{\gamma}_t \bar{g}_{rt} \,\mathrm{D}z_{rt}$ and $\pi_{ij} = -\psi(\theta_{ij} - \theta_i\theta_j)$. In this formulation we assume that θ_i^r, π_{ij}, and σ^2 are constants, so that (7.2) implies that the contemporaneous covariance matrix of demand disturbances is the same in each period.

The effect of the correction (8.5) is to make (8.6), which can also be written $\Sigma_i x_{it} = \Sigma_r w_{rt}$, hold. This is turn means that

[1]For more on technical change see, for example, Allen [2, ch. 13] and Becker [12]. Other minor changes in the model are also implied by this interpretation, but are outside the scope of this volume.

summation of (8.7) over i will yield $\Sigma_i \theta_i^r = 1$, which is the scalar version of (3.35), $\Sigma_i \pi_{ij} = 0$, and $\Sigma_i \varepsilon_{it} = 0$. These properties are similar to the "adding up" property of the Rotterdam model (see Brown and Deaton [16]) and imply that one (say the last) demand equation is a linear combination of the others, and hence can be deleted from the system.

Interpretation of this deletion is straightforward: eq. (7.1) describes the contribution of the ith input to the Divisia quantity index of inputs in differential terms; the total-input decision implies that when the first $n-1$ such contributions are determined, the last can be obtained as a residual. Consequently, the nth equation conveys no extra information. The correction (8.5) ensures that the same property is obtained in the finite change version.

If we were to assume that the coefficients $\psi^* \theta^*_{rs}$ in (7.3) were constant, (7.4) would imply that the variances and covariances of the supply disturbances depend on γ, which varies over time. By multiplying the finite change version of (7.3) by $\bar{\gamma}_t$, we obtain

$$w_{rt} = \sum_{s=1}^{m} \alpha_{rs} \left[\mathrm{D}y_{st} - \sum_{i=1}^{n} \theta_i^s \, \mathrm{D}p_{it} \right] + \varepsilon^{**}_{rt}, \qquad (8.8)$$

where we assume that $\alpha_{rs} = \bar{\gamma}_t \psi^*_t \theta^*_{rs}$ is constant. Eq. (7.4) then implies that $\mathrm{cov}(\varepsilon^{**}_{rt}, \varepsilon^{**}_{st}) = \sigma^2 \bar{\gamma}_t \psi^*_t \theta^*_{rs} = \sigma^2 \alpha_{rs}$ is also constant.

The specification (8.7) and (8.8) is consistent in the sense that it has homoscedastic disturbances under (7.2) and (7.4) and that the constraint $\Sigma_i \theta_i^r = 1$ will hold for each r. It is not the only such specification: in fact, multiplication of (8.7) and (8.8) by any power k of $\bar{\gamma}_t$ will lead to a consistent specification:

$$(\bar{\gamma}_t^k x_{it}) = \sum_{r=1}^{m} \theta_i^r (\bar{\gamma}_t^k w_{rt}) + \sum_{j=1}^{n} (\bar{\gamma}_t^{2k} \pi_{ijt}) (\mathrm{D}p_{jt}/\bar{\gamma}_t^k) + (\bar{\gamma}_t^k \varepsilon_{it}), \qquad (8.9)$$

$$(\bar{\gamma}_t^k w_{rt}) = \sum_{s=1}^{m} (\bar{\gamma}_t^{2k} \alpha_{rst}) \times \left[(\mathrm{D}y_{st}/\bar{\gamma}_t^k) - \sum_{i=1}^{n} \theta_i^s \, (\mathrm{D}p_{it}/\bar{\gamma}_t^k) \right] + (\bar{\gamma}_t^k \varepsilon^{**}_{rt}), \qquad (8.10)$$

where it is now assumed that $\bar{\gamma}_t^{2k}\alpha_{rst}$, θ_i^r, and $\bar{\gamma}_t^{2k}\pi_{ijt}$ are each constant.

Note that θ_{rs}^* is constant in each of these formulations, since $\Sigma_r \Sigma_s \bar{\gamma}_t^{2k}\alpha_{rst}$ is constant and equal to $\bar{\gamma}_t^{2k+1}\psi_t^*$ by (4.8). This means that the elements of $\boldsymbol{\Theta}^*$ can be obtained by dividing the corresponding elements of the matrix of output price parameters by their sum. It also follows that ψ_t^* is inversely proportional to $\bar{\gamma}_t^{2k+1}$ in the formulation (8.10); whether this is true and for what k are empirical matters.

In all these formulations the marginal coefficients θ_i^r are also postulated to be constant, as is π_{ij} in (8.7). These assumptions are misspecifications which are similar to the misspecification in the Rotterdam model which occurs when its coefficients are taken to be constant. One justification for permitting this misspecification in the Rotterdam model is that the expectations of the resulting estimators will be weighted averages of the actual values taken by the corresponding coefficients (see Theil [80, ch. 14]); a similar but more complex argument applies here. Evidence which will be presented in Chapter 9 is consistent with this thesis.

The other coefficients which we have considered in previous chapters can be estimated using estimates of the above system, but the resulting estimates will generally not be constant. Thus, the estimated version of θ_i can be obtained from

$$\theta_{it} = \sum_{r=1}^{m} \bar{g}_{rt}\theta_i^r, \tag{8.11}$$

which is the finite change analog of (3.26). The estimated version of ψ can be obtained from

$$\frac{\bar{\gamma}_t}{\psi_t} = 1 + \frac{1}{\psi_t^*}\sum_{r=1}^{m}\sum_{s=1}^{m} \bar{g}_{rt}\bar{g}_{st}\theta^{*rs}, \tag{8.12}$$

which is the finite change analog of (4.28), and the estimated version of θ_{ij} can be obtained from

$$\theta_{ijt} = -\frac{1}{\psi_t}\pi_{ij} + \theta_{it}\theta_{jt}, \tag{8.13}$$

which is derived from $\pi_{ij} = -\psi(\theta_{ij} - \theta_i\theta_j)$.

Note that (8.12) provides estimates of ψ in each period, so that ψ is identified for the multiproduct firm. This is in contrast to the situation in the Rotterdam model, where the corresponding coefficient is the income flexibility. There, neither the income flexibility nor the coefficients corresponding to θ_{ij} are identified unless some particular structure is imposed on the utility function. The reason for this is that utility is specified only up to a monotone increasing transformation, which can be interpreted as meaning that utility cannot be measured. The difference is that in the firm output can be measured, and it is through coefficients associated with the outputs that ψ is identified in (8.12).

8.2. Conditions to be tested

The theory of the multiproduct firm leads to several classes of hypotheses which there is reason to test. The first such class is that of basic hypotheses, i.e., those which economic theory predicts should hold for any profit maximizing firm. Just as in consumption theory, there are two of these: homogeneity and symmetry.[2]

In addition to these basic hypotheses, there are hypotheses which need not hold for any given firm. These are concerned with the specific structure of the individual firm, and serve both to represent simplified structures and, if true, to reduce the

[2]An additional basic hypothesis which can be considered is the firm's analog of Slutsky negativity: this amounts to a positive definite matrix $[\alpha_{rs}]$ and a negative semidefinite matrix $[\pi_{ij}]$. For the data used in the next chapter these conditions are met when symmetry is imposed, so there is no reason to consider them explicitly. See Clements [25] for a technique which can be used when the data do not automatically satisfy these conditions.

number of parameters to be estimated. I have chosen to consider output independence (or nonjointness of production) and input–output separability among such structural simplifications.[3]

These hypotheses lend themselves naturally to the nested structure shown in fig. 8.1, where there are six models. The first model is unconstrained; the second has homogeneity imposed; and the third in addition has symmetry imposed. The fourth, fifth, and sixth models all have homogeneity and symmetry imposed, and in addition output independence, input–output separability, or both. The natural procedure is to test and impose these restrictions in sequence as shown in fig. 8.1.

The model consisting of (8.7) and (8.8) does not contain constant terms, just as the Rotterdam model of consumption behavior does not contain constant terms. With some data (see Theil [78, ch. 5]) it has seemed desirable to add constant terms to the Rotterdam model; the interpretation of these terms is that they represent systematic changes in tastes over time. In a similar way, we may want to add constant terms to the model of the multiproduct firm: these terms would then represent systematic changes in the firm's technology. The question of whether constant terms should be added to the model is not nested with the previous hypotheses. Instead, we have another system of six models similar to that shown in fig. 8.1, but with constant terms added to each. The implication is that the necessity for constant terms should be tested at each stage.

The most important implications of the theory of rational random behavior are that demand and supply disturbances should be normally distributed and independent of each other.[4]

[3]Other possible hypotheses are homotheticity in inputs, outputs, or both, and input independence. These are difficult to impose in the model (8.7) and (8.8). Homotheticity in inputs could be studied in a model based on (3.54); input independence is somewhat trickier, because this identifies ψ in a second way in addition to the one described at the end of section 8.1. Block independence of inputs or outputs can also be imposed.

[4]We have already used the particular covariance structure given in (7.2) and (7.4) to produce homoscedastic disturbances in the system (8.7) and (8.8). It is possible to impose this covariance structure in the course of estimation using techniques akin to those used by Theil and Laitinen [82]. However, these techniques are complex, and the results presented in the next chapter suggest that this would not be very fruitful.

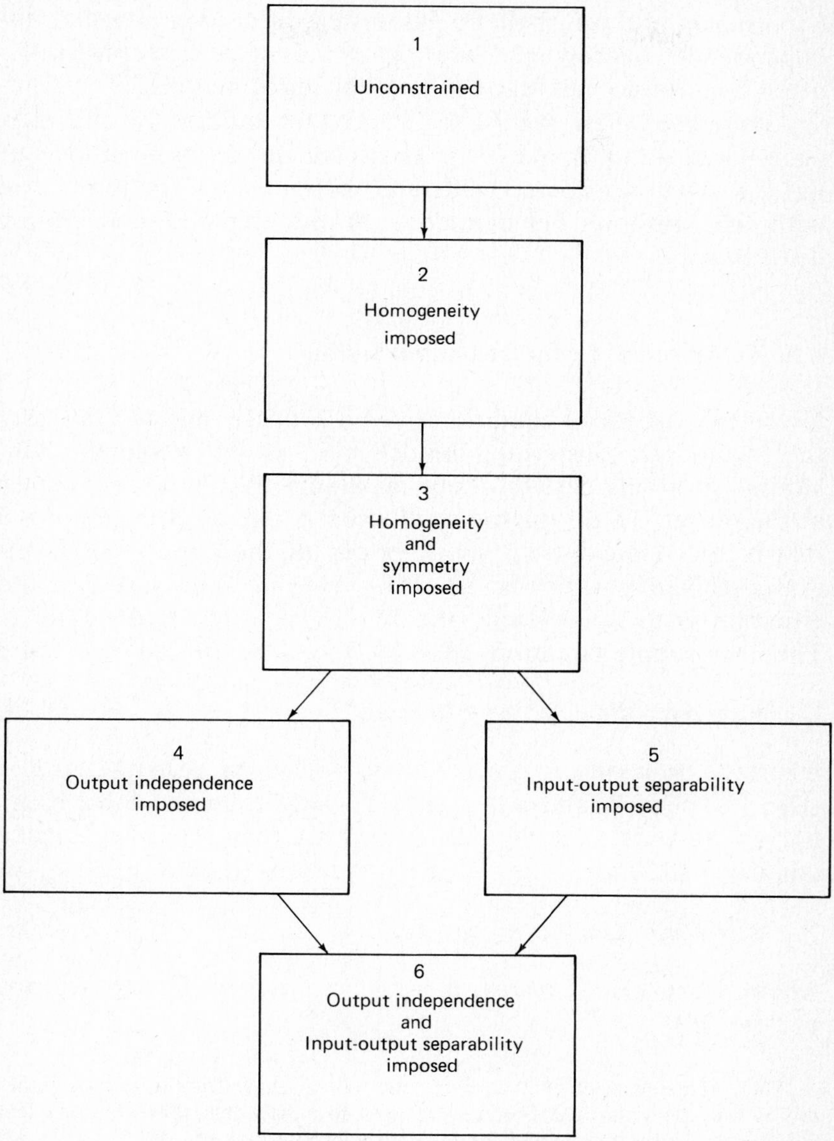

Figure 8.1. Structure of hypothesis testing.

In the next section we shall take normality as a maintained hypothesis, but we shall be interested in testing whether independence is acceptable. This again cannot be nested with the other hypotheses and leads to another set of models.

Altogether, then, we have twenty-four models to consider, each based on (8.7) and (8.8). These are the six basic models of fig. 8.1, each considered with and without constant terms and with and without independence of the demand and supply disturbances.

8.3. Techniques of estimation and testing

Given the variety of conditions we wish to test and the fact that the symmetry constrained models all involve nonlinear constraints, it seems best to adopt maximum likelihood techniques at the outset. To do this we shall write $\boldsymbol{A} = [\alpha_{rs}]$, $\boldsymbol{B}$ as the $m \times n$ matrix of coefficients of input prices in the supply equations (8.8),[5] $\boldsymbol{C} = [\theta_i^r]$, which is $n-1$ by m, since the last demand equation is to be deleted, and $\boldsymbol{D} = [\pi_{ij}]$, which is $n-1$ by n. Then the supply equations (8.8) for $r = 1, \ldots, m$ can be written

$$\boldsymbol{w}_t = \boldsymbol{A}\boldsymbol{y}_t + \boldsymbol{B}\boldsymbol{p}_t + \boldsymbol{\varepsilon}_t^{**} = \boldsymbol{M}\boldsymbol{u}_t + \boldsymbol{\varepsilon}_t^{**}, \tag{8.14}$$

where $\boldsymbol{w}_t = (w_{1t}, \ldots, w_{mt})'$, $\boldsymbol{y}_t = (\mathrm{D}y_{1t}, \ldots, \mathrm{D}y_{mt})'$, $\boldsymbol{p}_t = (\mathrm{D}p_{1t}, \ldots, \mathrm{D}p_{nt})'$, and $\boldsymbol{\varepsilon}_t^{**} = (\varepsilon_{1t}^{**}, \ldots, \varepsilon_{mt}^{**})'$. In the third member we have $\boldsymbol{M} = [\boldsymbol{A}\ \boldsymbol{B}]$ and $\boldsymbol{u}_t' = (\boldsymbol{y}_t'\ \boldsymbol{p}_t')$. Similarly, the demand equations (8.7) for $i = 1, \ldots, n-1$ can be written

$$\boldsymbol{x}_t = \boldsymbol{C}\boldsymbol{w}_t + \boldsymbol{D}\boldsymbol{p}_t + \boldsymbol{\varepsilon}_t = \boldsymbol{N}\boldsymbol{v}_t + \boldsymbol{\varepsilon}_t, \tag{8.15}$$

where $x_t = (x_{1t}, \ldots, x_{n-1,t})'$, $\boldsymbol{\varepsilon}_t = (\varepsilon_{1t}, \ldots, \varepsilon_{n-1,t})'$, $\boldsymbol{N} = [\boldsymbol{C}\ \boldsymbol{D}]$, and $\boldsymbol{v}_t' = (\boldsymbol{w}_t'\ \boldsymbol{p}_t')$.

[5]The (r, i)th element of $\boldsymbol{B}$ corresponds to $-\Sigma_s \alpha_{rs}\theta_i^s$; for the unconstrained model the elements of $\boldsymbol{B}$ are not required to satisfy this constraint, but can vary freely. In the model with homogeneity imposed we require $\boldsymbol{A\iota}^* + \boldsymbol{B\iota} = \boldsymbol{0}$, while in the symmetry constrained models the above constraint is imposed: see table 8.1 below.

Next we write

$$\mathscr{V}\begin{pmatrix}\boldsymbol{\varepsilon}_t^{**}\\ \boldsymbol{\varepsilon}_t\end{pmatrix}=\boldsymbol{\Sigma};\qquad \mathscr{V}(\boldsymbol{\varepsilon}_t^{**})=\boldsymbol{\Omega}^*;\qquad \mathscr{V}(\boldsymbol{\varepsilon}_t)=\boldsymbol{\Omega},\tag{8.16}$$

as our covariance structure. The hypothesis of independent demand and supply disturbances under the assumption of normality amounts to

$$\boldsymbol{\Sigma}=\begin{bmatrix}\boldsymbol{\Omega}^* & 0\\ 0 & \boldsymbol{\Omega}\end{bmatrix}.\tag{8.17}$$

Under the additional assumption that the disturbances are independent in different periods, we then obtain as the logarithm of the likelihood function

$$\begin{aligned}L=&-\frac{T(m+n-1)}{2}\log 2\pi-\frac{T}{2}\log|\boldsymbol{\Sigma}|\\ &-\frac{1}{2}\sum_{t=1}^{T}\begin{bmatrix}\boldsymbol{w}_t-\boldsymbol{M}\boldsymbol{u}_t\\ \boldsymbol{x}_t-\boldsymbol{N}\boldsymbol{v}_t\end{bmatrix}'\boldsymbol{\Sigma}^{-1}\begin{bmatrix}\boldsymbol{w}_t-\boldsymbol{M}\boldsymbol{u}_t\\ \boldsymbol{x}_t-\boldsymbol{N}\boldsymbol{v}_t\end{bmatrix},\end{aligned}\tag{8.18}$$

where T is the number of observations.

For any one of the twenty-four particular forms of this model, we wish to find the values of the parameters which will maximize this function. To do this we seek to equate the derivatives of L to zero. As is usually the case, when we take the derivatives of (8.18) with respect to $\boldsymbol{\Sigma}^{-1}$, we obtain[6]

$$\hat{\boldsymbol{\Sigma}}=\frac{1}{T}\sum_{t=1}^{T}\begin{bmatrix}\boldsymbol{w}_t-\boldsymbol{M}\boldsymbol{u}_t\\ \boldsymbol{x}_t-\boldsymbol{N}\boldsymbol{v}_t\end{bmatrix}\begin{bmatrix}\boldsymbol{w}_t-\boldsymbol{M}\boldsymbol{u}_t\\ \boldsymbol{x}_t-\boldsymbol{N}\boldsymbol{v}_t\end{bmatrix}'\tag{8.19}$$

as the conditional estimate of $\boldsymbol{\Sigma}$ given $\boldsymbol{M}$ and $\boldsymbol{N}$ when $\boldsymbol{\Sigma}$ is not constrained. When $\boldsymbol{\Sigma}$ is constrained by (8.17), substitution of

[6]This follows from $\partial(\log|\boldsymbol{\Sigma}^{-1}|)/\partial\boldsymbol{\Sigma}^{-1}=\boldsymbol{\Sigma}'$ and $\partial(\boldsymbol{a}'\boldsymbol{\Sigma}^{-1}\boldsymbol{a})/\partial\boldsymbol{\Sigma}^{-1}=\boldsymbol{a}\boldsymbol{a}'$; see Theil [76, ch. 1]. Note that it is not necessary to impose symmetry on $\hat{\boldsymbol{\Sigma}}$ because the estimate which emerges is symmetric in any case.

(8.17) into (8.18) shows that the diagonal blocks of $\hat{\boldsymbol{\Sigma}}(\hat{\boldsymbol{\Omega}}^*$ and $\hat{\boldsymbol{\Omega}})$ are the same as in (8.19), but the off-diagonal blocks become zero.

For the unconstrained model (model 1 in fig. 8.1), the elements of $\boldsymbol{M}$ and $\boldsymbol{N}$ are permitted to vary freely when we seek the maximum of (8.18). In order to apply any of the constraints, it is convenient to regard the elements of $\boldsymbol{M}$ and $\boldsymbol{N}$ as functions of a vector $\boldsymbol{\mu}$ which contains a smaller number of parameters. The parameter matrices for each of the six basic models are given in table 8.1 for $m = n = 2$ in partitioned form:[7]

$$\begin{bmatrix} \boldsymbol{M} \\ \boldsymbol{N} \end{bmatrix} = \begin{bmatrix} \boldsymbol{A} & \boldsymbol{B} \\ \boldsymbol{C} & \boldsymbol{D} \end{bmatrix}. \tag{8.20}$$

For illustrative purposes, consider the third model in which symmetry is imposed. Here the vector of free parameters is $\boldsymbol{\mu} = (\alpha_{11}, \alpha_{12}, \alpha_{22}, \theta_1^1, \theta_1^2, \pi_{11})$. Symmetry is imposed on $\boldsymbol{A}$ by requiring that the off-diagonal elements are equal. Symmetry of $\boldsymbol{D}$ is guaranteed when homogeneity is imposed because $n = 2$. Note that none of the elements of $\boldsymbol{B}$ is a free parameter in this model because symmetry requires that $\boldsymbol{B} = -\boldsymbol{AK}'$.

Now for given $\boldsymbol{\Sigma}$ we consider (8.18) as a function of $\boldsymbol{\mu}$ and take the derivative with respect to the ith element of $\boldsymbol{\mu}$:

$$\frac{\partial L}{\partial \mu_i} = \sum_{t=1}^{T} \begin{bmatrix} \boldsymbol{w}_t - \boldsymbol{M}\boldsymbol{u}_t \\ \boldsymbol{x}_t - \boldsymbol{N}\boldsymbol{v}_t \end{bmatrix}' \boldsymbol{\Sigma}^{-1} \begin{bmatrix} \dfrac{\partial \boldsymbol{M}}{\partial \mu_i} \boldsymbol{u}_t \\ \dfrac{\partial \boldsymbol{N}}{\partial \mu_i} \boldsymbol{v}_t \end{bmatrix}. \tag{8.21}$$

The first-order conditions for a maximum of L which are required in addition to (8.19) are then obtained by setting (8.21) equal to zero for each μ_i. The second-order condition (again for given $\boldsymbol{\Sigma}$) for a maximum of L is that the matrix formed of

[7]When constant terms are added to these models, the only difference is that an additional column of free parameters is added; correspondingly, an extra variable always equal to one is added to $\boldsymbol{u}_t$ and $\boldsymbol{v}_t$.

elements

$$\frac{\partial^2 L}{\partial \mu_i\, \partial \mu_j} = -\sum_{t=1}^{T} \begin{bmatrix} \dfrac{\partial \boldsymbol{M}}{\partial \mu_j} \boldsymbol{u}_t \\ \dfrac{\partial \boldsymbol{N}}{\partial \mu_j} \boldsymbol{v}_t \end{bmatrix}' \boldsymbol{\Sigma}^{-1} \begin{bmatrix} \dfrac{\partial \boldsymbol{M}}{\partial \mu_i} \boldsymbol{u}_t \\ \dfrac{\partial \boldsymbol{N}}{\partial \mu_i} \boldsymbol{v}_t \end{bmatrix}$$

$$+\sum_{t=1}^{T} \begin{bmatrix} \boldsymbol{w}_t - \boldsymbol{M}\boldsymbol{u}_t \\ \boldsymbol{x}_t - \boldsymbol{N}\boldsymbol{v}_t \end{bmatrix}' \boldsymbol{\Sigma}^{-1} \begin{bmatrix} \dfrac{\partial^2 \boldsymbol{M}}{\partial \mu_i\, \partial \mu_j} \boldsymbol{u}_t \\ \dfrac{\partial^2 \boldsymbol{N}}{\partial \mu_i\, \partial \mu_j} \boldsymbol{v}_t \end{bmatrix} \tag{8.22}$$

Table 8.1
Relation of basic and derived parameters: Two outputs, two inputs.

1 Unconstrained	α_{11}	α_{12}	β_{11}	β_{12}
	α_{21}	α_{22}	β_{21}	β_{22}
	θ_1^1	θ_1^2	π_{11}	π_{12}
2 Homogeneity imposed	α_{11}	α_{12}	β_{11}	$-(\alpha_{11}+\alpha_{12}+\beta_{11})$
	α_{21}	α_{22}	β_{21}	$-(\alpha_{21}+\alpha_{22}+\beta_{21})$
	θ_1^1	θ_1^2	π_{11}	$-\pi_{11}$
3 Symmetry imposed	α_{11}	α_{12}	$-\alpha_{11}\theta_1^1-\alpha_{12}\theta_1^2$	$-\alpha_{11}(1-\theta_1^1)-\alpha_{12}(1-\theta_1^2)$
	α_{12}	α_{22}	$-\alpha_{12}\theta_1^1-\alpha_{22}\theta_1^2$	$-\alpha_{12}(1-\theta_1^1)-\alpha_{22}(1-\theta_1^2)$
	θ_1^1	θ_1^2	π_{11}	$-\pi_{11}$
4 Output independence imposed	α_{11}	0	$-\alpha_{11}\theta_1^1$	$-\alpha_{11}(1-\theta_1^1)$
	0	α_{22}	$-\alpha_{22}\theta_1^2$	$-\alpha_{22}(1-\theta_1^2)$
	θ_1^1	θ_1^2	π_{11}	$-\pi_{11}$
5 Input–Output separability imposed	α_{11}	α_{12}	$-(\alpha_{11}+\alpha_{12})\theta_1^1$	$-(\alpha_{11}+\alpha_{12})(1-\theta_1^1)$
	α_{12}	α_{22}	$-(\alpha_{12}+\alpha_{22})\theta_1^1$	$-(\alpha_{12}+\alpha_{22})(1-\theta_1^1)$
	θ_1^1	θ_1^1	π_{11}	$-\pi_{11}$
6 Output independence and input–output separability imposed	α_{11}	0	$-\alpha_{11}\theta_1^1$	$-\alpha_{11}(1-\theta_1^1)$
	0	α_{22}	$-\alpha_{22}\theta_1^1$	$-\alpha_{22}(1-\theta_1^1)$
	θ_1^1	θ_1^1	π_{11}	$-\pi_{11}$

be negative definite. The expectation of the sum in the second line of (8.22) is zero; consequently the information matrix has elements

$$-\mathscr{E}\left(\frac{\partial^2 L}{\partial \mu_i\, \partial \mu_j}\right) = \sum_{t=1}^{T} \begin{bmatrix} \dfrac{\partial \boldsymbol{M}}{\partial \mu_j} \boldsymbol{u}_t \\ \dfrac{\partial \boldsymbol{N}}{\partial \mu_j} \boldsymbol{v}_t \end{bmatrix}' \boldsymbol{\Sigma}^{-1} \begin{bmatrix} \dfrac{\partial \boldsymbol{M}}{\partial \mu_i} \boldsymbol{u}_t \\ \dfrac{\partial \boldsymbol{N}}{\partial \mu_i} \boldsymbol{v}_t \end{bmatrix}. \tag{8.23}$$

Given values of the parameters which maximize L, the inverse of the matrix with elements (8.23) will yield an asymptotic estimate of the covariance matrix of the estimators of $\boldsymbol{\mu}$, from which standard errors may be obtained.

For a given vector $\boldsymbol{\mu}$ we define $\boldsymbol{a}$ as the vector with ith element $\partial L/\partial \mu_i$ given in (8.21) and $\boldsymbol{E}$ as the square matrix whose (i, j)th element is $-\mathscr{E}(\partial^2 L/\partial \mu_i\, \partial \mu_j)$ given in (8.23). Then our iterative procedure for finding the maximum of the logarithmic likelihood function (8.18) consists of the following steps. First we compute $\hat{\boldsymbol{\Sigma}}$ using (8.19) with $\boldsymbol{M}$ and $\boldsymbol{N}$ evaluated at the given $\boldsymbol{\mu}$. If we wish to impose (8.17) we simply force the off-diagonal blocks of $\hat{\boldsymbol{\Sigma}}$ to be zero. Then we use (8.21) and (8.23) to compute $\boldsymbol{a}$ and $\boldsymbol{E}$, after which we obtain

$$\Delta\boldsymbol{\mu} = \boldsymbol{E}^{-1}\boldsymbol{a}. \tag{8.24}$$

If the elements of $\Delta\boldsymbol{\mu}$ are sufficiently small in absolute value compared to the elements of $\boldsymbol{\mu}$, we accept the given $\boldsymbol{\mu}$ as the vector of likelihood maximizing estimates and $\boldsymbol{E}^{-1}$ as its asymptotic covariance matrix. Otherwise we compute a new vector $\boldsymbol{\mu}$ as $\boldsymbol{\mu} + \Delta\boldsymbol{\mu}$ and proceed again.

Given likelihood maximizing estimates $\hat{\boldsymbol{\mu}}$ and $\hat{\boldsymbol{\Sigma}}$, eq. (8.19) implies that the sum in the second line of (8.18) can be written as

$$\tfrac{1}{2}\,\mathrm{tr}[\hat{\boldsymbol{\Sigma}}^{-1}(T\hat{\boldsymbol{\Sigma}})] = -\frac{T(m+n-1)}{2}. \tag{8.25}$$

Thus, the value of the logarithm of the maximized likelihood function is

$$L_{\max} = -\frac{T(m+n-1)}{2}\log 2\pi e - \frac{T}{2}\log|\hat{\boldsymbol{\Sigma}}|. \tag{8.26}$$

This value for different nested models can be used to perform a test of the hypothesis that the more restrictive model holds, against the alternative that the other does. This is based on the fact that minus twice the logarithm of the ratio of the value of the maximized likelihood function for the more restrictive model to the value for the less restrictive model is distributed asymptotically as a χ^2 variate. The number of degrees of freedom of this variate is determined by the difference between the numbers of free parameters in the two models.[8]

The number of free parameters can be determined, in the case of two outputs and two inputs, from table 8.1. Thus, for the unconstrained model twelve free parameters appear there. In addition, there are variances and covariances; if the input and output disturbances are independent these amount to the variances of the two output disturbances, their covariance, and the variance of the input disturbance. Thus, we obtain sixteen free parameters for the unconstrained model without constant terms and with independence of the input and output disturbances. This number is entered in table 8.2, together with similar entries for the twenty-three other models. For each of the six basic models, adding a constant terms adds three free parameters, while allowing the input and output disturbances to be correlated adds two, which represent the covariances of the input disturbance with the output disturbances.

Now hypothesis testing is straightforward. Suppose we wish to test the compound hypothesis that homogeneity and symmetry hold, no constant terms are needed, and the demand and supply disturbances are uncorrelated. As an alternative hypothesis we take the case where none of these conditions holds. What we

[8]For a description of the large sample properties of maximum likelihood estimators and the asymptotic distribution of the likelihood ratio, see Theil [76, section 8.5].

Table 8.2
The number of free parameters: Two outputs, two inputs.

Basic model	Dependent disturbances		Independent disturbances	
	Constant	No constant	Constant	No constant
1	21	18	19	16
2	18	15	16	13
3	15	12	13	10
4	14	11	12	9
5	14	11	12	9
6	13	10	11	8

then need to do is to estimate the first basic model with dependent disturbances and a constant term, and the third basic model, where homogeneity and symmetry have been imposed, without constant terms and with independent disturbances. Each of these models will yield a maximized value of the logarithmic likelihood function according to (8.26). We subtract the second (restricted) value from the first (unrestricted) one and multiply by two to obtain a test statistic which is asymptotically distributed as a χ^2 variate. Assuming there are two inputs and two outputs, we can consult table 8.2 to see that the unrestricted model has twenty-one free parameters, while the restricted one has ten. Thus, the test statistic is asymptotically distributed as $\chi^2(11)$.

CHAPTER 9

Application to hypothetical data

In principle the procedures described in Chapter 8 can now be applied to data. However, the requirements which such a set of data must fulfill before it matches the assumptions of the model are rather stringent. Strictly, what is needed is a time series of observations of quantities and prices for some multiproduct firm which regards its input and output prices as exogenous; that is, a competitive, profit maximizing multiproduct firm.[1] The typical firm for which data of this sort are available is in a regulated industry (railroads and utilities are the outstanding examples), and hence these assumptions do not apply.[2]

Another sort of data which could be used with this model also includes a time series of input and output prices, but has quantity data which are averages of the inputs and outputs of a large number of relatively homogeneous firms. An example of this would be average farm data from an area where crop and livestock choices are reasonably homogeneous.[3] Undoubtedly

[1]According to the developments of the last chapter, we should also assume that the technology of the firm remains fixed over the duration of this time series. This is implausible, but what exactly should be done to cope with violation of this assumption cannot be decided except with regard to particular data.

[2]It can generally be assumed that U.S. railroads minimize costs, but the requirement that they provide services on demand at the prices established by the Interstate Commerce Commission generally means that output prices and marginal costs will not be the same. Rate-of-return regulation, which applies to many utilities, implies that not even cost minimizing behavior can be assumed.

[3]Data of this sort are actually closer to the per capita data typically used in the Rotterdam model than the single firm data suggested in the paragraph above. This suggests that a statistical aggregation argument akin to that of Barnett [8] might be used to justify such an approach. Note, however, that the number of firms in an industry is generally much smaller than the number of consumers in an economy.

such data could be developed from existing sources with sufficient effort, but it does not appear to be available now.

As a consequence, it was decided that the appropriate first step toward implementation of the econometric model of Chapter 8 is with hypothetical data. An advantage of this approach is that it permits assessment of the properties of the model. In particular, it is possible to assess whether the known misspecification in this model affects either the testing or the estimation techniques associated with the model. It is also possible to compare the known properties of the hypothetical data with the results of estimation and testing.

Section 9.1 describes four cost functions, and section 9.2 describes how these functions were used to generate hypothetical data. In section 9.3 we discuss numerical problems which were encountered when maximum likelihood estimation was attempted, as well as the techniques which were used to solve these problems. In section 9.4 we describe the results of hypothesis testing, and in section 9.5 the parameter estimates are compared with the coefficients to which they correspond.

9.1. Four cost functions

In order to assess the capability of the hypothesis-testing procedure described in Chapter 8, I decided to use four cost functions, each defined for two outputs and two input prices. The first cost function is[4]

$$C_1(z, \boldsymbol{p}) = (p_1 z_1^{\alpha_1} + p_2 z_2^{\alpha_2})^{\tau_0}\, p_1^{\tau_1} p_2^{\tau_2}, \tag{9.1}$$

where the α's and τ's are parameters satisfying $\alpha_1, \alpha_2 > 1/\tau_0$; τ_0, τ_1, $\tau_2 > 0$; and $\tau_0 + \tau_1 + \tau_2 = 1$. This cost function is neither

[4]Strictly speaking, each of the variables p_1, p_2, z_1, and z_2 should be multiplied by a constant which serves to equate the dimension of cost (say, dollars/year) to the dimension of the expression on the right. By suitable choice of units these constants can be made to take the numeric value 1, so I have suppressed them for simplicity.

output independent nor input–output separable, and consequently it corresponds to the third basic model of Chapter 8.

The second cost function is

$$C_2(z, p) = (p_1^{\tau_0} z_1^{\alpha_1} + p_2^{\tau_0} z_2^{\alpha_2}) p_1^{\tau_1} p_2^{\tau_2}, \tag{9.2}$$

where again the α's and τ's are parameters. For this function the parameters must satisfy $\alpha_1, \alpha_2 > 1$; $\tau_0, \tau_1, \tau_2 > 0$; and $\tau_0 + \tau_1 + \tau_2 = 1$. This cost function is output independent since it can be written as the sum of two functions, one involving only the first output and a second involving only the second. It is not input–output separable, so it corresponds to the fourth basic model in Chapter 8.

The third cost function is

$$C_3(z, p) = (z_1^{\alpha_1} + z_2^{\alpha_2})^{\tau_0} p_1^{\tau_1} p_2^{\tau_2}, \tag{9.3}$$

where the α's and τ's are parameters which satisfy $\alpha_1, \alpha_2 > 1/\tau_0 > 1$; $\tau_1, \tau_2 > 0$; and $\tau_1 + \tau_2 = 1$. Since this cost function can be decomposed into a function of the input prices and a function of the outputs, it is input–output separable (see (4.34)). It is not output independent, so it corresponds to the fifth basic model in Chapter 8. Note that the multiplicative decomposability of (9.3) also implies that this cost function is homothetic in inputs (see (4.42)).

The fourth cost function is

$$C_4(z, p) = (z_1^{\alpha_1} + z_2^{\alpha_2}) p_1^{\tau_1} p_2^{\tau_2}, \tag{9.4}$$

where the parameters satisfy $\alpha_1, \alpha_2 > 1$; $\tau_1, \tau_2 > 0$; and $\tau_1 + \tau_2 = 1$. Since this cost function is both additively separable between the outputs and multiplicatively separable between the outputs and the input prices, it is both output independent and input–output separable, and hence corresponds to the sixth basic model in Chapter 8. This cost function is also homothetic in inputs; we showed in section 4.6 that this is necessary for any cost function which is both output independent and input–output separable.

If $\alpha_1 = \alpha_2 = \alpha$ for any of these four cost functions, it is the cost function corresponding to a firm which exhibits homogeneous production, and hence is homothetic in both inputs and outputs. The elasticities of cost of the four cost functions are constant and equal respectively to $\alpha\tau_0$, α, $\alpha\tau_0$, and α in this case. If $\alpha_1 \neq \alpha_2$ for any of these cost functions, then it is not homothetic in outputs, and C_1 and C_2 are not homothetic in inputs either.

In order to generate data from these cost functions, it is necessary to specify values of the parameters for each. The values chosen were intended to make the "firms" corresponding to the cost functions behave as similarly as possible. Thus, α_1 and α_2 were chosen in each case in such a way that γ, the elasticity of cost, varies between 1.1 and 1.2, with the first value corresponding to specialization in production of z_2. In addition, τ_1, τ_2, and τ_0 (where it appears) were chosen in such a way as to make the factor shares of q_1 and q_2 approximately two-thirds and one-third, respectively.

The actual specifications of these parameters, together with the values of the coefficients which were derived in Chapters 3 and 4, are presented in tables 9.1 and 9.2. The coefficients and the equilibrium position for each cost function are evaluated at $y_1 = y_2 = p_1 = p_2 = 1$.

There are several points about these tables which should be noted. First, the two cost functions which are not output independent, C_1 and C_3, yield identical values for cost, revenue, profit, γ, and output levels. This occurs because when $p_1 = p_2 = 1$, eqs. (9.1) and (9.3) imply that C_1 and C_3, regarded as functions of output only, are identical. A similar comment applies to C_2 and C_4, the two cost functions which are output independent.

The output independent cost functions have a level of operation which is about one-tenth that of the cost functions which are not output independent. This occurs because the matrix $\boldsymbol{\Theta}^*$ for C_1 and C_3 indicates that the two outputs are very strong specific substitutes: the measure (6.29) which we described in Chapter 6 as a measure of output interaction takes the value 1.017 for $\boldsymbol{\Theta}^*$, as evaluated in table 9.2. For the case of two

Table 9.1
Parameter and variable values of four cost functions at unit prices.

Parameter or variable	Nonseparable		Input–output separable	
	Not independent	Output independent	Not independent	Output independent
	C_1	C_2	C_3	C_4
R	9.0229	0.7874	9.0229	0.7874
C	7.9113	0.6854	7.9113	0.6854
π	1.1117	0.1020	1.1117	0.1020
γ	1.1405	1.1489	1.1405	1.1489
z_1	3.8463	0.4019	3.8463	0.4019
z_2	5.1766	0.3855	5.1766	0.3855
g_1	0.4263	0.5104	0.4263	0.5104
g_2	0.5737	0.4896	0.5737	0.4896
q_1	4.7672	0.4416	5.1423	0.4455
q_2	3.1441	0.2438	2.7690	0.2399
f_1	0.6026	0.6443	0.65[a]	0.65[a]
f_2	0.3974	0.3557	0.35[a]	0.35[a]
α_1	2.4[a]	1.2[a]	2.4[a]	1.2[a]
α_2	2.2[a]	1.1[a]	2.2[a]	1.1[a]
τ_0	0.5[a]	0.5[a]	0.5[a]	–
τ_1	0.4[a]	0.4[a]	0.65[a]	0.65[a]
τ_2	0.1[a]	0.1[a]	0.35[a]	0.35[a]

[a]These coefficients and parameters are constant.

outputs, positive values of the off-diagonal elements of $\boldsymbol{\Theta}^*$ imply that the matrix $\partial^2 C/\partial z\,\partial z'$ has negative off-diagonal elements. This in turn means that an increase in the production of either output reduces the marginal cost of the other.

In contrast to this, note that the matrix $\boldsymbol{\Theta}$ for the input–output separable cost functions C_3 and C_4 is almost diagonal: the measure (6.28) of input interaction is 2.8×10^{-6} for C_3 and 7.0×10^{-7} for C_4, as evaluated in table 9.2. For C_1 and C_2 it takes the larger values 0.106 and 0.021 respectively. In the latter two functions the inputs are specific complements, while in the former they are specific substitutes in a minor way.

Table 9.2
Coefficient values of four cost functions at unit prices.

	Nonseparable		Input–output separable	
	Not independent	Output independent	Not independent	Output independent
Coefficient	C_1	C_2	C_3	C_4
ψ^*	7.2833	7.4481	7.2833	7.4481
θ^*_{11}	0.1769	0.3426	0.1769	0.3426
θ^*_{12}	0.2122	0.0[a]	0.2122	0.0[a]
θ^*_{22}	0.3988	0.6574	0.3988	0.6574
ψ	0.9963	0.9981	0.9963	0.9981
θ_{11}	0.5084	0.5963	0.6508	0.6504
θ_{12}	0.1153	0.0589	−0.0008	−0.0004
θ_{22}	0.2610	0.2859	0.3508	0.3504
θ^1_1	1.1974	0.9[a]	0.65[a]	0.65[a]
θ^1_2	−0.1974	0.1[a]	0.35[a]	0.35[a]
θ^2_1	0.1974	0.4[a]	0.65[a]	0.65[a]
θ^2_2	0.8026	0.6[a]	0.35[a]	0.35[a]
θ_1	0.6237	0.6552	0.65[a]	0.65[a]
θ_2	0.3763	0.3448	0.35[a]	0.35[a]
π_{11}	−0.1190	−0.1667	−0.2275[a]	−0.2275[a]

[a]These coefficients are constant.

Finally, note that for C_1 the coefficient θ^1_2 takes a negative value, which indicates that an increase in the production of z_1, with z_2 and the input prices remaining constant, will result in a decrease in the demand for q_2: with respect to z_1, q_2 is an inferior input, although it has a Divisia elasticity θ_2/f_2 only slightly below unity.

9.2. Generation of hypothetical data

To generate data from these functions it is necessary to begin with exogenous input and output price data. For this purpose I took Theil's [78, ch. 5] four-good Dutch consumer data, which is in the form of logarithmic price changes. These were converted to a set of four price indexes for years 0–31, with each index in year 0 set to unity.[5] These indexes are shown in table 9.3. The price log changes, which are the relevant variables for estimation and are the same for each set of data which was generated, are also reproduced in table 9.3.

It should be noted that there is a considerable amount of relative price variation in these price indexes. Comparing year 0 values to year 31 values indicates that the first output price has been reduced almost 30 percent while the second is almost unchanged. The first input price has been reduced by slightly under 10 percent, while the second has increased by almost 50 percent. On the surface this suggests that a firm which manufactures z_1 and z_2 ought to shift from z_1 to z_2 and from q_2 to q_1 over the entire period covered by these indexes, but we shall see that this is somewhat misleading.

Given these price series, I calculated profit maximizing levels of inputs and outputs for each cost function and each year. The method used to find the profit maximizing levels of outputs was similar to that described in Chapter 8 for finding the maximum of the likelihood function. For given $\boldsymbol{z}$ ($\boldsymbol{p}$ is exogenously given), we calculated

$$\boldsymbol{a} = \frac{\partial C}{\partial \boldsymbol{z}} - \boldsymbol{y}, \tag{9.5}$$

which should be zero at the point of maximum profit (see (4.1)). Then we computed

$$\boldsymbol{E} = \frac{\partial^2 C}{\partial \boldsymbol{z}\, \partial \boldsymbol{z}'} \tag{9.6}$$

[5]Because it seems likely that output data of a firm will be less aggregated than input data, I took the two price change series which showed greater variation as output price changes and the other two as input price changes. The reason for choosing existing price data rather than generating new "data" was to avoid unrealistic behavior of these "exogenous" variables.

Table 9.3
Input and output price indexes and price changes.[a]

	Price indexes				Price changes			
	Outputs		Inputs		Outputs		Inputs	
t	y_{1t}	y_{2t}	p_{1t}	p_{2t}	Dy_{1t}	Dy_{2t}	Dp_{1t}	Dp_{2t}
0	1.0000	1.0000	1.0000	1.0000				
1	0.9080	0.9536	0.9878	0.9918	−0.0965	−0.0475	−0.0123	−0.0082
2	0.9117	0.9591	0.9900	0.9905	0.0041	0.0057	0.0023	−0.0013
3	0.9164	0.9913	0.9816	0.9789	0.0051	0.0331	−0.0086	−0.0118
4	0.8533	0.9255	0.9210	0.9703	−0.0713	−0.0687	−0.0637	−0.0088
5	0.8487	0.8929	0.9179	0.9755	−0.0055	−0.0359	−0.0034	0.0053
6	0.8493	0.9013	0.9126	0.9828	0.0008	0.0094	−0.0058	0.0074
7	0.8487	0.8999	0.8692	0.9852	−0.0007	−0.0016	−0.0487	0.0025
8	0.7836	0.8432	0.8587	0.9724	−0.0799	−0.0650	−0.0121	−0.0131
9	0.7337	0.7420	0.8395	0.9453	−0.0658	−0.1279	−0.0226	−0.0283
10	0.6523	0.6404	0.7890	0.9155	−0.1176	−0.1473	−0.0621	−0.0320
11	0.6031	0.6333	0.7506	0.8875	−0.0783	−0.0111	−0.0499	−0.0310
12	0.5874	0.6363	0.7389	0.8676	−0.0265	0.0047	−0.0157	−0.0227

13	0.5679	0.6131	0.6999	0.8431	−0.0337	−0.0371	−0.0542	−0.0287
14	0.5180	0.6072	0.6805	0.8120	−0.0919	−0.0097	−0.0281	−0.0376
15	0.5569	0.6508	0.6887	0.8288	0.0724	0.0693	0.0120	0.0205
16	0.5811	0.6788	0.6914	0.8289	0.0425	0.0421	0.0038	0.0002
17	0.6120	0.6701	0.6939	0.8315	0.0518	−0.0128	0.0037	0.0031
18	0.6715	0.7528	0.7207	0.8773	0.0927	0.1163	0.0378	0.0536
19	0.7331	0.8120	0.7884	0.9655	0.1409	0.0758	0.0898	0.0958
20	0.7031	0.8453	0.7972	1.0026	−0.0948	0.0401	0.0111	0.0377
21	0.6920	0.8348	0.7923	0.9994	−0.0159	−0.0125	−0.0061	−0.0032
22	0.6980	0.8647	0.8107	1.0675	0.0086	0.0352	0.0229	0.0659
23	0.6960	0.8757	0.8144	1.1046	−0.0029	0.0127	0.0046	0.0342
24	0.6911	0.9109	0.8084	1.1375	−0.0071	0.0394	−0.0074	0.0293
25	0.6975	0.9551	0.8667	1.2123	0.0092	0.0474	0.0696	0.0637
26	0.6927	0.9353	0.9009	1.2753	−0.0068	−0.0210	0.0387	0.0507
27	0.6923	0.9526	0.8993	1.2912	−0.0007	0.0183	−0.0017	0.0124
28	0.7029	0.9430	0.8965	1.3516	0.0152	−0.0101	−0.0032	0.0457
29	0.7085	0.9622	0.9007	1.3851	0.0080	0.0202	0.0047	0.0245
30	0.7149	0.9910	0.9082	1.4276	0.0090	0.0295	0.0083	0.0302
31	0.7231	1.0245	0.9201	1.4853	0.0114	0.0332	0.0130	0.0396

[a]The source of the logarithmic price changes is Theil [78, table 5.2].

and

$$\Delta z = E^{-1} a. \tag{9.7}$$

If the elements of Δz were small in absolute value compared to the elements of z, we accepted z as the profit maximizing vector of outputs. Otherwise we computed a new z from $z + \Delta z$ and repeated the procedure until z converged.[6]

Once the profit maximizing vector of output levels was known, it was possible to find the cost minimizing values of inputs by application of Shephard's lemma (2.29). In addition, I calculated the values in each year of f_i, g_r, γ, ψ, ψ^*, θ^*_{rs}, θ^r_i, π_{ij}, θ_i, and θ_{ij} using the procedure described in section 4.5.

Conversion of this data to a form suitable for estimation of the various forms of the model (8.7) and (8.8) was accomplished in the following way. The observable values $\bar{g}_{rt}$, $\bar{f}_{it}$, and $\bar{\gamma}_t$ were calculated from (8.1) and (8.3) using the values obtained previously.[7] The levels of outputs and inputs were converted to logarithmic changes.

For C_1 this data in undisturbed form is presented in table 9.4. This cost function is sufficiently complex that it is of interest to use these data to explore the effects of specification error alone without disturbances. For all four cost functions, pseudorandom normal disturbances were generated according to (7.2) and (7.4), with the coefficients on the right in (7.2) and (7.4) interpreted as the mean values of the coefficients before and after the transition.[8] These disturbances were then divided by $\bar{g}_{rt}$ and $\bar{f}_{it}$,

[6]The criterion for convergence was that the absolute value of each element of Δz be less than 10^{-10} of the absolute value of the corresponding element of z. Convergence was quick in all cases.

[7]Note that this implies that $\bar{g}_{rt}$ and $\bar{f}_{it}$ are not disturbed. The reason for this is that finite disturbances added to the variables in log change form imply levels of inputs and outputs which gradually drift away from the optimum, itself changing, in a sort of random walk. The problem, of course, is that disturbances cannot be uncorrelated both in level and log change form. This is the reason why the data presented below are given strictly in log change form. Note also that this leads to $\bar{f}_{it}$ for C_3 and C_4, which do not change.

[8]For γ this is the geometric mean. For $\psi^*\theta^*_{rs}$ it is the arithmetic mean of the unnormalized coefficients, and similarly for $\pi_{ij} = -\psi(\theta_{ij} - \theta_i\theta_j)$. Note that this means that the disturbances which were generated satisfy the implications of the theory of rational random behavior, including independence of input and output disturbances.

respectively, before they were added to Dz_{rt} and Dq_{it} to obtain the disturbed values of the data. The resulting sets of data are presented for C_1, C_2, C_3, and C_4 in tables 9.5, 9.6, 9.7, and 9.8, respectively.

Several characteristics of these data sets deserve comment. First, the values given for $\bar{\gamma}_t$ and $\bar{g}_{1t}$ are highly and positively correlated for each set of data. This occurs because of the particular structure of these four cost functions, which causes γ to be a weighted average of the values 1.1 and 1.2. The weights are determined by the levels of z_1 and z_2.

Second, there is a qualitative difference between the output independent cost functions, C_2 and C_4, and the cost functions, C_1 and C_3, which are not output independent. The former functions permit a much broader variation in the relative levels of operation of the corresponding firms than the latter do; this is shown both by the relative stability of the output shares for C_1 and C_3 and by the fact that C_2 and C_4 frequently exhibit large changes of opposite signs in the levels of the two outputs, while the other two cost functions do not.

Third, it is instructive to consider the broad changes which occur between the beginning and the end of this data in response to the relative price changes which are shown in table 9.3. For C_1 the values of $\bar{g}_{rt}$ are nearly identical for $t = 1$ and $t = 31$ even though the relative price changes suggest there should be a shift toward the manufacture of z_2. The reason for this is the interaction noted in section 9.1 between inputs and outputs. The great increase in the relative price of q_2, which is negatively useful at the margin for the manufacture of z_1, counteracted the decrease in the relative price of z_1.

For C_2 the same argument applies to explain why the revenue share of z_1 increased when its relative price decreased. The input-output separable cost functions, C_3 and C_4, showed decreases in the revenue share of z_1 as we might ordinarily expect. The share of q_1 in cost increased for C_1 and C_2 and remained constant for C_3 and C_4; this is consistent with a shift toward use of q_1 in response to its lowered relative price.

As a result of the generally lowered prices and the tendency of the prices of inputs to rise in comparison to the prices of

Table 9.4
Input and output data from C_1: Nonseparable, nonindependent, no disturbances

		Outputs				Inputs			
t	$\bar{\gamma}_t$	$\bar{g}_{1t}$	$\bar{g}_{2t}$	Dz_{1t}	Dz_{2t}	$\bar{f}_{1t}$	$\bar{f}_{2t}$	Dq_{1t}	Dq_{2t}
1	1.1403	0.4237	0.5763	−0.3914	−0.4192	0.6013	0.3987	−0.4672	−0.4607
2	1.1399	0.4199	0.5801	0.0263	0.0350	0.5994	0.4006	0.0323	0.0410
3	1.1387	0.4079	0.5921	0.2053	0.2655	0.5936	0.4064	0.2554	0.3020
4	1.1385	0.4057	0.5943	−0.1727	−0.2451	0.5925	0.4075	−0.2093	−0.2984
5	1.1404	0.4248	0.5752	−0.1447	−0.2014	0.6018	0.3982	−0.1813	−0.2338
6	1.1413	0.4339	0.5661	0.0442	0.0478	0.6063	0.3937	0.0555	0.0485
7	1.1413	0.4338	0.5662	0.1977	0.1872	0.6063	0.3937	0.2413	0.1843
8	1.1419	0.4398	0.5602	−0.3927	−0.4449	0.6093	0.3907	−0.4748	−0.4928
9	1.1446	0.4678	0.5322	−0.4735	−0.5994	0.6231	0.3769	−0.5835	−0.6767
10	1.1490	0.5115	0.4885	−0.5004	−0.6336	0.6449	0.3551	−0.6074	−0.7264
11	1.1497	0.5189	0.4811	−0.0207	0.0161	0.6486	0.3514	−0.0169	0.0213
12	1.1475	0.4972	0.5028	0.0412	0.0799	0.6377	0.3623	0.0534	0.0981
13	1.1469	0.4904	0.5096	0.0684	0.0557	0.6344	0.3656	0.0835	0.0494

14	1.1454	0.4753	0.5247	−0.1264	−0.0710	0.6269	0.3731	−0.1422	−0.0598
15	1.1431	0.4522	0.5478	0.3665	0.4179	0.6154	0.3846	0.4448	0.4613
16	1.1419	0.4405	0.5595	0.2620	0.3083	0.6096	0.3904	0.3182	0.3453
17	1.1426	0.4475	0.5525	0.0941	0.0564	0.6131	0.3869	0.1039	0.0518
18	1.1427	0.4480	0.5520	0.4070	0.4813	0.6133	0.3867	0.4985	0.5332
19	1.1428	0.4493	0.5507	0.0980	0.0551	0.6139	0.3861	0.1088	0.0471
20	1.1419	0.4408	0.5592	−0.2849	−0.2421	0.6097	0.3903	−0.3231	−0.2589
21	1.1399	0.4196	0.5804	−0.0597	−0.0692	0.5993	0.4007	−0.0719	−0.0779
22	1.1400	0.4208	0.5792	−0.0981	−0.1282	0.5999	0.4001	−0.1138	−0.1585
23	1.1401	0.4220	0.5780	−0.0619	−0.0838	0.6005	0.3995	−0.0719	−0.1047
24	1.1393	0.4143	0.5857	0.0884	0.1113	0.5967	0.4033	0.1169	0.1146
25	1.1381	0.4019	0.5981	−0.2467	−0.2511	0.5906	0.4094	−0.2929	−0.2705
26	1.1389	0.4100	0.5900	−0.3871	−0.4734	0.5945	0.4055	−0.4739	−0.5355
27	1.1397	0.4184	0.5816	0.0437	0.0551	0.5987	0.4013	0.0569	0.0579
28	1.1406	0.4271	0.5729	−0.0822	−0.1578	0.6030	0.3970	−0.1036	−0.2033
29	1.1417	0.4383	0.5617	0.0200	0.0170	0.6085	0.3915	0.0268	0.0117
30	1.1413	0.4342	0.5658	0.0277	0.0311	0.6065	0.3935	0.0377	0.0279
31	1.1408	0.4289	0.5711	0.0067	0.0038	0.6039	0.3961	0.0125	−0.0045

Table 9.5
Input and output data from C_1: Nonseparable, nonindependent.

		Outputs				Inputs			
t	$\bar{\gamma}_t$	$\bar{g}_{1t}$	$\bar{g}_{2t}$	Dz_{1t}	Dz_{2t}	$\bar{f}_{1t}$	$\bar{f}_{2t}$	Dq_{1t}	Dq_{2t}
1	1.1403	0.4237	0.5763	−0.4402	−0.4569	0.6013	0.3987	−0.4682	−0.4592
2	1.1399	0.4199	0.5801	0.0535	0.0707	0.5994	0.4006	0.0193	0.0603
3	1.1387	0.4079	0.5921	0.2296	0.2545	0.5936	0.4064	0.2572	0.2994
4	1.1385	0.4057	0.5943	−0.1830	−0.2739	0.5925	0.4075	−0.2092	−0.2987
5	1.1404	0.4248	0.5752	−0.1390	−0.2190	0.6018	0.3982	−0.1764	−0.2412
6	1.1413	0.4339	0.5661	0.0576	0.0439	0.6063	0.3937	0.0578	0.0450
7	1.1413	0.4338	0.5662	0.2321	0.2169	0.6063	0.3937	0.2341	0.1954
8	1.1419	0.4398	0.5602	−0.3651	−0.4431	0.6093	0.3907	−0.4706	−0.4994
9	1.1446	0.4678	0.5322	−0.4294	−0.5811	0.6231	0.3769	−0.5897	−0.6666
10	1.1490	0.5115	0.4885	−0.4955	−0.6191	0.6449	0.3551	−0.6072	−0.7269
11	1.1497	0.5189	0.4811	−0.0001	0.0391	0.6486	0.3514	−0.0215	0.0299
12	1.1475	0.4972	0.5028	0.0498	0.0729	0.6377	0.3623	0.0513	0.1018
13	1.1469	0.4904	0.5096	0.0768	0.0740	0.6344	0.3656	0.0820	0.0520

14	1.1454	0.4753	0.5247	−0.1103	−0.0814	0.6269	0.3731	−0.1420	−0.0602
15	1.1431	0.4522	0.5478	0.3483	0.4076	0.6154	0.3846	0.4437	0.4631
16	1.1419	0.4405	0.5595	0.2528	0.2670	0.6096	0.3904	0.3087	0.3600
17	1.1426	0.4475	0.5525	0.0601	0.0421	0.6131	0.3869	0.1063	0.0480
18	1.1427	0.4480	0.5520	0.4532	0.5340	0.6133	0.3867	0.4943	0.5399
19	1.1428	0.4493	0.5507	0.0783	0.0097	0.6139	0.3861	0.0996	0.0617
20	1.1419	0.4408	0.5592	−0.2709	−0.2045	0.6097	0.3903	−0.3270	−0.2528
21	1.1399	0.4196	0.5804	−0.0425	−0.0289	0.5993	0.4007	−0.0779	−0.0689
22	1.1400	0.4208	0.5792	−0.1269	−0.1559	0.5999	0.4001	−0.1124	−0.1607
23	1.1401	0.4220	0.5780	−0.1109	−0.1251	0.6005	0.3995	−0.0776	−0.0961
24	1.1393	0.4143	0.5857	0.0509	0.0507	0.5967	0.4033	0.1141	0.1189
25	1.1381	0.4019	0.5981	−0.2665	−0.2706	0.5906	0.4094	−0.2849	−0.2821
26	1.1389	0.4100	0.5900	−0.3541	−0.4552	0.5945	0.4055	−0.4702	−0.5408
27	1.1397	0.4184	0.5816	0.0332	0.0795	0.5987	0.4031	0.0611	0.0517
28	1.1406	0.4271	0.5729	−0.1176	−0.1964	0.6030	0.3970	−0.0985	−0.2110
29	1.1417	0.4383	0.5617	0.0307	0.0031	0.6085	0.3915	0.0318	0.0041
30	1.1413	0.4342	0.5658	0.0132	0.0178	0.6065	0.3935	0.0371	0.0288
31	1.1408	0.4289	0.5711	0.0083	−0.0163	0.6039	0.3961	0.0167	−0.0109

Table 9.6
Input and output data from C_2: Nonseparable, output independent.

		Outputs				Inputs			
t	$\bar{\gamma}_t$	$\bar{g}_{1t}$	$\bar{g}_{2t}$	Dz_{1t}	Dz_{2t}	$\bar{f}_{1t}$	$\bar{f}_{2t}$	Dq_{1t}	Dq_{2t}
1	1.1477	0.4984	0.5016	−0.3931	−0.4476	0.6384	0.3616	−0.4771	−0.4265
2	1.1459	0.4807	0.5193	0.0185	0.1073	0.6295	0.3705	0.0139	0.0818
3	1.1406	0.4269	0.5731	0.0012	0.4448	0.6030	0.3970	0.2417	0.4375
4	1.1396	0.4166	0.5834	−0.0966	−0.4103	0.5979	0.4021	−0.1990	−0.4089
5	1.1482	0.5033	0.4967	−0.0545	−0.3883	0.6409	0.3591	−0.1388	−0.3753
6	1.1524	0.5454	0.4546	−0.0038	0.0801	0.6619	0.3381	0.0512	0.0616
7	1.1523	0.5450	0.4550	0.1987	0.2193	0.6617	0.3383	0.2398	0.1828
8	1.1551	0.5721	0.4279	−0.3848	−0.4982	0.6754	0.3246	−0.4470	−0.5553
9	1.1666	0.6845	0.3155	−0.2596	−0.9561	0.7331	0.2669	−0.4187	−0.8781
10	1.1817	0.8292	0.1708	−0.2817	−1.0039	0.8084	0.1916	−0.4159	−0.8113
11	1.1840	0.8514	0.1486	−0.1536	0.3414	0.8201	0.1799	−0.1457	0.0793
12	1.1779	0.7938	0.2062	−0.0726	0.2464	0.7897	0.2103	−0.0266	0.1582
13	1.1758	0.7737	0.2263	0.1007	0.0521	0.7791	0.2209	0.0996	0.0401

14	1.1699	0.7164	0.2836	−0.3543	0.2449	0.7494	0.2506	−0.2761	0.0871
15	1.1606	0.6267	0.3733	0.3136	0.4951	0.7031	0.2969	0.4066	0.5282
16	1.1554	0.5753	0.4247	0.1482	0.3570	0.6770:	0.3230	0.2792	0.4313
17	1.1585	0.6053	0.3947	0.2781	−0.2052	0.6923	0.3077	0.1793	−0.0934
18	1.1587	0.6077	0.3923	0.2652	0.7832	0.6935	0.3065	0.4237	0.6763
19	1.1592	0.6129	0.3871	0.2191	−0.2391	0.6962	0.3038	0.1787	−0.0775
20	1.1553	0.5737	0.4263	−0.5098	0.1782	0.6766	0.3234	−0.4387	0.0001
21	1.1458	0.4797	0.5203	−0.0157	−0.0334	0.6290	0.3710	−0.0766	−0.0757
22	1.1463	0.4851	0.5149	−0.0845	−0.1812	0.6317	0.3683	−0.1109	−0.1665
23	1.1469	0.4906	0.5094	−0.0277	−0.1704	0.6344	0.3656	−0.0759	−0.1032
24	1.1434	0.4557	0.5443	−0.0477	0.1686	0.6171	0.3829	0.0944	0.2279
25	1.1378	0.3991	0.6009	−0.2939	−0.2163	0.5892	0.4108	−0.2860	−0.2309
26	1.1415	0.4361	0.5639	−0.2675	−0.6298	0.6075	0.3925	−0.4485	−0.6997
27	1.1453	0.4741	0.5259	0.0595	0.1285	0.6263	0.3737	0.0515	0.0967
28	1.1492	0.5138	0.4862	0.0706	−0.4248	0.6461	0.3539	−0.0519	−0.3648
29	1.1544	0.5652	0.4348	−0.0340	0.0317	0.6719	0.3281	0.0265	0.0143
30	1.1525	0.5467	0.4533	−0.0022	0.0563	0.6625	0.3375	0.0238	0.0642
31	1.1501	0.5225	0.4775	−0.0567	0.0254	0.6504	0.3496	0.0079	0.0152

Table 9.7
Input and output data from C_3: Input–output separable, nonindependent.

		Outputs				Inputs			
t	$\bar{\gamma}_t$	$\bar{g}_{1t}$	$\bar{g}_{2t}$	Dz_{1t}	Dz_{2t}	$\bar{f}_{1t}$	$\bar{f}_{2t}$	Dq_{1t}	Dq_{2t}
1	1.1402	0.4233	0.5767	−0.4327	−0.4600	0.65[a]	0.35[a]	−0.4683	−0.4512
2	1.1398	0.4194	0.5806	0.0360	0.0831	0.65	0.35	0.0306	0.0396
3	1.1387	0.4082	0.5918	0.2130	0.2661	0.65	0.35	0.2869	0.2451
4	1.1380	0.4007	0.5993	−0.1894	−0.2186	0.65	0.35	−0.1861	−0.2611
5	1.1392	0.4133	0.5867	−0.1465	−0.2116	0.65	0.35	−0.1889	−0.2258
6	1.1399	0.4202	0.5798	0.0522	0.0608	0.65	0.35	0.0732	0.0376
7	1.1393	0.4136	0.5864	0.2165	0.2742	0.65	0.35	0.2691	0.2063
8	1.1393	0.4145	0.5855	−0.3762	−0.4405	0.65	0.35	−0.4748	−0.5091
9	1.1422	0.4432	0.5568	−0.4704	−0.5802	0.65	0.35	−0.6308	−0.6637
10	1.1463	0.4849	0.5151	−0.5097	−0.6202	0.65	0.35	−0.6541	−0.6742
11	1.1466	0.4874	0.5126	−0.0018	0.0710	0.65	0.35	0.0234	0.0025
12	1.1443	0.4641	0.5359	0.0459	0.0870	0.65	0.35	0.0821	0.0691
13	1.1434	0.4555	0.5445	0.0743	0.0891	0.65	0.35	0.0838	0.0681

14	1.1417	0.4386	0.5614	−0.1074	−0.0575	0.65	0.35	−0.0840	−0.1087
15	1.1395	0.4154	0.5846	0.3576	0.4187	0.65	0.35	0.4626	0.4668
16	1.1383	0.4033	0.5967	0.2275	0.2968	0.65	0.35	0.3459	0.3134
17	1.1390	0.4107	0.5893	0.0635	0.0129	0.65	0.35	0.0555	0.0854
18	1.1389	0.4097	0.5903	0.4598	0.5686	0.65	0.35	0.5444	0.5275
19	1.1388	0.4088	0.5912	0.0373	0.0207	0.65	0.35	0.0795	0.0472
20	1.1376	0.3970	0.6030	−0.2383	−0.1536	0.65	0.35	−0.2444	−0.2460
21	1.1353	0.3730	0.6270	−0.0414	−0.0277	0.65	0.35	−0.0809	−0.0597
22	1.1350	0.3696	0.6304	−0.1173	−0.1178	0.65	0.35	−0.0872	−0.1243
23	1.1344	0.3635	0.6365	−0.1104	−0.0948	0.65	0.35	−0.0595	−0.0718
24	1.1330	0.3495	0.6505	0.0584	0.1194	0.65	0.35	0.1882	0.1307
25	1.1315	0.3344	0.6656	−0.2471	−0.2808	0.65	0.35	−0.2814	−0.2722
26	1.1322	0.3417	0.6583	−0.3776	−0.4660	0.65	0.35	−0.5091	−0.5435
27	1.1328	0.3473	0.6527	0.0685	0.0814	0.65	0.35	0.0695	0.0980
28	1.1330	0.3494	0.6506	−0.1267	−0.1834	0.65	0.35	−0.1234	−0.1701
29	1.1334	0.3535	0.6465	0.0320	0.0311	0.65	0.35	0.0583	0.0078
30	1.1326	0.3455	0.6545	0.0252	0.0493	0.65	0.35	0.0687	0.0508
31	1.1317	0.3357	0.6643	0.0162	0.0237	0.65	0.35	0.0561	0.0038

[a]The factor shares are constant for this cost function. See the text for explanation.

Table 9.8
Input and output data from C_4: Input–output separable, output independent.

		Outputs				Inputs			
t	$\bar{\gamma}_t$	$\bar{g}_{1t}$	$\bar{g}_{2t}$	Dz_{1t}	Dz_{2t}	$\bar{f}_{1t}$	$\bar{f}_{2t}$	Dq_{1t}	Dq_{2t}
1	1.1475	0.4965	0.5035	−0.3981	−0.4372	0.65[a]	0.35[a]	−0.4555	−0.4559
2	1.1457	0.4786	0.5214	0.0231	0.0982	0.65	0.35	0.0186	0.0690
3	1.1407	0.4279	0.5721	0.0053	0.4368	0.65	0.35	0.3169	0.3137
4	1.1373	0.3938	0.6062	−0.1661	−0.2725	0.65	0.35	−0.2076	−0.2631
5	1.1429	0.4509	0.5491	−0.0677	−0.3661	0.65	0.35	−0.2271	−0.2537
6	1.1461	0.4823	0.5177	−0.0223	0.1126	0.65	0.35	0.0758	0.0543
7	1.1430	0.4518	0.5482	0.1331	0.3426	0.65	0.35	0.2691	0.2446
8	1.1435	0.4559	0.5441	−0.3894	−0.5034	0.65	0.35	−0.4976	−0.5123
9	1.1563	0.5836	0.4164	−0.2567	−0.9782	0.65	0.35	−0.6441	−0.6144
10	1.1734	0.7503	0.2497	−0.3188	−0.9335	0.65	0.35	−0.5579	−0.5891
11	1.1744	0.7600	0.2400	−0.1774	0.3746	0.65	0.35	−0.0674	−0.0665
12	1.1657	0.6763	0.3237	−0.0659	0.2288	0.65	0.35	0.0477	0.0633
13	1.1621	0.6410	0.3590	0.0700	0.1089	0.65	0.35	0.0840	0.0647

14	1.1544	0.5653	0.4347	−0.3478	0.2205	0.65	0.35	−0.0920	−0.0833
15	1.1439	0.4605	0.5395	0.3058	0.5207	0.65	0.35	0.4880	0.4838
16	1.1385	0.4056	0.5944	0.1432	0.3551	0.65	0.35	0.3463	0.3853
17	1.1418	0.4396	0.5604	0.2857	−0.2000	0.65	0.35	0.0198	0.0112
18	1.1414	0.4352	0.5648	0.2452	0.8079	0.65	0.35	0.5933	0.5934
19	1.1410	0.4308	0.5692	0.2048	−0.2135	0.65	0.35	0.0055	0.0344
20	1.1363	0.3831	0.6169	−0.5353	0.2371	0.65	0.35	−0.1054	−0.1174
21	1.1262	0.2796	0.7204	−0.0073	−0.0337	0.65	0.35	−0.0838	−0.0650
22	1.1250	0.2670	0.7330	−0.1925	−0.0177	0.65	0.35	−0.0499	−0.0981
23	1.1229	0.2451	0.7549	−0.1654	0.0058	0.65	0.35	−0.0407	−0.0495
24	1.1188	0.2017	0.7983	−0.1560	0.3063	0.65	0.35	0.2990	0.2726
25	1.1146	0.1574	0.8426	−0.3332	−0.1963	0.65	0.35	−0.2324	−0.2548
26	1.1166	0.1783	0.8217	−0.1985	−0.6743	0.65	0.35	−0.6275	−0.6526
27	1.1180	0.1930	0.8070	−0.0042	0.2182	0.65	0.35	0.1420	0.1126
28	1.1186	0.1999	0.8001	−0.0635	−0.2367	0.65	0.35	−0.1900	−0.2576
29	1.1198	0.2119	0.7881	−0.0228	0.0364	0.65	0.35	0.0847	0.0465
30	1.1175	0.1877	0.8123	−0.0619	0.1416	0.65	0.35	0.1225	0.1027
31	1.1149	0.1607	0.8393	−0.0756	0.0687	0.65	0.35	0.1069	0.0649

[a]The factor shares are constant for this cost function. See the text for explanation.

outputs, the changes in the four firms' levels of operations are primarily downwards. These changes are rather abrupt. This is a consequence both of the rather large price changes and the large value of ψ^* in these cost functions. It will be recalled from section 4.4 that ψ^* can be interpreted as the price elasticity of the firm's supply of outputs as a whole; for these cost functions it can be seen from table 9.2 that the initial values of this elasticity are in excess of seven.

9.3. Numerical methods

Given the data presented in section 9.2 and the estimation procedure described in section 8.3, it is now possible to apply the second to the first. The procedure for obtaining maximum likelihood estimates – briefly described in section 8.3 – appears to work, but is extremely inefficient in most cases. By "appears to work" I mean that each iteration produced, for each set of data and each model, a new set of parameter values which corresponded to a higher value of the likelihood function. By "inefficient" I mean that convergence was in many cases extremely slow. Consequently, a closer analysis of this procedure is warranted, as well as a discussion of several techniques which I used to improve the performance of the procedure.

Two cases for which the procedure was not inefficient were the unconstrained and the homogeneity constrained models when the covariance matrix was constrained by (8.17). In both cases, starting with initial values of zero for each parameter in μ, the procedure converged on the second iteration. The reason for this is straightforward: for the unconstrained model this procedure amounts to least squares applied individually to each equation, while for the homogeneity constrained model it amounts to least squares applied individually to each equation when the last coefficient (corresponding to $\mathrm{D}p_{nt}$) is dropped and each price change is deflated by subtracting $\mathrm{D}p_{nt}$.[9] The maximum likelihood estimates and the least squares estimates are identical in these cases because the models are fully linear. This can be verified by substituting (8.17) into (8.18) and consulting table 8.1.

When (8.17) applies, but any of the symmetry constrained models is estimated, the nonlinearity of the model then causes relatively slow convergence. The slowness can be mitigated in these cases by observing that the matrix with elements (8.23) will change relatively slowly also. As a consequence, I modified the procedure of section 8.3 so that the matrices $\boldsymbol{E}$ and $\boldsymbol{E}^{-1}$ were recalculated only when the value of the logarithmic likelihood had changed sufficiently.[10] This modification had the effect of making the average iteration relatively quick and inexpensive, so that even if many iterations were necessary, it was feasible to estimate these models.[11]

Unfortunately, this modification was not sufficient to permit estimation of any of the models when the independence condition (8.17) was relaxed. Since there is no important reason for avoiding the profit based model when this condition is relaxed, the following procedure was used. First, the output equations (8.8) were substituted into the input equations (8.7) to produce a new set of input equations which had only price changes as independent variables. This is a finite change version of the

[9]This is similar to the method Theil [78, ch. 5] has used to impose homogeneity in the Rotterdam model. When either (8.7) or (8.8) consists of more than one equation this is generalized least squares with identical explanatory variables for (8.7) or (8.8); the usual result that these estimators are equivalent to least squares estimators applies because (8.17) "separates" the estimators of the two subsystems. When (8.17) is not imposed, this result does not apply – see below.

[10]"Sufficiently" means an arbitrarily chosen increase of 0.5, or any decrease. It is interesting that when a decrease occurred the next iteration, calculated with a new $\boldsymbol{E}$, always showed improvement above the previously achieved maximum.

[11]The number of iterations required ranged from 3 to over 500; it was generally higher when the model did not fit the data well, as, for example, when the data from C_1 were fitted to the model which is output independent and input–output separable.

procedure which was used to obtain (6.3) from the original supply and demand systems. Given these equations, it is then possible to apply an analysis like that of section 8.3 to the profit based system without considering any constraint on the covariance matrix.

The resulting procedure, for unconstrained and homogeneity constrained models, yields least squares estimates on the second iteration in the same way that the original procedure does when the covariance matrix is constrained. The same modification permitted the average iteration to be inexpensive enough to obtain estimates in most cases.[12]

The coefficient estimates which were obtained from this system could then be used to compute estimates of the parameters of (8.7) and (8.8). Using these estimates as the original vector $\boldsymbol{\mu}$, the original procedure could be invoked and typically converged immediately.[13]

9.4. Results of testing

The hypothesis-testing procedure described in section 8.2 requires for each set of data that twenty-four models be fitted by maximum likelihood. For the purposes of hypothesis testing the only important results are the maximum values attained by the likelihood function. The logarithms of these values are conveniently calculated using (8.26); since the logarithms are more directly useful, they are presented below.

[12]In the cases where convergence could not be completed (basic models 4 or 5 with data generated from C_1), the estimates current at the end of iteration (25 inversions of $\boldsymbol{E}$) were used to compute estimates for the original procedure; from this starting point the original procedure converged.

[13]In fact, the two models are identical when there is no constraint on the covariance matrix; the apparent difference amounts to rewriting the same likelihood function in terms of different parameters. The maximum achieved by the likelihood function is the same for the two procedures. In a few cases iteration was necessary in the second procedure: I suspect a minor programming error in the conversion from one set of estimates to the other.

9.4.1. The undisturbed data

For the data in table 9.4, which were derived from the cost function C_1, these logarithmic likelihood values are presented in table 9.9. The values in the first two columns, which correspond to the models in which no constraint is imposed on the covariance matrix $\boldsymbol{\Sigma}$, are substantially higher than the corresponding values in the last two columns, where the constraint (8.17) has been imposed. The smallest difference, 20.65, is for the sixth model with no constant terms; this corresponds to a value 41.30 of a test statistic which (see table 8.2) is asymptotically distributed as $\chi^2(2)$. Since the 1% significance point of $\chi^2(2)$ is 9.21, this means that independence of the input and output disturbances must be unambiguously rejected, no matter which of the six basic models with or without constant terms is considered.

It will be recalled that the data of table 9.4 in fact had no random disturbances added. This means that the "disturbances" considered in the paragraph above are caused by the two sources of misspecification in the model (8.7) and (8.8), namely the assumed linearity of response of the firm to finite changes in the explanatory variables and the assumption of constant coefficients. What we reject, therefore, is the hypothesis that the errors caused by misspecification in the demand system are independent of those in the supply system.

Table 9.9
Logarithms of the likelihood maxima for the data of table 9.4.

Basic model	Dependent disturbances		Independent disturbances	
	Constant	No constant	Constant	No constant
1	456.64	456.37	341.69	341.31
2	450.27	450.23	334.74	334.40
3	450.05	449.95[a]	334.34	333.74
4	380.24	380.16	264.34	263.92
5	423.65	423.52	301.37	299.08
6	255.69	254.42	234.96	233.77

[a]This value corresponds to the preferred model for these data.

Next, consider the models with constant terms included (first and third columns) in comparison to those without constant terms (second and fourth columns). The largest pairwise difference between the logarithmic likelihood values for these models is 2.29 for the fifth basic model with independent input and output disturbances. This corresponds to a value 4.58 of a test statistic which is asymptotically distributed as $\chi^2(3)$. The 5 percent significance point of $\chi^2(3)$ is 7.81; consequently, there is no reason to reject the hypothesis that the constant terms are zero in any of the six basic models with or without independence of the input and output disturbances.

We conclude that we can confine our attention to the six basic models without constant terms and with an unconstrained covariance matrix. The logarithms of the likelihood maxima corresponding to these models are given in the second column of table 9.9. Comparing the first and second models, we obtain a value 12.28 for a test statistic which is asymptotically distributed as $\chi^2(3)$. Since the 1 percent significance point of $\chi^2(3)$ is 11.34, this suggests that homogeneity must be rejected for these data. Laitinen [49] has shown that an asymptotic test statistic which is algebraically related to this likelihood ratio test statistic is biased toward rejection of the null hypothesis. This test statistic is distributed as Hotelling's T^2 (see Anderson [3, ch. 5]); re-examination in the light of this interpretation indicates that homogeneity is acceptable at the 1 percent but not at the 5 percent significance level.[14]

Given homogeneity, the test for symmetry involves comparison of the logarithms of the likelihood maxima for the second and third models. The implied value of the test statistic is 0.56, which cannot be construed as evidence against symmetry.

[14]Appropriate reinterpretation of Anderson's [3, section 5.2] results establishes that if λ is the likelihood ratio (equal to $\exp[-6.14] = 2.15 \times 10^{-3}$ in this case), then $T(\lambda^{-2/T} - 1)$ is distributed as Hotelling's T^2, which is itself distributed in this case as $(81/25)F(3, 25)$. The 5 and 1 percent significance points of this F distribution are 2.99 and 4.68; therefore the 5 and 1 percent significance points of the T^2 variate are 9.69 and 15.16. The value of the test statistic is 15.07.

The fourth, fifth, and sixth models are all special forms and lead to test statistics of 139.58, 52.86, and 391.04, respectively, when compared to the third model. Under their respective null hypotheses, these statistics are to be viewed as realizations of random variables which are distributed asymptotically as $\chi^2(1)$, $\chi^2(1)$, and $\chi^2(2)$, respectively. The evidence for rejection of each of these three models is very strong.

A final overall test can be made by comparing the value of the logarithm of the likelihood maximum for the third model in the second column to that of the least constrained model. This comparison yields a value 13.38 of a test statistic which is distributed asymptotically as $\chi^2(9)$. The 5 percent significance point of $\chi^2(9)$ is 16.92, so the overall hypothesis that the former model is correct cannot be rejected. The conclusion we reach is that the data of table 9.4 are barely consistent with homogeneity and symmetry, but definitely not with input–output separability, output independence, or both.

9.4.2. *The data with disturbances*

The logarithms of the likelihood maxima associated with the data of table 9.5 are presented in table 9.10. Analysis of these results is similar to that of the results in table 9.9, and the model

Table 9.10
Logarithms of the likelihood maxima for the data of table 9.5.

Basic model	Dependent disturbances		Independent disturbances	
	Constant	No constant	Constant	No constant
1	298.44	295.03	287.33	283.29
2	295.72	292.51	285.25	281.06
3	294.85	291.88[a]	284.78	280.10
4	231.15	228.38	220.37	216.78
5	277.69	273.57	264.11	260.42
6	215.00	213.30	201.00	198.94

[a]This value corresponds to the preferred model for these data.

chosen is the same. The value of the overall test statistic for this model and this data is 13.12, slightly smaller than the value for the previous data.

There are several minor differences between tables 9.9 and 9.10. First, although the hypothesis of independent demand and supply disturbances has to be rejected for both sets of data, the rejection is stronger for the undisturbed data. This is natural, since the disturbances which were added to the other data were consistent with this hypothesis.

Second, for the disturbed data even the asymptotic test statistic is consistent with homogeneity, so there is no need to invoke the finite sample T^2. On the other hand, the disturbed data appear, using the asymptotic test at the 5 percent significance level, to require constant terms in some models. This test statistic can also be converted to a finite sample statistic which is distributed as Hotelling's T^2, and a test based on this statistic indicates no necessity for constant terms.

The logarithms of the likelihood maxima for the data of tables 9.6, 9.7, and 9.8 are presented in tables 9.11, 9.12, and 9.13, respectively. These results all differ somewhat from the foregoing ones in that the hypothesis of independent input and output disturbances can be accepted in each case. Referring to table 9.2, it can be seen that the coefficients θ_i' and π_{11} are constant for the cost functions C_3 and C_4 which were used to generate the

Table 9.11
Logarithms of the likelihood maxima for the data of table 9.6.

Basic model	Dependent disturbances		Independent disturbances	
	Constant	No constant	Constant	No constant
1	215.29	214.00	213.09	211.73
2	210.92	210.36	208.57	207.98
3	210.70	210.04	208.31	207.66
4	210.53	209.84	208.15	207.47[a]
5	187.06	186.36	152.04	150.44
6	178.07	177.24	151.79	149.97

[a]This value corresponds to the preferred model for these data.

Table 9.12
Logarithms of the likelihood maxima for the data of table 9.7

Basic model	Dependent disturbances		Independent disturbances	
	Constant	No constant	Constant	No constant
1	279.72	277.11	279.60	277.08
2	275.42	273.40	275.26	273.36
3	275.07	272.90	274.95	272.89
4	220.08	217.49	219.94	217.48
5	274.90	272.89	274.86	272.88[a]
6	220.03	217.45	219.81	217.41

[a]This value corresponds to the preferred model for these data.

data of tables 9.7 and 9.8. This means that for these data the demand system (8.7) is specified correctly; since the disturbances which were added satisfy the independence hypothesis, there is nothing in these data to cause correlation of the demand and supply residuals.

For the data of table 9.6, which were generated using the cost function C_2, the coefficients θ_i^r are constant, but the coefficient π_{11} is not. This means that the demand system is misspecified for these data, but evidently not sufficiently to cause correlation of the demand and supply residuals.

For each of these bodies of data there is no evidence that

Table 9.13
Logarithms of the likelihood maxima for the data of table 9.8.

Basic model	Dependent disturbances		Independent disturbances	
	Constant	No constant	Constant	No constant
1	228.09	225.32	227.11	224.04
2	220.98	219.46	219.74	218.24
3	220.39	219.01	219.16	217.78
4	219.95	218.70	218.72	217.48
5	220.26	218.99	219.05	217.49
6	219.90	218.70	218.61	217.19[a]

[a]This value corresponds to the preferred model for these data.

constant terms are required. There is a tendency for the three sets of data to reject homogeneity based on the asymptotic test. As before, this tendency is reduced but not eliminated when the small sample test is used. Symmetry is acceptable for all three bodies of data.

For the data of tables 9.6 and 9.7, which are output independent and input–output separable, respectively, the corresponding hypotheses are acceptable. The further hypotheses that the data of table 9.6 are input–output separable and the data of table 9.7 are output independent are rejected at any reasonable significance level. The data of table 9.8, on the contrary, are consistent with both input–output separability and output independence. The overall tests yield values 15.64, 13.88, and 21.80 for test statistics which are asymptotically distributed as χ^2 with 12, 12, and 13 degrees of freedom for the data of tables 9.6, 9.7, and 9.8, respectively. The 5 percent significance points of $\chi^2(12)$ and $\chi^2(13)$ are 21.03 and 22.36, so the models marked in these tables are each acceptable according to the overall tests.

9.5. Results of estimation

In the previous section we analyzed tables 9.9–9.13 to obtain for each body of data a preferred model, which is marked in the table in each case. This is the simplest of the twenty-four available models which is consistent with the given data. Associated with each preferred model are estimates of the parameters of the model.

For the data of tables 9.4 and 9.5 the preferred model is the third basic model with an unconstrained covariance matrix and no constant terms. The values of the parameter estimates for this model are presented in table 9.14 for both of these bodies of data. For comparison, the average values of the corresponding coefficients of C_1, the cost function from which these data were generated, are also given together with measures of their variability in the sample.

The parameter estimates for the two bodies of data are very similar, and each gives a qualitatively, and to a considerable degree quantitatively, accurate description of the behavior associated with the cost function C_1. The standard errors of the estimates associated with the undisturbed data are misleadingly low. Those associated with the disturbed data are more satisfactory; in almost all cases (θ^*_{12} and θ^*_{22} are the exceptions) the estimates associated with these data are within two standard errors of the mean values of the corresponding coefficients.

The estimates associated with the preferred models for the data of tables 9.6–9.8 are presented in table 9.15, together with the mean values of the corresponding coefficients. The quality of these estimates is similar to that of the estimates based on the data from table 9.5. In only one case (the estimate of θ^*_{22} associated with the data of table 9.7) is the parameter estimate more than two standard errors from the mean value of the coefficient.

Table 9.14
Parameter estimates for the preferred models based on data from C_1.

	Estimate[a]		
Parameter	Undisturbed data	Disturbed data	Mean value[b]
$\bar{\gamma}_t \psi^*_t$	8.093 (0.048)	8.115 (0.160)	8.238 (0.156)
θ^*_{11}	0.1953 (0.0020)	0.1903 (0.0056)	0.1892 (0.0272)
θ^*_{12}	0.2200 (0.0003)	0.2208 (0.0031)	0.2137 (0.0040)
θ^*_{22}	0.3646 (0.0025)	0.3681 (0.0076)	0.3834 (0.0350)
θ^1_1	1.2334 (0.0023)	1.2364 (0.0374)	1.1904 (0.0157)
θ^1_2	−0.2334 (0.0023)	−0.2364 (0.0374)	−0.1904 (0.0157)
θ^2_1	0.1492 (0.0011)	0.1475 (0.0259)	0.1904 (0.0157)
θ^2_2	0.8508 (0.0011)	0.8525 (0.0259)	0.8096 (0.0157)
π_{11}	−0.1079 (0.0079)	−0.0878 (0.0329)	−0.1165 (0.0057)

[a]Values in parentheses are standard errors.

[b]Mean based on the calculated values of the coefficients in the thirty-two years for which the price indexes in table 9.3 exist. Values in parentheses are the sample standard deviations.

Table 9.15
Parameter estimates for the preferred models based on data from C_2, C_3 and C_4.

Para-meter	Data from table 9.6		Data from table 9.7		Data from table 9.8	
	Estimate[a]	Mean value[b]	Estimate[a]	Mean value[b]	Estimate[a]	Mean value[b]
$\bar{\gamma}_t \psi_t^*$	7.757 (0.293)	8.270 (0.645)	8.279 (0.162)	8.451 (0.232)	8.439 (0.343)	9.093 (0.888)
θ_{11}^*	0.4446 (0.0213)	0.4065 (0.1366)	0.1623 (0.0077)	0.1580 (0.0336)	0.3021 (0.0199)	0.2659 (0.1519)
θ_{12}^*	c	c	0.2159 (0.0067)	0.2051 (0.0097)	c	c
θ_{22}^*	0.5554 (0.0213)	0.5935 (0.1366)	0.4059 (0.0117)	0.4317 (0.0527)	0.6978 (0.0199)	0.7341 (0.1519)
θ_1^1	0.8832 (0.0101)	0.9	0.6486 (0.0033)	0.65	0.6467 (0.0024)	0.65
θ_2^1	0.1168 (0.0101)	0.1	0.3514 (0.0033)	0.35	0.3533 (0.0024)	0.35
θ_1^2	0.4059 (0.0084)	0.4	c	c	c	c
θ_2^2	0.5941 (0.0084)	0.6	c	c	c	c
π_{11}	−0.1224 (0.0582)	−0.1581 (0.0193)	−0.2361 (0.0413)	−0.2275	−0.2126 (0.0312)	−0.2275

[a]Values in parentheses are standard errors.
[b]Mean based on the calculated values of the coefficient in the thirty-two years for which the price indexes in table 9.3 exist. Values in parentheses are the sample standard deviations for those coefficients which vary.
[c]The parameter or coefficient does not exist in this model.

CHAPTER 10

Conclusions and suggestions for further research

In this volume I have developed a comprehensive theory of the long-run behavior of the competitive multiproduct firm. I have also developed and, to a limited degree, tested an econometric model based on this theory. In this final chapter I shall review briefly the research presented here, draw what conclusions can be drawn, and suggest the course which future research in this area ought to take.

10.1. Summary and conclusions

The bulk of the theoretical work in this volume was the application to the multiproduct firm of the differential approach to microeconomic theory. This led in Chapter 3 to a differential system of input demand equations for the cost minimizing firm. In Chapter 4 the analysis was extended to the competitive profit maximizing firm and led to a differential system of output supply equations. Interpretation of these systems of equations then permitted straightforward and detailed analysis of the comparative statics of the multiproduct firm.

A parallel analysis was carried out in Chapter 5 for the revenue maximizing firm. This yielded alternative systems of output supply and input demand equations, also in differential form. In Chapter 6 these different but equivalent systems were compared, which in effect allowed us to look at the relationships among cost minimizing, revenue maximizing, and profit maximizing behaviors of the firm.

This also permitted assessment of the economic meaning of the duality of production, cost, revenue, and profit functions; we used this duality to explore the effects of various specialized assumptions which have been made about the firm in econometric contexts. The most common of these are input–output separability and homotheticity. We also introduced the concepts of input independence and output independence; the latter has a very strong interpretation in that it is equivalent to production which is nonjoint.

In addition to this, we presented in Chapter 2 a discussion of the various forms which a multiproduct production function can take. In Chapter 7 we applied the theory of rational random behavior to the multiproduct firm to obtain a theoretical basis for adding disturbances to the differential demand and supply equations which were derived earlier.

In Chapter 8 we turned to econometric specification. This consisted first of the specification of a system of demand and supply equations involving finite (rather than infinitesimal) changes in the observable variables. This system, although different in detail, is closely equivalent to the Rotterdam model of consumer demand. In particular, the additional assumptions which are made and the misspecification to which these assumptions lead are very similar for the two models.

With this model as a basis, we then discussed techniques of estimation and testing of hypotheses, a subject which is more complex than it is for the Rotterdam model. In Chapter 9 we applied these techniques to hypothetical data generated from known technologies.

One conclusion to be drawn from this test of the model is that the hypothesis-testing techniques work very well with respect to specialized forms of the firms and not so well (but still adequately) with respect to tests of basic economic implications. In particular, the hypothetically generated data had a moderate but persistent tendency to require rejection of homogeneity even when a small sample test was employed. Given the fact that the data is certainly consistent with homogeneity, this leads to the speculation that it is the misspecification in the model which causes these rejections. A further speculation is that the same misspecification causes the conditional (on homogeneity) test for symmetry to be biased toward acceptance of the null hypothesis: this tendency is evident in the results presented in Chapter 9 and is also consistent with the general experience researchers have had with the Rotterdam model.

A second conclusion to be drawn from the results of Chapter 9 is that the parameter estimates which emerge from the testing and estimation procedures can be accepted with some confidence if they are interpreted correctly. If the parameters are regarded as constant characteristics of the firm, the demand and supply equations which we estimated are not integrable: they are not consistent with some given cost or production function except under extremely restrictive assumptions. Consequently, these parameter estimates should in general be regarded as estimates of the average values of coefficients which vary; under this interpretation the parameter estimates reflect the average behavior of the firm with adequate accuracy.

Another conclusion we can draw is that it is optimistic to expect this model to support the predictions of the theory of rational random behavior. In general we can expect the misspecification in the model to mask such behavior so that it cannot be detected even if it is present.

Our general conclusion is that the theoretical treatment of the multiproduct firm, which is the main subject of this volume, is useful not just because good theory is always useful, but also because it leads to a viable econometric model: a model which permits useful measurement, on the average, of the multiproduct firm, and which permits economically interesting hypotheses to be tested.

10.2. Directions for future research

Although the theory presented here has been comprehensive within its limits, those limits are somewhat restrictive. The two major assumptions which we have maintained throughout are that the firm is able to practice long-run optimization and that it deals in competitive markets for its factors and products. Neither of these assumptions is fully consistent with available data, and consequently the econometric model considered in Chapters 8 and 9 must be considered somewhat limited in its applicability.

It is thus desirable, both from an economic and an econometric point of view, that these assumptions be relaxed. This is not, however, as simple a task as it might first appear. Consider first the problem of short-run cost minimization when we assume that some of the firm's inputs cannot be freely adjusted. If the availability of these inputs is in fact rigid, so that the amount available to the firm at any one time is fixed, then the firm's problem amounts to finding the optimal mix of the variable inputs. This problem has been considered by Clements [25] under the further assumption that the production function is of the form (1.3), an assumption which can be relaxed without great difficulty. It has also been considered by Pfouts [60] and several other authors under the assumption that production is nonjoint, except for jointness induced in the short run by limited availability of the fixed inputs.

The natural assumption to make for econometric estimation of such models is that the fixed input is exogenously determined; in the context of a single decision this is undoubtedly correct if the other assumptions are valid. However, when the data are in time series form, this assumption is untenable: if the fixed inputs vary over time, the variation must, except in rare cases, be in accord with the long-run benefit of the firm and must consequently be endogenous. Moreover, since the long run for such input decisions must be longer than the period from which a given data point is obtained, such long-run adjustment must be dynamic in nature.

In fact, of course, the assumption that "fixed inputs" are fixed should be questioned as well. Short and long runs in economic theory are not fixed lengths of time: the long run is the period of time required to adjust all variables to their optimal levels, while the short run for any variable is a period short enough that, for practical purposes, no change in its level can be achieved. Clearly, if there is period-to-period change in the volume of some input the period is longer than the short run, even though it may not be long enough to permit full adjustment of the input.

This means that the model which should be developed as an extension of the long-run model is a "medium-run" model, in which only partial adjustment of some (perhaps all) inputs is permitted. Since partial adjustment implies some time elasticity of adjustment, such a model must also be dynamic.

The problems of noncompetitive organization of markets in the context of the multiproduct firm are also greater than might be first thought. Consider the case of a multiproduct firm which has a monopoly. The first question which has to be asked is which of its products the firm has a monopoly in. If the firm's production is joint among all its outputs, one might argue that a monopoly in one should be accompanied by a monopoly in the others. However, there is now a considerable literature (e.g. [10, 11, 58, and 59]) devoted to the problem of natural monopoly in the multiproduct firm which indicates clearly that this argument is wrong. Also, production need not be joint: I am sure that there is no jointness in the production of computers and computer cards. This indicates that the appropriate model of a monopolistic multiproduct firm is one in which some output markets are competitive and some are not.

A knottier problem is the fact that most noncompetitive firms are subject to regulation of various kinds. This means that the implications of pure monopoly do not hold for these firms any more than the implications of pure competition. Since regulation takes so many forms, it appears likely that the econometric problems which arise from noncompetitive markets will have to be addressed on a case-by-case basis.

None of the foregoing is meant to imply that further progress in this area is impossibly difficult, nor are these problems inherently multiproduct ones. The problems of regulated behavior and of less than full adjustment of inputs can occur just as well in a single product context. However, in the world of real firms the multiproduct firm appears to be the rule rather than the exception. Consequently, it appears better to make progress, both in theory and measurement, by studying these problems in the context of the multiproduct firm, and also in the context of specific data.

Appendix to Chapter 2

A.1. First-order derivatives of the output homogeneous production function

For arbitrary z and q with positive elements we have from (2.9) $\bar{z}_r = z_r \, \mathrm{d}(\boldsymbol{q}, z)$; so taking logarithms and using (2.14) we have

$$\log \bar{z}_r = \log z_r + h(\boldsymbol{q}, z). \tag{A.1}$$

Then, taking derivatives with respect to $\log z_s$ and $\log q_i$, we find

$$\frac{\partial \log \bar{z}_r}{\partial \log z_s} = \delta_{rs} + \frac{\partial h}{\partial \log z_s}, \tag{A.2}$$

$$\frac{\partial \log \bar{z}_r}{\partial \log q_i} = \frac{\partial h}{\partial \log q_i}, \tag{A.3}$$

where δ_{rs} is a Kronecker delta.

By the definition of $\bar{z}$ we have $h_b(\boldsymbol{q}, \bar{z}) \equiv 0$, so the derivative of this relation with respect to $\log q_i$ is

$$\frac{\partial h_b}{\partial \log q_i} + \sum_{r=1}^{m} \frac{\partial h_b}{\partial \log \bar{z}_r} \frac{\partial \log \bar{z}_r}{\partial \log q_i} = 0.$$

Substitution from (A.3) and solving for $\partial h / \partial \log q_i$ then yields

$$\frac{\partial h}{\partial \log q_i} = A \frac{\partial h_b}{\partial \log q_i}, \tag{A.4}$$

where

$$A = -\frac{1}{\sum_{r=1}^{m} \partial h_b/\partial \log \bar{z}_r}. \tag{A.5}$$

The derivative of $h_b(\boldsymbol{q}, \bar{z}) \equiv 0$ with respect to $\log z_s$ similarly leads, using (A.2), to $\Sigma_r\, \partial h_b/\partial \log \bar{z}_r[\delta_{rs} + \partial h/\partial \log z_s] = 0$ which yields

$$\frac{\partial h}{\partial \log z_s} = A \frac{\partial h_b}{\partial \log \bar{z}_s}. \tag{A.6}$$

Note that A is positive by our assumptions of section 2.1 so that (A.4) and (A.6) imply that the first derivatives of $h(\cdot)$ have the same signs as the corresponding derivatives of $h_b(\cdot)$. Also, the sum of (A.6) over r together with (A.5) confirms the property (2.16).

A.2. Second-order derivatives

We differentiate (A.5) with respect to $\log q_i$ to obtain

$$\frac{\partial A}{\partial \log q_i} = A^2 \sum_{r=1}^{m} \frac{\partial^2 h_b}{\partial \log \bar{z}_r\, \partial \log q_i} + A^2 \sum_{r=1}^{m} \sum_{s=1}^{m} \frac{\partial^2 h_b}{\partial \log \bar{z}_r\, \partial \log \bar{z}_s} \frac{\partial \log \bar{z}_s}{\partial \log q_i}.$$

Next we substitute from (A.3) and write the resulting expression in matrix notation as

$$\frac{\partial A}{\partial \log \boldsymbol{q}} = A^2 \boldsymbol{H}_b^* \boldsymbol{\iota}^* + A^2 (\boldsymbol{\iota}^{*\prime} \boldsymbol{H}_b^{**} \boldsymbol{\iota}^*) \frac{\partial h}{\partial \log \boldsymbol{q}}, \tag{A.7}$$

where $\boldsymbol{H}_b^*$ is the $n \times m$ matrix of derivatives $\partial^2 h_b/\partial \log q_i\, \partial \log \bar{z}_r$ and $\boldsymbol{H}_b^{**}$ is the $m \times m$ matrix of derivatives $\partial^2 h_b/\partial \log \bar{z}_r\, \partial \log \bar{z}_s$.

Similarly, we differentiate (A.5) with respect to $\log z_s$ to obtain

$$\frac{\partial A}{\partial \log z_s} = A^2 \sum_{r=1}^{m} \sum_{t=1}^{m} \frac{\partial^2 h_b}{\partial \log \bar{z}_r\, \partial \log \bar{z}_t} \frac{\partial \log \bar{z}_t}{\partial \log z_s},$$

and then substitute from (A.2) and write the result in matrix form

$$\frac{\partial A}{\partial \log \boldsymbol{z}} = A^2 \boldsymbol{H}_b^{**} \boldsymbol{\iota}^* + A^2(\boldsymbol{\iota}^{*\prime} \boldsymbol{H}_b^{**} \boldsymbol{\iota}^*) \frac{\partial h}{\partial \log \boldsymbol{z}}. \tag{A.8}$$

When we now consider the derivative of (A.4) with respect to $\log q_i$, the left side is the (i, j)th element of $\boldsymbol{H}$ (see (2.17)), while the right side is

$$A \frac{\partial^2 h_b}{\partial \log q_i\, \partial \log q_j} + A \sum_{r=1}^{m} \frac{\partial^2 h_b}{\partial \log q_i\, \partial \log \bar{z}_r} \frac{\partial \log \bar{z}_r}{\partial \log q_j} + \frac{\partial h_b}{\partial \log q_i} \frac{\partial A}{\partial \log q_j}. \tag{A.9}$$

We define $\boldsymbol{H}_b$ as the $n \times n$ matrix with elements $\partial^2 h_b / \partial \log q_i\, \partial \log q_j$. Next, we use (A.3) in the sum in (A.9) and write the whole in matrix form as

$$\boldsymbol{H} = A\boldsymbol{H}_b + A\boldsymbol{H}_b^{*} \boldsymbol{\iota}^* \frac{\partial h}{\partial \log \boldsymbol{q}'} + \frac{\partial h_b}{\partial \log \boldsymbol{q}} \frac{\partial A}{\partial \log \boldsymbol{q}'}. \tag{A.10}$$

Finally, we use the transpose of (A.7) and (A.4) in the form $\partial h / \partial \log \boldsymbol{q} = A\, \partial h_b / \partial \log \boldsymbol{q}$ and divide by A to obtain

$$A^{-1}\boldsymbol{H} = \boldsymbol{H}_b + \boldsymbol{H}_b^{*} \boldsymbol{\iota}^* \frac{\partial h}{\partial \log \boldsymbol{q}'} + \frac{\partial h}{\partial \log \boldsymbol{q}} \boldsymbol{\iota}^{*\prime} \boldsymbol{H}_b^{*\prime} + (\boldsymbol{\iota}^{*\prime} \boldsymbol{H}_b^{**} \boldsymbol{\iota}^*) \frac{\partial h}{\partial \log \boldsymbol{q}} \frac{\partial h}{\partial \log \boldsymbol{q}'}. \tag{A.11}$$

In a similar way we take the derivative of (A.4) with respect to $\log z_r$, obtaining on the left the (i, r)th element of $\boldsymbol{H}^*$ and on the right

$$A \sum_{s=1}^{n} \frac{\partial^2 h_b}{\partial \log q_i \, \partial \log \bar{z}_s} \frac{\partial \log \bar{z}_s}{\partial \log z_r} + \frac{\partial h_b}{\partial \log q_i} \frac{\partial A}{\partial \log z_r}.$$

Again, we substitute from (A.2) and put into matrix notation to obtain

$$\boldsymbol{H}^* = A\boldsymbol{H}_b^* + A\boldsymbol{H}_b^* \boldsymbol{\iota}^* \, \partial h/\partial \log \boldsymbol{z}' + (\partial h_b/\partial \log \boldsymbol{q})(\partial A/\partial \log \boldsymbol{z}').$$

Now substitution from the transpose of (A.8) and (A.4) followed by division by A yields

$$A^{-1}\boldsymbol{H}^* = \boldsymbol{H}_b^* + \boldsymbol{H}_b^* \boldsymbol{\iota}^* \frac{\partial h}{\partial \log \boldsymbol{z}'} + \frac{\partial h}{\partial \log \boldsymbol{q}} \boldsymbol{\iota}^{*\prime} \boldsymbol{H}_b^{**}$$
$$+ (\boldsymbol{\iota}^{*\prime} \boldsymbol{H}_b^{**} \boldsymbol{\iota}^*) \frac{\partial h}{\partial \log \boldsymbol{q}} \frac{\partial h}{\partial \log \boldsymbol{z}'}. \qquad \text{(A.12)}$$

Finally, we consider the derivative of (A.6) with respect to $\log z_r$ which yields the (s, r)th element of $\boldsymbol{H}^{**}$ on the left and

$$A \sum_{t=1}^{m} \frac{\partial^2 h_b}{\partial \log \bar{z}_s \, \partial \log \bar{z}_t} \frac{\partial \log \bar{z}_t}{\partial \log z_r} + \frac{\partial h_b}{\partial \log \bar{z}_s} \frac{\partial A}{\partial \log z_r}$$

on the right. We substitute from (A.2) and write this in matrix form as

$$\boldsymbol{H}^{**} = A\boldsymbol{H}_b^{**} + A\boldsymbol{H}_b^{**} \boldsymbol{\iota}^* \, \partial h/\partial \log \boldsymbol{z}'$$
$$+ (\partial h_b/\partial \log \bar{\boldsymbol{z}})(\partial A/\partial \log \boldsymbol{z}').$$

Next we substitute from the transpose of (A.8), use (A.6) in the form $\partial h/\partial \log \boldsymbol{z} = A \, \partial h_b/\partial \log \bar{\boldsymbol{z}}$, and divide by A to obtain

$$A^{-1}\boldsymbol{H}^{**} = \boldsymbol{H}_b^{**} + \boldsymbol{H}_b^{**} \boldsymbol{\iota}^* \frac{\partial h}{\partial \log \boldsymbol{z}'} + \frac{\partial h}{\partial \log \boldsymbol{z}} \boldsymbol{\iota}^{*\prime} \boldsymbol{H}_b^{**}$$
$$+ (\boldsymbol{\iota}^{*\prime} \boldsymbol{H}_b^{**} \boldsymbol{\iota}^*) \frac{\partial h}{\partial \log \boldsymbol{z}} \frac{\partial h}{\partial \log \boldsymbol{z}'}. \qquad \text{(A.13)}$$

It should be noted that since $h_b(\cdot)$ has continuous first and second derivatives, it follows that so does $h(\cdot)$. In addition, when $h(\boldsymbol{q}, \boldsymbol{z}) = 0$ so that $d(\boldsymbol{q}, \boldsymbol{z}) = 1$, we have $z_r = \bar{z}_r$ for each r so that the matrices $\boldsymbol{H}_b$, $\boldsymbol{H}_b^*$, and $\boldsymbol{H}_b^{**}$ are evaluated at the same point as $\boldsymbol{H}$, $\boldsymbol{H}^*$, and $\boldsymbol{H}^{**}$. The same is true of the vectors of first derivatives. Also, postmultiplication of (A.12) and (A.13) by $\boldsymbol{\iota}^*$ confirms (2.27) and (2.26) in view of (2.16) written as $(\partial h/\partial \log \boldsymbol{z})'\boldsymbol{\iota}^* = -1$.

Finally, note that when $\boldsymbol{H}_b^* = \boldsymbol{0}$, which occurs if $h_b(\cdot)$ is written in the input–output separable form (2.35), then the first two terms on the right in (A.12) vanish, so that (A.12) becomes

$$A^{-1}\boldsymbol{H}^* = \frac{\partial h}{\partial \log \boldsymbol{q}} \left[\boldsymbol{\iota}^{*\prime}\boldsymbol{H}_b^{**} + (\boldsymbol{\iota}^{*\prime}\boldsymbol{H}_b^{**}\boldsymbol{\iota}^*) \frac{\partial h}{\partial \log \boldsymbol{z}'} \right], \tag{A.14}$$

which is the product of a column vector postmultiplied by a row vector as asserted in (2.37).

A.3. Derivatives of the input homogeneous production function

The first and second derivatives of the input homogeneous production function can be derived in a manner completely analogous to the way the derivatives of the output homogeneous production function were obtained. From (2.5) and (2.11) we obtain $\log \bar{q}_i = \log q_i - h_Q(\boldsymbol{q}, \boldsymbol{z})$ for arbitrary positive[1] $\boldsymbol{q}$ and $\boldsymbol{z}$. The derivatives of $\log \bar{q}_i$ can then be obtained, while for any other representation of the production function we have $h_b(\bar{\boldsymbol{q}}, \boldsymbol{z}) \equiv 0$ by the definition of $\bar{\boldsymbol{q}}$. Proceeding in this fashion, we obtain

$$\frac{\partial h_Q}{\partial \log q_i} = B \frac{\partial h_b}{\partial \log \bar{q}_i}, \tag{A.15}$$

$$\frac{\partial h_Q}{\partial \log z_r} = B \frac{\partial h_b}{\partial \log z_r}, \tag{A.16}$$

[1]By "positive $\boldsymbol{q}$" here and throughout the appendix we mean a vector $\boldsymbol{q}$ each of whose elements is strictly positive.

where

$$B = \frac{1}{\sum_{i=1}^{n} \partial h_b/\partial \log \bar{q}_i}. \tag{A.17}$$

The sign of B is positive, so the signs of the first derivatives of $h_Q(\cdot)$ are the same as those of $h(\cdot)$ and $h_b(\cdot)$, while summation of (A.15) over i confirms (2.13), the input homogeneous property of $h_Q(\cdot)$.

Continuing in the same fashion, we obtain

$$B^{-1}\boldsymbol{H}_Q = \bar{\boldsymbol{H}}_b - \frac{\partial h_Q}{\partial \log \boldsymbol{q}}\boldsymbol{\iota}'\bar{\boldsymbol{H}}_b - \bar{\boldsymbol{H}}_b\boldsymbol{\iota}\frac{\partial h_Q}{\partial \log \boldsymbol{q}'} + \boldsymbol{\iota}'\bar{\boldsymbol{H}}_b\boldsymbol{\iota}\frac{\partial h_Q}{\partial \log \boldsymbol{q}}\frac{\partial h_Q}{\partial \log \boldsymbol{q}'}, \tag{A.18}$$

$$B^{-1}\boldsymbol{H}_Q^* = \bar{\boldsymbol{H}}_b^* - \frac{\partial h_Q}{\partial \log \boldsymbol{q}}\boldsymbol{\iota}'\bar{\boldsymbol{H}}_b^* - \bar{\boldsymbol{H}}_b\boldsymbol{\iota}\frac{\partial h_Q}{\partial \log \boldsymbol{z}'} + \boldsymbol{\iota}'\bar{H}_b\boldsymbol{\iota}\frac{\partial h_Q}{\partial \log \boldsymbol{q}}\frac{\partial h_Q}{\partial \log \boldsymbol{z}'}, \tag{A.19}$$

$$B^{-1}\boldsymbol{H}_Q^{**} = \bar{\boldsymbol{H}}_b^{**} - \frac{\partial h_Q}{\partial \log \boldsymbol{z}}\boldsymbol{\iota}'\bar{\boldsymbol{H}}_b^* - \bar{\boldsymbol{H}}_b^{*\prime}\boldsymbol{\iota}\frac{\partial h_Q}{\partial \log \boldsymbol{z}'} + \boldsymbol{\iota}'\bar{\boldsymbol{H}}_b\boldsymbol{\iota}\frac{\partial h_Q}{\partial \log \boldsymbol{z}}\frac{\partial h_Q}{\partial \log \boldsymbol{z}'}, \tag{A.20}$$

where $\bar{\boldsymbol{H}}_b$, $\bar{\boldsymbol{H}}_b^*$, and $\bar{\boldsymbol{H}}_b^{**}$ are the matrices whose elements are the derivatives $\partial^2 h_b/\partial \log \bar{q}_i\, \partial \log \bar{q}_j$, $\partial^2 h_b/\partial \log \bar{q}_i\, \partial \log z_r$, and $\partial^2 h_b/\partial \log z_r\, \partial \log z_s$, respectively. When the firm's inputs and outputs are on the efficient production surface, so that $h_b(\boldsymbol{q}, \boldsymbol{z}) = 0 = h_Q(\boldsymbol{q}, \boldsymbol{z})$, we have $\bar{\boldsymbol{q}} = \boldsymbol{q}$ and hence the matrices $\bar{\boldsymbol{H}}_b$, $\bar{\boldsymbol{H}}_b^*$, and $\bar{\boldsymbol{H}}_b^{**}$ are evaluated at the same point as $\boldsymbol{H}_Q$, $\boldsymbol{H}_Q^*$, and $\boldsymbol{H}_Q^{**}$.

Premultiplication of (A.18) and (A.19) by $\boldsymbol{\iota}'$ yields zero vectors, which confirms (2.22) and (2.23). Also, when $h_b(\cdot)$ is input–output separable, $\bar{\boldsymbol{H}}_b^*$ is a zero matrix, which implies that (A.19) can be written

$$B^{-1}\boldsymbol{H}_Q^* = \left[\boldsymbol{\iota}'\bar{\boldsymbol{H}}_b\boldsymbol{\iota}\frac{\partial h_Q}{\partial \log \boldsymbol{q}} - \bar{\boldsymbol{H}}_b\boldsymbol{\iota}\right]\frac{\partial h_Q}{\partial \log \boldsymbol{z}'}, \tag{A.21}$$

which confirms the form of (2.36).

A.4. Homotheticity in inputs

When the firm is homothetic in inputs, we have $h(\phi^*(\alpha, z)\boldsymbol{q}, \alpha z) = 0$ for positive α whenever $h(\boldsymbol{q}, z) = 0$. We take the derivative with respect to α to obtain

$$\sum_{i=1}^{n} \frac{\partial h}{\partial(\phi^* q_i)} q_i \frac{\partial \phi^*}{\partial \alpha} + \sum_{r=1}^{m} \frac{\partial h}{\partial(\alpha z_r)} z_r = 0. \tag{A.22}$$

When we evaluate this at $\alpha = 1$, we then obtain

$$\frac{\partial \phi^*}{\partial \alpha} = -\frac{\sum_{r=1}^{m} \partial h/\partial \log z_r}{\sum_{i=1}^{n} \partial h/\partial \log q_i} = \frac{1}{\sum_{i=1}^{n} \partial h/\partial \log q_i}, \tag{A.23}$$

which follows from $\phi^*(1, z) = 1$ and (2.16). Thus, if we define

$$u^*(z) = \left(\frac{\partial \phi^*}{\partial \alpha}\right)^{-1}, \tag{A.24}$$

where the derivative is evaluated at $\alpha = 1$, we have established the first part of (2.39). For the second part we follow a parallel procedure using $h_Q(\phi^*(\alpha, z)\boldsymbol{q}, \alpha z) = 0$; eq. (A.22) and the first two members of (A.23) then hold if h is replaced by h_Q; application of (2.13) and (A.24) then completes the proof.

For the second derivatives we note that $h(\boldsymbol{q}, d(\boldsymbol{q}, z)z) \equiv 0$ holds by the definition of $d(\cdot)$ for arbitrary positive $\boldsymbol{q}$ and z. If the firm is homothetic in inputs, we then obtain $h(\phi^*(\alpha, d(\boldsymbol{q}, z)z)\boldsymbol{q}, \alpha d(\boldsymbol{q}, z)z) \equiv 0$ for arbitrary positive $\boldsymbol{q}$, z, and

α. Thus, we can take the derivative of this expression with respect to q_i to obtain

$$\frac{\partial h}{\partial(\phi^* q_i)}\phi^* + \frac{\partial d}{\partial q_i}\left[\sum_{j=1}^{n}\sum_{r=1}^{m}\frac{\partial h}{\partial(\phi^* q_j)}\frac{\partial \phi^*}{\partial(dz_r)}q_j z_r + \sum_{r=1}^{m}\frac{\partial h}{\partial(\alpha d z_r)}\alpha z_r\right] = 0, \tag{A.25}$$

which holds for arbitrary positive $\boldsymbol{q}$, $\boldsymbol{z}$, and α. In particular, we can now choose $\boldsymbol{q}$ and $\boldsymbol{z}$ so that the firm's production is efficient, i.e., so that $d(\boldsymbol{q}, \boldsymbol{z}) = 1$ or $h(\boldsymbol{q}, \boldsymbol{z}) = 0$. This implies that (A.25) can be simplified to

$$\frac{\partial h}{\partial(\phi^* q_i)}\phi^* + \frac{\partial d}{\partial q_i}\left[\sum_{j=1}^{n}\sum_{r=1}^{m}\frac{\partial h}{\partial(\phi^* q_j)}\frac{\partial \phi^*}{\partial z_r}q_j z_r + \sum_{r=1}^{m}\frac{\partial h}{\partial(\alpha z_r)}\alpha z_r\right] = 0. \tag{A.26}$$

The derivatives of $h(\cdot)$ now have $\phi^*\boldsymbol{q}$ and $\alpha \boldsymbol{z}$ as arguments, while ϕ^* and $\partial\phi^*/\partial z_r$ are functions of α and $\boldsymbol{z}$. This expression holds for any positive α; we take the derivative of (A.26) with respect to α to obtain

$$\phi^*\left[\frac{\partial \phi^*}{\partial \alpha}\sum_{j=1}^{n}\frac{\partial^2 h}{\partial(\phi^* q_i)\,\partial(\phi^* q_j)}q_j + \sum_{r=1}^{m}\frac{\partial^2 h}{\partial(\phi^* q_i)\,\partial(\alpha z_r)}z_r\right] + \frac{\partial h}{\partial(\phi^* q_i)}\frac{\partial \phi^*}{\partial \alpha} + \frac{\partial d}{\partial q_i}e(\alpha, \boldsymbol{q}, \boldsymbol{z}) = 0. \tag{A.27}$$

Here $e(\alpha, \boldsymbol{q}, \boldsymbol{z})$ is the derivative with respect to α of the term in brackets in (A.26), which does not depend on i. Next we evaluate (A.27) at $\alpha = 1$ to obtain

$$\left[\frac{\partial \phi^*}{\partial \alpha}\sum_{j=1}^{n}\frac{\partial^2 h}{\partial q_i\,\partial q_j}q_j + \sum_{r=1}^{m}\frac{\partial^2 h}{\partial q_i\,\partial z_r}z_r\right] + \frac{\partial h}{\partial q_i}\frac{\partial \phi^*}{\partial \alpha} + \frac{\partial d}{\partial q_i}e(1, \boldsymbol{q}, \boldsymbol{z}) = 0. \tag{A.28}$$

where $\partial\phi^*/\partial\alpha$ is evaluated at $\alpha = 1$. Now, note that since $\partial h/\partial q_i = (1/q_i)\,\partial h/\partial \log q_i$, we have

$$\frac{\partial^2 h}{\partial q_i\,\partial q_j} = \frac{1}{q_i q_j}\left[-\delta_{ij}\frac{\partial h}{\partial \log q_i} + \frac{\partial^2 h}{\partial \log q_i\,\partial \log q_j}\right], \tag{A.29}$$

$$\frac{\partial^2 h}{\partial q_i\,\partial z_r} = \frac{1}{q_i z_r}\frac{\partial^2 h}{\partial \log q_i\,\partial \log z_r}. \tag{A.30}$$

Substitution of these results into (A.28) using (2.25) then yields

$$\frac{\partial\phi^*}{\partial\alpha}\sum_{j=1}^{n}\frac{\partial^2 h}{\partial \log q_i\,\partial \log q_j}\frac{1}{q_i} + \frac{\partial d}{\partial q_i}\,e(1, \boldsymbol{q}, \boldsymbol{z}) = 0. \tag{A.31}$$

Now division by $\partial\phi^*/\partial\alpha$, multiplication by q_i, and use of $q_i\,\partial d/\partial q_i = \partial h/\partial \log q_i$, which holds when $d(\boldsymbol{q}, \boldsymbol{z}) = 1$, establishes the first part of (2.45), where $a^* = -e(1, \boldsymbol{q}, \boldsymbol{z})/(\partial\phi^*/\partial\alpha)$ does not depend on i.

A.5. Homotheticity in outputs

When the firm's technology is homothetic in outputs we have $h(\alpha\boldsymbol{q}, \phi(\alpha, \boldsymbol{q})\boldsymbol{z}) = 0$ for positive α whenever $h(\boldsymbol{q}, \boldsymbol{z}) = 0$. Again we take the derivative with respect to α to obtain

$$\sum_{i=1}^{n}\frac{\partial h}{\partial(\alpha q_i)}q_i + \sum_{r=1}^{m}\frac{\partial h}{\partial(\phi z_r)}z_r\frac{\partial\phi}{\partial\alpha} = 0. \tag{A.32}$$

Evaluating this at $\alpha = 1$ we then obtain, using (2.16),

$$\frac{\partial\phi}{\partial\alpha} = -\frac{\sum_{i=1}^{n}\partial h/\partial \log q_i}{\sum_{r=1}^{m}\partial h/\partial \log z_r} = \sum_{i=1}^{n}\frac{\partial h}{\partial \log q_i}, \tag{A.33}$$

which establishes the first part of (2.41) if we define $u(q)$ as $\partial\phi/\partial\alpha$ evaluated at $\alpha = 1$. We can rewrite (A.32) and the first two members of (A.33) with h_Q in place of h; application of (2.13) then establishes the second part of (2.41).

For the second derivative condition which holds when production is homothetic in outputs, we again use $h(\boldsymbol{q}, d(\boldsymbol{q}, z)z) \equiv 0$ to obtain $h(\alpha\boldsymbol{q}, \phi(\alpha, \boldsymbol{q})d(\boldsymbol{q}, z)z) \equiv 0$ which holds for arbitrary positive $\boldsymbol{q}$, z, and α. The derivative of this with respect to z_r is

$$\frac{\partial h}{\partial(\phi d z_r)} \phi d + \sum_{s=1}^{m} \frac{\partial h}{\partial(\phi d z_s)} \phi z_s \frac{\partial d}{\partial z_r} = 0. \tag{A.34}$$

Again, we now choose $\boldsymbol{q}$ and z so $d(\boldsymbol{q}, z) = 1$ and $h(\boldsymbol{q}, z) = 0$. We can then simplify (A.34) to

$$\phi \frac{\partial h}{\partial(\phi z_r)} + \frac{\partial d}{\partial z_r} \sum_{s=1}^{m} \frac{\partial h}{\partial(\phi z_s)} \phi z_s = 0, \tag{A.35}$$

where now the arguments of the derivatives of $h(\cdot)$ are $\alpha\boldsymbol{q}$ and ϕz. This equation holds for arbitrary positive α, so we can take the derivative with respect to α to obtain

$$\phi\left[\sum_{i=1}^{n} \frac{\partial^2 h}{\partial(\phi z_r)\,\partial(\alpha q_i)} q_i + \frac{\partial\phi}{\partial\alpha} \sum_{s=1}^{m} \frac{\partial^2 h}{\partial(\phi z_r)\,\partial(\phi z_s)} z_s\right] + \frac{\partial\phi}{\partial\alpha} \frac{\partial h}{\partial(\phi z_r)} + \frac{\partial d}{\partial z_r} e^*(\alpha, \boldsymbol{q}, z) = 0, \tag{A.36}$$

where $e^*(\alpha, \boldsymbol{q}, z)$ is the derivative with respect to α of the sum in (A.35), which does not depend on r. Again, we evaluate this at $\alpha = 1$ to obtain

$$\left[\sum_{i=1}^{n} \frac{\partial^2 h}{\partial z_r\,\partial q_i} q_i + \frac{\partial\phi}{\partial\alpha} \sum_{s=1}^{m} \frac{\partial^2 h}{\partial z_r\,\partial z_s} z_s\right] + \frac{\partial\phi}{\partial\alpha} \frac{\partial h}{\partial z_r} + \frac{\partial d}{\partial z_r} e^*(1, \boldsymbol{q}, z) = 0. \tag{A.37}$$

Now, $\partial h/\partial z_r = (1/z_r)\,\partial h/\partial \log z_r$ implies

$$\frac{\partial^2 h}{\partial z_r\, \partial z_s}=\frac{1}{z_r z_s}\left[-\delta_{rs}\frac{\partial h}{\partial \log z_r}+\frac{\partial^2 h}{\partial \log z_r\, \partial \log z_s}\right]. \tag{A.38}$$

Substitution of this result and (A.30) into (A.37) and use of (2.24) then gives

$$\sum_{i=1}^{n}\frac{1}{z_r}\frac{\partial^2 h}{\partial \log z_r\, \partial \log q_i}+\frac{\partial d}{\partial z_r}e^*(1,\boldsymbol{q},\boldsymbol{z})=0. \tag{A.39}$$

Next, we multiply (A.39) by z_r, use $z_r\,\partial d/\partial z_r=\partial h/\partial \log z_r$, which holds when $d(\boldsymbol{q},\boldsymbol{z})=1$, sum over r using (2.16), and use (2.25) to obtain $e^*(1,\boldsymbol{q},\boldsymbol{z})=0$. This, in conjunction with (A.39), establishes the first part of (2.46).

The second parts of (2.45) and (2.46) can be established using lines of argument which are essentially the same as were used to establish the first parts of (2.46) and (2.45), respectively. The only important difference is that the starting point is $h_Q(\boldsymbol{q}/d_Q(\boldsymbol{q},\boldsymbol{z}),\boldsymbol{z})\equiv 0$, which also holds for any positive values of the inputs and outputs.

A.6. Homogeneous production

If production is homothetic in both inputs and outputs and $u(\boldsymbol{q})=\boldsymbol{u}^*(\boldsymbol{z})=k$ for some constant k, we then have $\Sigma_i\,\partial h/\partial \log q_i=\Sigma_i\,(q_i/d)\,\partial d/\partial q_i=k$ or

$$\sum_{i=1}^{n} q_i\frac{\partial d}{\partial q_i}=kd \tag{A.40}$$

for any $\boldsymbol{q}$ and $\boldsymbol{z}$ satisfying $d(\boldsymbol{q},\boldsymbol{z})=1$. Since d and $\partial d/\partial q_i$ are both homogeneous of degree -1 in z, we have

$$\frac{\partial d(\boldsymbol{q},\beta\boldsymbol{z})}{\partial q_i}=\frac{1}{\beta}\frac{\partial d(\boldsymbol{q},\boldsymbol{z})}{\partial q_i};\qquad d(\boldsymbol{q},\beta\boldsymbol{z})=\frac{1}{\beta}d(\boldsymbol{q},\boldsymbol{z}). \tag{A.41}$$

Since $d(\boldsymbol{q},\boldsymbol{z})=\beta$ implies $d(\boldsymbol{q},\beta\boldsymbol{z})=1$, (A.40) then implies that

$\Sigma_i q_i \, \partial d(\boldsymbol{q}, \beta z)/\partial q_i = kd(\boldsymbol{q}, \beta z)$; application of (A.41) then indicates that (A.40) can be extended to any positive $\boldsymbol{q}$ and z.

Now we use Euler's theorem to establish that $d(\boldsymbol{q}, z)$ is homogeneous of degree k in $\boldsymbol{q}$; from this the first parts of (2.42) and (2.43) can be established directly. The second parts can be established similarly. The first part of (2.47) follows directly from the homogeneity of $d(\boldsymbol{q}, z)$ in $\boldsymbol{q}$ in exactly the same way that (2.26) and (2.27) follow from the homogeneity of $d(\boldsymbol{q}, z)$ in z; the second part of (2.48) follows from the homogeneity of $d_Q(\boldsymbol{q}, z)$ in z when production is homogeneous.

A.7. Input–output homotheticity

When (2.44) holds, we also have $u^*(\alpha z) = u(\phi^*(\alpha, z)\boldsymbol{q})$ because the firm is homothetic in inputs. Suppose we choose some particular vector z of outputs, so $\phi^*(\alpha, z) = v(\alpha)$ can be regarded as an increasing function of α alone, as can $u^*(\alpha z) = w(\alpha)$. If $u^*(z) = w_0$, we then have for any $\boldsymbol{q}$ on the isoquant $u(\boldsymbol{q}) = w_0$, $u(v(\alpha)\boldsymbol{q}) = w(\alpha)$ or, since $v(\alpha)$ is increasing in α, $u(\beta\boldsymbol{q}) = w(v^{-1}(\beta))$, which implies that $u(\beta\boldsymbol{q}) = w_1$ is also an isoquant for $w_1 = w(v^{-1}(\beta))$. Consequently the function $u(\cdot)$ is homothetic in the usual sense. A parallel argument establishes that $u^*(\cdot)$ is also homothetic.

Since $u^*(\cdot)$ is homothetic, there is an increasing function $s(\cdot)$ such that $s(u^*(z))$ is linearly homogeneous. From (2.44) we obtain $s(u(\boldsymbol{q})) = s(u^*(z))$, which implies that $d(\boldsymbol{q}, z) = s(u(\boldsymbol{q}))/s(u^*(z))$ is the output distance function and $h(\boldsymbol{q}, z) = \log[s(u(\boldsymbol{q}))] - \log[s(u^*(z))]$ is the output homogeneous production function. Differentiation of this with respect to $\log q_i$ and then with respect to $\log z_r$ yields a zero result, which establishes the first part of (2.50). The second part of (2.49) can be established similarly.

Appendix to Chapter 3

B.1. The fundamental matrix equation

The derivative of (3.2) with respect to $\log z_r$ is

$$p_i q_i \frac{\partial \log q_i}{\partial \log z_r} - \rho \frac{\partial h}{\partial \log q_i} \frac{\partial \log \rho}{\partial \log z_r} - \rho \sum_{j=1}^{n} \frac{\partial^2 h}{\partial \log q_i \, \partial \log q_j} \frac{\partial \log q_j}{\partial \log z_r}$$

$$- \rho \frac{\partial^2 h}{\partial \log q_i \, \partial \log z_r} = 0. \tag{B.1}$$

The second term on the left equals $-p_i q_i \, \partial \log \rho / \partial \log z_r$ in view of (3.2). Using (3.8) and $f_i = p_i q_i / C$, we can write (B.1), when divided by C, for all pairs (i, r) in matrix form as

$$(\boldsymbol{F} - \gamma \boldsymbol{H}) \frac{\partial \log \boldsymbol{q}}{\partial \log \boldsymbol{z}'} - \boldsymbol{F}\boldsymbol{\iota} \frac{\partial \log \rho}{\partial \log \boldsymbol{z}'} = \gamma \boldsymbol{H}^*. \tag{B.2}$$

Next we differentiate (3.2) with respect to $\log p_j$:

$$\delta_{ij} p_i q_i + p_i q_i \frac{\partial \log q_i}{\partial \log p_j} - \rho \frac{\partial h}{\partial \log q_i} \frac{\partial \log \rho}{\partial \log p_j}$$

$$- \rho \sum_{k=1}^{n} \frac{\partial^2 h}{\partial \log q_i \, \partial \log q_k} \frac{\partial \log q_k}{\partial \log p_j} = 0.$$

The third term, using (3.2), equals $-p_i q_i \, \partial \log \rho / \partial \log p_j$ so after dividing by C we can write this for all pairs (i, j) as

$$(\boldsymbol{F} - \gamma \boldsymbol{H}) \frac{\partial \log \boldsymbol{q}}{\partial \log \boldsymbol{p}'} - \boldsymbol{F}\boldsymbol{\iota} \frac{\partial \log \rho}{\partial \log \boldsymbol{p}'} = -\boldsymbol{F}. \tag{B.3}$$

Now we take the derivative of $h(\boldsymbol{q}, \boldsymbol{z})=0$ with respect to $\log z_r$, holding prices and other outputs constant, to obtain

$$\sum_{i=1}^{n} \frac{\partial h}{\partial \log q_i} \frac{\partial \log q_i}{\partial \log z_r} + \frac{\partial h}{\partial \log z_r} = 0. \tag{B.4}$$

We multiply this by γ and use (3.15) and (3.21) to write it for all r as

$$\boldsymbol{\iota}'\boldsymbol{F} \frac{\partial \log \boldsymbol{q}}{\partial \log \boldsymbol{z}'} = \gamma \boldsymbol{g}'. \tag{B.5}$$

Differentiation of $h(\boldsymbol{q}, \boldsymbol{z})=0$ with respect to $\log p_i$ yields

$$\sum_{j=1}^{n} \frac{\partial h}{\partial \log q_j} \frac{\partial \log q_j}{\partial \log p_i} = 0 \tag{B.6}$$

which, after substitution from (3.15) and multiplication by γ, can be written for all i as

$$\boldsymbol{\iota}'\boldsymbol{F} \frac{\partial \log \boldsymbol{q}}{\partial \log \boldsymbol{p}'} = \boldsymbol{0}. \tag{B.7}$$

Finally, we premultiply (B.2) and (B.3) by $\boldsymbol{F}^{-1}$ and combine the results with (B.5) and (B.7) into the partitioned matrix equation

$$\begin{bmatrix} \boldsymbol{F}^{-1}(\boldsymbol{F} - \gamma \boldsymbol{H})\boldsymbol{F}^{-1} & \boldsymbol{\iota} \\ \boldsymbol{\iota}' & 0 \end{bmatrix} \begin{bmatrix} \boldsymbol{F} \dfrac{\partial \log \boldsymbol{q}}{\partial \log \boldsymbol{z}'} & \boldsymbol{F} \dfrac{\partial \log \boldsymbol{q}}{\partial \log \boldsymbol{p}'} \\ -\dfrac{\partial \log \rho}{\partial \log \boldsymbol{z}'} & -\dfrac{\partial \log \rho}{\partial \log \boldsymbol{p}'} \end{bmatrix}$$

$$= \begin{bmatrix} \gamma \boldsymbol{F}^{-1}\boldsymbol{H}^* & -\boldsymbol{I} \\ \gamma \boldsymbol{g}' & \boldsymbol{0} \end{bmatrix}, \tag{B.8}$$

which is the fundamental matrix equation of the cost minimizing multiproduct firm. Using (3.29), the inverse of the partitioned matrix on the left can be written

$$\begin{bmatrix} \boldsymbol{F}^{-1}(\boldsymbol{F}-\gamma\boldsymbol{H})\boldsymbol{F}^{-1} & \boldsymbol{\iota} \\ \boldsymbol{\iota}' & 0 \end{bmatrix}^{-1} = \begin{bmatrix} \psi(\boldsymbol{\Theta}-\boldsymbol{\theta}\boldsymbol{\theta}') & \boldsymbol{\theta} \\ \boldsymbol{\theta}' & -1/\psi \end{bmatrix}, \tag{B.9}$$

where $\boldsymbol{\theta} = \boldsymbol{\Theta}\boldsymbol{\iota}$. Premultiplication of (B.8) by (B.9) then leads to (3.27) and (3.28), as well as expressions for the derivatives of the Lagrange multiplier ρ:

$$\frac{\partial \log \rho}{\partial \log \boldsymbol{p}'} = \boldsymbol{\theta}', \tag{B.10}$$

$$\frac{\partial \log \rho}{\partial \log \boldsymbol{z}'} = \frac{\gamma}{\psi}\boldsymbol{g}' - \gamma\boldsymbol{\theta}'\boldsymbol{F}^{-1}\boldsymbol{H}^*. \tag{B.11}$$

The marginal coefficient θ_i^r can be written using (3.25) as

$$\frac{p_i q_i}{\partial C/\partial z_r}\frac{\partial \log q_i}{\partial \log z_r}\frac{1}{z_r} = \frac{Cf_i}{\rho g_r}\frac{\partial \log q_i}{\partial \log z_r} = \frac{f_i}{\gamma g_r}\frac{\partial \log q_i}{\partial \log z_r}. \tag{B.12}$$

The third member of (B.12) is a multiple $1/\gamma g_r$ of $f_i\,\partial \log q_i/\partial \log z_r$, which is the (i, r)th element of (3.28); this establishes (3.33) and (3.47). The equivalence of $\boldsymbol{\Theta\iota}$ and $\boldsymbol{Kg}$ is established by postmultiplying (3.47) by $\boldsymbol{g}$ and using (2.27).

B.2. Allen partial elasticities of substitution

Allen's [1] definition of the partial elasticity of substitution between the ith and jth inputs can be written in our notation as a multiple $1/(\gamma q_i q_j)$ of the (i, j)th element of the inverse of the bordered Hessian of the production function:

$$\begin{bmatrix} \partial^2 h/\partial \boldsymbol{q}\,\partial \boldsymbol{q}' & \boldsymbol{p} \\ \boldsymbol{p}' & 0 \end{bmatrix}^{-1}. \tag{B.13}$$

Since $\partial h/\partial q_i = (1/q_i)\,\partial h/\partial \log q_i$, the (i, j)th element of $\partial^2 h/\partial \boldsymbol{q}\,\partial \boldsymbol{q}'$ can be written

$$\frac{\partial^2 h}{\partial q_i\,\partial q_j} = \frac{1}{q_i q_j}\left(\frac{\partial^2 h}{\partial \log q_i\,\partial \log q_j} - \delta_{ij}\frac{\partial h}{\partial \log q_i}\right).$$

Using $p_i q_i/C = f_i$ and (3.15), this can be written for all pairs (i, j) as

$$\frac{\partial^2 h}{\partial \boldsymbol{q}\,\partial \boldsymbol{q}'} = \frac{1}{C^2}\boldsymbol{P}\boldsymbol{F}^{-1}\left[\boldsymbol{H} - \frac{1}{\gamma}\boldsymbol{F}\right]\boldsymbol{F}^{-1}\boldsymbol{P} = -\frac{1}{\gamma\psi C^2}\boldsymbol{P}\boldsymbol{\Theta}^{-1}\boldsymbol{P}, \qquad \text{(B.14)}$$

where $\boldsymbol{P}$ is the diagonal matrix of input prices, and the second step is based on (3.29). Substitution of this into (B.13) then yields

$$\begin{bmatrix} -\dfrac{1}{\gamma\psi C^2}\boldsymbol{P}\boldsymbol{\Theta}^{-1}\boldsymbol{P} & \boldsymbol{p} \\ \boldsymbol{p}' & 0 \end{bmatrix}^{-1} = \begin{bmatrix} -\gamma\psi C^2 \boldsymbol{P}^{-1}(\boldsymbol{\Theta} - \boldsymbol{\theta}\boldsymbol{\theta}')\boldsymbol{P}^{-1} & \boldsymbol{P}^{-1}\boldsymbol{\theta} \\ \boldsymbol{\theta}'\boldsymbol{P}^{-1} & \dfrac{1}{\gamma\psi C^2} \end{bmatrix}, \qquad \text{(B.15)}$$

so that the (i, j)th element referred to above is $(-\gamma\psi C^2) \times (\theta_{ij} - \theta_i\theta_j)/p_i p_j$. Now, multiplication of this by $1/(\gamma q_i q_j)$ yields (3.40).

B.3. Derivation of eq. (3.41)

Using (3.8), (3.20), and (3.21) we can write

$$\gamma g_r = \frac{\partial \log C}{\partial \log z_r} = -\gamma \frac{\partial h}{\partial \log z_r}, \qquad \text{(B.16)}$$

which shows that $\partial^2 C/\partial \log z_r\,\partial \log z_s$ is equal to

$$-\gamma \frac{\partial h}{\partial \log z_r} \frac{\partial \log \gamma}{\partial \log z_s} - \gamma \frac{\partial^2 h}{\partial \log z_r \, \partial \log z_s}$$

$$-\gamma \sum_{i=1}^{n} \frac{\partial^2 h}{\partial \log z_r \, \partial \log q_i} \frac{\partial \log q_i}{\partial \log z_s}.$$

We use (3.21) to write this in matrix form as

$$\frac{\partial^2 \log C}{\partial \log \boldsymbol{z} \, \partial \log \boldsymbol{z}'} = \gamma \boldsymbol{g} \frac{\partial \log \gamma}{\partial \log \boldsymbol{z}'} - \gamma \boldsymbol{H}^{**} - \gamma \boldsymbol{H}^{*\prime} \frac{\partial \log \boldsymbol{q}}{\partial \log \boldsymbol{z}'}, \tag{B.17}$$

where $\boldsymbol{H}^{**}$ and $\boldsymbol{H}^{*}$ are defined in (2.18) and (2.19). We have $\partial \log \gamma / \partial \log \boldsymbol{z}' = \partial \log \rho / \partial \log \boldsymbol{z}' - \partial \log C / \partial \log \boldsymbol{z}'$ in view of (3.8) so that (B.11) and (B.16) yield

$$\frac{\partial \log \gamma}{\partial \log \boldsymbol{z}'} = \gamma \left(\frac{1}{\psi} - 1 \right) \boldsymbol{g}' - \gamma \boldsymbol{\theta}' \boldsymbol{F}^{-1} \boldsymbol{H}^{*}. \tag{B.18}$$

Now we use (B.17), (B.18), and (3.28) to write

$$\frac{\partial^2 \log C}{\partial \log \boldsymbol{z} \, \partial \log \boldsymbol{z}'} = \gamma^2 \left(\frac{1}{\psi} - 1 \right) \boldsymbol{g}\boldsymbol{g}' - \gamma^2 (\boldsymbol{g}\boldsymbol{\theta}' \boldsymbol{F}^{-1} \boldsymbol{H}^{*} + \boldsymbol{H}^{*\prime} \boldsymbol{F}^{-1} \boldsymbol{\theta} \boldsymbol{g}')$$
$$- \gamma \boldsymbol{H}^{**} - \gamma^2 \psi \boldsymbol{H}^{*\prime} \boldsymbol{F}^{-1} (\boldsymbol{\Theta} - \boldsymbol{\theta}\boldsymbol{\theta}') \boldsymbol{F}^{-1} \boldsymbol{H}^{*}. \tag{B.19}$$

Pre- and postmultiplication of (B.19) by $\boldsymbol{\iota}^{*\prime}$ and $\boldsymbol{\iota}^{*}$, respectively, yields, in view of $\boldsymbol{H}^{*}\boldsymbol{\iota}^{*} = \boldsymbol{0}$ and $\boldsymbol{H}^{**}\boldsymbol{\iota}^{*} = \boldsymbol{0}$ (see (2.27) and (2.26)) and $\boldsymbol{g}'\boldsymbol{\iota}^{*} = 1$, $\gamma^2(1/\psi - 1)$ on the right, which establishes (3.41). Note that this result cannot conveniently be established without (2.26) and (2.27) which hold in general only for the output homogeneous production function.

Appendix to Chapter 4

C.1. Derivatives of cost

Shephard's lemma (2.29) written in vector form is $\partial C/\partial \boldsymbol{p} = \boldsymbol{q}$, yielding $\partial^2 C/\partial \boldsymbol{p}\, \partial \boldsymbol{p}' = \partial \boldsymbol{q}/\partial \boldsymbol{p}'$ after differentiation with respect to $\boldsymbol{p}'$. But $\partial \boldsymbol{q}/\partial \boldsymbol{p}' = C\boldsymbol{P}^{-1}\boldsymbol{F}\, (\partial \log \boldsymbol{q}/\partial \log \boldsymbol{p}')\boldsymbol{P}^{-1}$, so that (3.27) implies

$$\frac{\partial^2 C}{\partial \boldsymbol{p}\, \partial \boldsymbol{p}'} = -\psi C\boldsymbol{P}^{-1}(\boldsymbol{\Theta} - \boldsymbol{\theta}\boldsymbol{\theta}')\boldsymbol{P}^{-1}, \tag{C.1}$$

which yields (4.25) directly. Differentiation of $\partial C/\partial \boldsymbol{p} = \boldsymbol{q}$ with respect to $\boldsymbol{z}'$ gives $\partial^2 C/\partial \boldsymbol{p}\, \partial \boldsymbol{z}' = \partial \boldsymbol{q}/\partial \boldsymbol{z}'$ and hence, using (3.33),

$$\frac{\partial^2 C}{\partial \boldsymbol{p}\, \partial \boldsymbol{z}'} = \boldsymbol{P}^{-1}\boldsymbol{K}\boldsymbol{Y}, \tag{C.2}$$

which yields (4.26). Here $\boldsymbol{Y}$ is the diagonal $m \times m$ matrix with the output prices y_r (when they are defined) or marginal costs $\partial C/\partial z_r$ (when output prices are not defined) on the diagonal.

Differentiation of $\partial C/\partial z_r = (C/z_r)\, \partial \log C/\partial \log z_r$ by z_s gives

$$\frac{\partial^2 C}{\partial z_r\, \partial z_s} = \frac{C}{z_r z_s}\left[\frac{\partial^2 \log C}{\partial \log z_r\, \partial \log z_s} + \frac{\partial \log C}{\partial \log z_r}\frac{\partial \log C}{\partial \log z_s} - \delta_{rs}\frac{\partial \log C}{\partial \log z_r}\right].$$

Using (4.3), (4.5), and (B.16) we can write this result for all pairs

(r, s) as

$$\frac{\partial^2 C}{\partial z\,\partial z'} = \frac{1}{\gamma R} \boldsymbol{Y}\boldsymbol{G}^{-1} \left[\frac{\partial^2 \log C}{\partial \log \boldsymbol{z}\,\partial \log \boldsymbol{z}'} + \gamma^2 \boldsymbol{g}\boldsymbol{g}' - \gamma \boldsymbol{G}\right] \boldsymbol{G}^{-1}\boldsymbol{Y}. \tag{C.3}$$

C.2. Derivation of the supply equations

We obtain $\Sigma_t\,(\partial^2 C/\partial z_r\,\partial z_t)(\partial z_t/\partial y_s) = \delta_{rs}$ by differentiating (4.1) with respect to y_s. We write this as

$$\sum_{t=1}^{m} \frac{\partial^2 C}{\partial z_r\,\partial z_t}\, z_t\, \frac{\partial \log z_t}{\partial \log y_s} = \delta_{rs} y_s. \tag{C.4}$$

We have $z_t = Rg_t/y_t$ from (4.3), so that (C.4) for all pairs (r, s) can be written as

$$R\,\frac{\partial^2 C}{\partial \boldsymbol{z}\,\partial \boldsymbol{z}'}\,\boldsymbol{Y}^{-1}\boldsymbol{G}\,\frac{\partial \log \boldsymbol{z}}{\partial \log \boldsymbol{y}'} = \boldsymbol{Y}. \tag{C.5}$$

Now (4.6) permits us to define $\psi^*\boldsymbol{\Theta}^*$ by (4.27) and ψ^* by

$$\psi^* = \frac{1}{R}\boldsymbol{y}' \left(\frac{\partial^2 C}{\partial \boldsymbol{z}\,\partial \boldsymbol{z}'}\right)^{-1} \boldsymbol{y} > 0, \tag{C.6}$$

so that (C.5) implies

$$\boldsymbol{G}\,\frac{\partial \log \boldsymbol{z}}{\partial \log \boldsymbol{y}'} = \psi^*\boldsymbol{\Theta}^*. \tag{C.7}$$

Note that (4.27) and (C.6) together imply (4.8), and that the symmetry of $\boldsymbol{\Theta}^*$ is implied by that of $\partial^2 C/\partial \boldsymbol{z}\,\partial \boldsymbol{z}'$.

Next we differentiate (4.1) with respect to p_i,

$$\frac{\partial^2 C}{\partial z_r\,\partial p_i} + \sum_{s=1}^{m} \frac{\partial^2 C}{\partial z_r\,\partial z_s}\,\frac{\partial z_s}{\partial p_i} = 0,$$

which implies

$$\frac{\partial \boldsymbol{z}}{\partial \boldsymbol{p}'} = -\left(\frac{\partial^2 C}{\partial \boldsymbol{z}\, \partial \boldsymbol{z}'}\right)^{-1} \frac{\partial^2 C}{\partial \boldsymbol{z}\, \partial \boldsymbol{p}'} = -\left(\frac{\partial^2 C}{\partial \boldsymbol{z}\, \partial \boldsymbol{z}'}\right)^{-1} \boldsymbol{YK'P}^{-1}, \tag{C.8}$$

where the last step is based on (C.2). We premultiply (C.8) by $(1/R)\boldsymbol{Y}$ and postmultiply by $\boldsymbol{P}$ and use (4.3) and (4.27) to obtain

$$\boldsymbol{G} \frac{\partial \log \boldsymbol{z}}{\partial \log \boldsymbol{p}'} = -\psi^* \boldsymbol{\Theta}^* \boldsymbol{K}'. \tag{C.9}$$

Now (4.7) may be obtained by taking the differential of $\log \boldsymbol{z}$, premultiplying by $\boldsymbol{G}$, and substituting from (C.7) and (C.9).

Inversion of (4.27) and application of (C.3) yield

$$(\psi^* \boldsymbol{\Theta}^*)^{-1} = \frac{1}{\gamma} \boldsymbol{G}^{-1} \left[\frac{\partial^2 \log C}{\partial \log \boldsymbol{z}\, \partial \log \boldsymbol{z}'} + \gamma^2 \boldsymbol{g}\boldsymbol{g}' - \gamma \boldsymbol{G}\right] \boldsymbol{G}^{-1}, \tag{C.10}$$

which we pre- and postmultiply by $\boldsymbol{g}'$ and $\boldsymbol{g}$, respectively, using (B.19), $\boldsymbol{H}^*\boldsymbol{\iota}^* = \boldsymbol{0}$, and $\boldsymbol{H}^{**}\boldsymbol{\iota}^* = \boldsymbol{0}$ to obtain

$$\frac{1}{\psi^*} \boldsymbol{g}' \boldsymbol{\Theta}^{*-1} \boldsymbol{g} = \frac{\gamma}{\psi} - 1 > 0, \tag{C.11}$$

where the inequality is based on the positive definiteness of $\boldsymbol{\Theta}^*$.

Next we prove the following lemma.

Lemma 1. For any symmetric positive definite matrix $\boldsymbol{A}$ which is normalized so that its elements add up to one, $\boldsymbol{\iota}'\boldsymbol{A}\boldsymbol{\iota} = 1$, and for any conformable vector $\boldsymbol{a}$ whose elements add up to one, $\boldsymbol{\iota}'\boldsymbol{a} = 1$, the quadratic form $\boldsymbol{a}'\boldsymbol{A}^{-1}\boldsymbol{a}$ satisfies $\boldsymbol{a}'\boldsymbol{A}^{-1}\boldsymbol{a} \geq 1$, with equality if and only if $\boldsymbol{a} = \boldsymbol{A}\boldsymbol{\iota}$.

To show this, first assume $\boldsymbol{a} = \boldsymbol{A}\boldsymbol{\iota}$. Then $\boldsymbol{a}'\boldsymbol{A}^{-1}\boldsymbol{a} = \boldsymbol{\iota}'\boldsymbol{A}\boldsymbol{A}^{-1}\boldsymbol{A}\boldsymbol{\iota} = 1$. If $\boldsymbol{a} \neq \boldsymbol{A}\boldsymbol{\iota}$, then $\boldsymbol{a} = \boldsymbol{A}(\boldsymbol{\iota} + \boldsymbol{v})$ for some vector $\boldsymbol{v} \neq \boldsymbol{0}$ which satisfies $\boldsymbol{\iota}'\boldsymbol{A}\boldsymbol{v} = 0$ since $1 = \boldsymbol{\iota}'\boldsymbol{a} = \boldsymbol{\iota}'\boldsymbol{A}(\boldsymbol{\iota} + \boldsymbol{v}) = 1 + \boldsymbol{\iota}'\boldsymbol{A}\boldsymbol{v}$. Then $\boldsymbol{a}'\boldsymbol{A}^{-1}\boldsymbol{a} =$

$(\boldsymbol{\iota}+\boldsymbol{v})'\boldsymbol{A}\boldsymbol{A}^{-1}\boldsymbol{A}(\boldsymbol{\iota}+\boldsymbol{v})=\boldsymbol{\iota}'\boldsymbol{A}\boldsymbol{\iota}+\boldsymbol{v}'\boldsymbol{A}\boldsymbol{v}>1$, since $\boldsymbol{A}$ is positive definite.

Applying this lemma to (C.11) we see that $\boldsymbol{g}'\boldsymbol{\Theta}^{*-1}\boldsymbol{g}\geq 1$ holds with equality if and only if $\boldsymbol{g}=\boldsymbol{\Theta}^*\boldsymbol{\iota}^*$. Thus, $\psi^*(\gamma/\psi-1)\geq 1$ which, with the inequality in (C.11), implies (4.9). Also, the first two parts of (C.11) written in scalar form are the same as (4.28).

C.3. Output independence and input–output separability

It is straightforward to show that when the cost function is subject to constraints (4.34) and (4.38) it must take the form (4.43). Therefore we confine ourselves to the properties of the firm when its production is homothetic in inputs and is input–output separable.

Under these assumptions the firm's production constraint can be written in the form (2.35), and we can write $h_c(\alpha \boldsymbol{z})=h_a(\phi^*(\alpha,\boldsymbol{z})\boldsymbol{q})$ for any positive α whenever $h_c(\boldsymbol{z})=h_a(\boldsymbol{q})$. An argument precisely similar to that used in Appendix A to establish that the function $u(\cdot)$ in (2.44) is homothetic can be used to establish that $h_a(\cdot)$ is homothetic. Thus, under these circumstances $h_a(\cdot)$ in (2.35) can be taken without loss of generality to be homogeneous of degree one.

Using this form of the production constraint, the Lagrangian function for cost minimization is $L(\boldsymbol{q},\lambda)=\Sigma_i p_i q_i+\lambda(h_c(\boldsymbol{z})-h_a(\boldsymbol{q}))$. The first-order conditions take the form

$$p_i=\lambda\frac{\partial h_a}{\partial q_i}. \tag{C.12}$$

Multiplying by q_i and summing over i yields

$$C=\lambda\sum_{i=1}^{n} q_i\frac{\partial h_a}{\partial q_i}=\lambda h_a(\boldsymbol{q})=\lambda h_c(\boldsymbol{z}), \tag{C.13}$$

where we have used the homogeneity of $h_a(\cdot)$ for the second equal sign and (2.35) for the third. We differentiate (C.12) with respect to z_r, keeping other outputs and all input prices constant, to obtain

$$\frac{\partial \lambda}{\partial z_r}\frac{\partial h_a}{\partial q_i}+\lambda \sum_{j=1}^{n} \frac{\partial^2 h_a}{\partial q_i\, \partial q_j}\frac{\partial q_j}{\partial z_r}=0. \tag{C.14}$$

Now, since $h_a(\cdot)$ is homogeneous, $\Sigma_i\, q_i\, \partial h_a/\partial q_i = h_a(\boldsymbol{q})$ and consequently $\Sigma_i\, q_i\, \partial^2 h_a/\partial q_i\, \partial q_j + \partial h_a/\partial q_j = \partial h_a/\partial q_j$ so that

$$\sum_{i=1}^{n} q_i \frac{\partial^2 h_a}{\partial q_i\, \partial q_j}=0. \tag{C.15}$$

Now we multiply (C.14) by q_i and sum over i to find

$$\frac{\partial \lambda}{\partial z_r} h_a(\boldsymbol{q})+\lambda \sum_{j=1}^{n}\frac{\partial q_j}{\partial z_r}\sum_{i=1}^{n} q_i \frac{\partial^2 h_a}{\partial q_i\, \partial q_j}=0. \tag{C.16}$$

By (C.15) the sum in (C.16) is zero, and $h_a(\boldsymbol{q})>0$ for positive $\boldsymbol{q}$, so we must have $\partial \lambda/\partial z_r = 0$. Thus, λ is a function only of the input prices $\boldsymbol{p}$, which in conjunction with (C.13) shows that (4.42) holds. Note that $h_c(\cdot)$ in (2.35) and in (4.42) are the same function when $h_a(\cdot)$ in (2.35) is interpreted as linearly homogeneous.

It is somewhat more difficult to show that when the cost function has the structure (4.42) then the production function takes the form (2.35). To show this we will need a lemma which will be proved in section C.4. This lemma is an extension of a well-known property of the homothetic single product production function.

Lemma 2: An input–output separable multiproduct production function is homothetic in inputs if and only if its elasticity of scale can be written as a function of its output levels alone.

Now, it follows immediately from (4.34) that the production function corresponding to (4.42) is input–output separable. The derivative of (4.42) with respect to z_r is $\partial C/\partial z_r = \lambda(\boldsymbol{p})\,\partial h_c/\partial z_r$, which implies that $\partial \log C/\partial \log z_r = \partial \log h_c/\partial \log z_r$. Now (3.13) implies that $\gamma = \Sigma_r\, \partial \log h_c/\partial \log z_r$, which is a function of the outputs alone; since γ is the reciprocal of the elasticity of scale, application of the lemma then shows that the multiproduct production function is homothetic in inputs. The general duality of cost and production functions then guarantees that the production function can be written as (2.35) with $h_a(\cdot)$ linear homogeneous and $h_c(\cdot)$ the same function as in (4.42), since otherwise a different cost function would be associated with the production function.

C.4. Proof of lemma 2

If the firm is homothetic in inputs, then (2.39) applies; since $\Sigma_i\, \partial h/\partial \log q_i$ is equal to the elasticity of scale (see (3.9)), we have $1/\gamma = u^*(\boldsymbol{z})$ as asserted. This proves necessity. For sufficiency, we first establish a simple lemma on homothetic functions.

Lemma 3. A function $f(\boldsymbol{x})$ is homothetic if $f(\boldsymbol{x}) = f(\boldsymbol{x}^*)$ implies that $\Sigma_i\, x_i\, \partial f/\partial x_i = \Sigma_i\, x_i^*\, \partial f/\partial x_i^*$ holds for all vectors $\boldsymbol{x}$ and $\boldsymbol{x}^*$ in the domain of $f(\cdot)$, where $\partial f/\partial x_i$ is evaluated at $\boldsymbol{x}$ and $\partial f/\partial x_i^*$ is evaluated at $\boldsymbol{x}^*$.

To prove this lemma we note that $f(\cdot)$ is homothetic if there is an increasing function $s(\cdot)$ such that $s(f(\cdot))$ is linearly homogeneous. A function with this property is obtained as follows. Let $\bar{\boldsymbol{x}}$ be an arbitrary fixed point in the domain of $f(\cdot)$. Then we define $s(w) = v$, where v satisfies $f(v\bar{\boldsymbol{x}}) = w$. It then follows that $s(f(\boldsymbol{x})) = v$, where $f(v\bar{\boldsymbol{x}}) = f(\boldsymbol{x})$ for any $\boldsymbol{x}$ in the domain of $f(\cdot)$. From the condition of the lemma we obtain

$$\sum_i x_i \frac{\partial f}{\partial x_i} = \sum_i v\bar{x}_i \frac{\partial f}{\partial (v\bar{x}_i)}. \tag{C.17}$$

Now we note that v is a function of $\boldsymbol{x}$ and that $\bar{\boldsymbol{x}}$ is fixed. We differentiate $f(v\bar{\boldsymbol{x}})=f(\boldsymbol{x})$ with respect to x_i to obtain $\Sigma_j\, \partial f/\partial(v\bar{x}_j)\bar{x}_j\, \partial v/\partial x_i = \partial f/\partial x_i$, which we multiply by x_i and sum over i:

$$\left[\sum_i x_i \frac{\partial v}{\partial x_i}\right]\left[\sum_j \bar{x}_j \frac{\partial f}{\partial(v\bar{x}_j)}\right] = \sum_i x_i \frac{\partial f}{\partial x_i}. \tag{C.18}$$

Substituting on the right from (C.17) we find $\Sigma_i\, x_i\, \partial v/\partial x_i = v$ so that $v(\boldsymbol{x}) = s(f(\boldsymbol{x}))$ is linearly homogeneous as required.

Now we assume that the firm is input–output separable, so that its production function can be written as in (2.35), and that its elasticity of scale can be written as a function of its outputs only. Suppose that $h_a(\boldsymbol{q}) = h_a(\bar{\boldsymbol{q}})$. Then we can produce the same bundle of outputs with either $\boldsymbol{q}$ or $\bar{\boldsymbol{q}}$. We evaluate the elasticity of scale as in section 3.2 by considering the total differential of the production function

$$\sum_{r=1}^{m} z_r \frac{\partial h_c}{\partial z_r}\, \mathrm{d}(\log z_r) = \sum_{i=1}^{n} q_i \frac{\partial h_a}{\partial q_i}\, \mathrm{d}(\log q_i). \tag{C.19}$$

To evaluate the elasticity of scale, we wish to make the inputs change proportionately and consider the effect on the outputs when they are also constrained to change proportionately. This implies that $\mathrm{d}(\log z_r) = \mathrm{d}(\log z)$ on the left and $\mathrm{d}(\log q_i) = \mathrm{d}(\log q)$ on the right can each be factored from its respective sum, yielding

$$\frac{1}{\gamma} = \frac{\mathrm{d}(\log z)}{\mathrm{d}(\log q)} = \frac{\sum_{i=1}^{n} q_i\, (\partial h_a/\partial q_i)}{\sum_{r=1}^{m} z_r\, (\partial h_c/\partial z_r)}. \tag{C.20}$$

In a similar way, when the input vector $\bar{q}$ is used, we obtain

$$\frac{1}{\bar{\gamma}} = \frac{\mathrm{d}(\log z)}{\mathrm{d}(\log \bar{q})} = \frac{\sum_{i=1}^{n} \bar{q}_i\, (\partial h_a/\partial \bar{q}_i)}{\sum_{r=1}^{m} z_r\, (\partial h_c/\partial z_r)}. \tag{C.21}$$

Since z is the same in both cases and the elasticity of scale does not depend on $\boldsymbol{q}$ (i.e., $\gamma = \bar{\gamma}$), these expressions must be equal, which yields

$$\sum_{i=1}^{n} q_i \frac{\partial h_a}{\partial q_i} = \sum_{i=1}^{n} \bar{q}_i \frac{\partial h_a}{\partial \bar{q}_i}, \tag{C.22}$$

whenever $h_a(\boldsymbol{q}) = h_a(\bar{\boldsymbol{q}})$. Now we apply lemma 3 above to show that $h_a(\cdot)$ is homothetic.

It is straightforward to show that the definition of homotheticity in inputs given above (2.38) holds when $h_a(\cdot)$ in (2.35) is homothetic. In that case there is an increasing function $s(\cdot)$ such that $s(h_a(\cdot))$ is linearly homogeneous. Let z and $\boldsymbol{q}$ be such that $s(h_c(z)) = s(h_a(\boldsymbol{q}))$, and suppose that we multiply z by α and $\boldsymbol{q}$ by ϕ^* so that $s(h_c(\alpha z)) = s(h_a(\phi^* \boldsymbol{q}))$ also holds. Then $s(h_a(\phi^* \boldsymbol{q})) = \phi^* s(h_a(\boldsymbol{q})) = \phi^* s(h_c(z))$ so that $\phi^* = s(h_c(\alpha z))/s(h_c(z))$ is a function of α and z as required.

It should be noted that this argument also establishes that the definition of homotheticity in inputs given in section 2.4 reduces to the usual definition of homotheticity when the firm produces only one product.

Appendix to Chapter 5

D.1. The second-order condition for revenue maximization

The vector $\boldsymbol{q}$ is regarded as given for revenue maximization, so the differential of the constraint $h(\boldsymbol{q}, \boldsymbol{z}) = 0$ which is relevant for the second-order condition is $\Sigma_r\,(\partial h/\partial \log z_r)\,\mathrm{d}(\log z_r) = 0$. In view of (3.21), this is equivalent to $\Sigma_r\, g_r\, \mathrm{d}(\log z_r) = 0$. This means that the necessary second-order condition is that for all vectors $\boldsymbol{x}$ satisfying $\boldsymbol{x}'\boldsymbol{g} = 0$ the quadratic form $\boldsymbol{x}'(\boldsymbol{G} + \boldsymbol{H}^{**})\boldsymbol{x}$ must be negative. Since $\boldsymbol{\iota}^{*\prime}\boldsymbol{g} = 1$, this is not contradicted by $\boldsymbol{\iota}^{*\prime}(\boldsymbol{G} + \boldsymbol{H}^{**})\boldsymbol{\iota}^* = 1$.

We let $\boldsymbol{G}^{1/2}$ be the diagonal matrix with positive square roots of the revenue shares g_r on the diagonal, and consider the equation

$$[\boldsymbol{G}^{-1/2}(\boldsymbol{G} + \boldsymbol{H}^{**})\boldsymbol{G}^{-1/2} - \mu_r \boldsymbol{I}]\boldsymbol{G}^{1/2}\bar{\boldsymbol{x}}_r^* = \boldsymbol{0}, \tag{D.1}$$

which can be solved for the m characteristic roots μ_r of $\boldsymbol{G}^{-1/2}(\boldsymbol{G} + \boldsymbol{H}^{**})\boldsymbol{G}^{-1/2}$ and the corresponding characteristic vectors written as $\boldsymbol{G}^{1/2}\bar{\boldsymbol{x}}_r^*$. We assume that the characteristic vectors are normalized in the usual way, so that $\bar{\boldsymbol{x}}_r^{*\prime}\boldsymbol{G}^{1/2}\boldsymbol{G}^{1/2}\bar{\boldsymbol{x}}_r^* = \bar{\boldsymbol{x}}_r^{*\prime}\boldsymbol{G}\bar{\boldsymbol{x}}_r^* = 1$ for each r and $\bar{\boldsymbol{x}}_r^{*\prime}\boldsymbol{G}\bar{\boldsymbol{x}}_s^* = 0$ for $r \neq s$. We premultiply (D.1) by $\boldsymbol{G}^{1/2}$ to obtain

$$[(\boldsymbol{G} + \boldsymbol{H}^{**}) - \mu_r \boldsymbol{G}]\bar{\boldsymbol{x}}_r^* = \boldsymbol{0}, \tag{D.2}$$

which shows that solution of (D.1) amounts to finding the characteristic roots and vectors of $\boldsymbol{G} + \boldsymbol{H}^{**}$ relative to $\boldsymbol{G}$.

Substitution of $\boldsymbol{\iota}^*$ into (D.2) and use of (2.26) establishes that $\bar{x}_1^* = \iota^*$ is a characteristic vector in (D.2) with corresponding root $\mu_1 = 1$. Next, consider any other characteristic vector $\bar{x}_r^*$ for $r = 2, \ldots, m$. From the normalization we have $\bar{x}_r^{*\prime}G\bar{x}_1^* = \bar{x}_r^{*\prime}G\iota^* = \bar{x}_r^{*\prime}g = 0$. Therefore, if the necessary second-order condition holds, we have $\bar{x}_r^{*\prime}(G + H^{**})\bar{x}_r^* < 0$, which shows that the associated characteristic root μ_r is negative. This establishes that $G^{-1/2}(G + H^{**})G^{-1/2}$ and therefore $G + H^{**}$ are nonsingular.

Next we take the inverse of the matrix on the left in brackets in (D.1) to obtain $[G^{1/2}(G + H^{**})^{-1}G^{1/2} - (1/\mu_r)I]G^{1/2}\bar{x}_r^* = 0$ which holds for the μ_r's and $\bar{x}_r^*$'s of the last paragraph. We premultiply this by $G^{1/2}$ and use (5.16) to obtain

$$\left(\bar{\Theta}^* - \frac{1}{\mu_r} G\right) \bar{x}_r^* = 0. \tag{D.3}$$

Since the signs of the characteristic roots have not been changed, this establishes that $\bar{\Theta}^*$ has one positive root (unity) and $m - 1$ negative roots with respect to G. Next, we substitute $\mu_1 = 1$ and $\bar{x}_1^* = \iota^*$ into (D.3) to establish (5.17). Finally, we note that $(\bar{\Theta}^* - gg')\iota^* = 0$ follows from (5.17). For any other $\bar{x}_r^*$, $r = 2, \ldots, m$, we have

$$\bar{x}_r^{*\prime}(\bar{\Theta}^* - gg')\bar{x}_r^* = \bar{x}_r^{*\prime}\bar{\Theta}^*\bar{x}_r^* - (\bar{x}_r^{*\prime}g)^2. \tag{D.4}$$

The second term on the right is zero, since each but the first $\bar{x}_r^*$ is orthogonal to g. The first term is equal, by (D.3), to $(1/\mu_r)\bar{x}_r^{*\prime}G\bar{x}_r^*$, which is negative. This establishes that $\bar{\Theta}^* - gg'$ is negative semidefinite of rank $m - 1$.

D.2. The fundamental matrix equation of the revenue maximizing firm

We take the derivative of (5.2) with respect to $\log q_i$ to obtain

$$y_r z_r \frac{\partial \log z_r}{\partial \log q_i} + \bar{\rho} \frac{\partial h}{\partial \log z_r} \frac{\partial \log \bar{p}}{\partial \log q_i} + \bar{\rho} \frac{\partial^2 h}{\partial \log z_r \, \partial \log q_i}$$

$$+ \bar{\rho} \sum_{s=1}^{m} \frac{\partial^2 h}{\partial \log z_r \, \partial \log z_s} \frac{\partial \log z_s}{\partial \log q_i} = 0.$$

We substitute from (5.2) into the second term on the left, obtaining $-y_r z_r\, \partial \log \bar{p}/\partial \log q_i$ for this term. Now we divide by $\bar{p}$, use (5.3) and $g_r = y_r z_r/R$, and write the result for all pairs (r, i) in matrix form as

$$(\boldsymbol{G}+\boldsymbol{H}^{**})\frac{\partial \log \boldsymbol{z}}{\partial \log \boldsymbol{q}'}-\boldsymbol{g}\frac{\partial \log R}{\partial \log \boldsymbol{q}'}=-\boldsymbol{H}^{*\prime}. \tag{D.5}$$

Next we differentiate (5.2) with respect to $\log y_s$:

$$\delta_{rs} y_r z_r + y_r z_r \frac{\partial \log z_r}{\partial \log y_s} + \bar{p}\frac{\partial h}{\partial \log z_r}\frac{\partial \log \bar{p}}{\partial \log y_s}$$
$$+\bar{p}\sum_{t=1}^{m}\frac{\partial^2 h}{\partial \log z_r\, \partial \log z_t}\frac{\partial \log z_t}{\partial \log y_s}=0.$$

We substitute from (5.2) into the third term on the left, divide by $\bar{p}$, use (5.3), and write the result in matrix form for all pairs (r, s) as

$$(\boldsymbol{G}+\boldsymbol{H}^{**})\frac{\partial \log \boldsymbol{z}}{\partial \log \boldsymbol{y}'}-\boldsymbol{g}\frac{\partial \log R}{\partial \log \boldsymbol{y}'}=-\boldsymbol{G}. \tag{D.6}$$

Now we substitute from (3.15) into (5.9), which was obtained by differentiating $h(\boldsymbol{q}, \boldsymbol{z})=0$ with respect to $\log q_i$, and write the result for all i as

$$\boldsymbol{g}'\frac{\partial \log \boldsymbol{z}}{\partial \log \boldsymbol{q}'}=\frac{1}{\gamma}\boldsymbol{f}'. \tag{D.7}$$

We differentiate $h(\boldsymbol{q}, \boldsymbol{z})=0$ with respect to $\log y_s$ to obtain

$$\sum_{r=1}^{m}\frac{\partial h}{\partial \log z_r}\frac{\partial \log z_r}{\partial \log y_s}=0.$$

Substitution from (3.21) and multiplication by -1 then yields for all s:

$$\boldsymbol{g}'\frac{\partial \log \boldsymbol{z}}{\partial \log \boldsymbol{y}'}=\boldsymbol{0}. \tag{D.8}$$

Finally, we premultiply (D.5) and (D.6) by $-\boldsymbol{G}^{-1}$ and combine the results with (D.7) and (D.8) into the partitioned matrix equation

$$\begin{bmatrix} -\boldsymbol{G}^{-1}(\boldsymbol{G}+\boldsymbol{H}^{**})\boldsymbol{G}^{-1} & \boldsymbol{\iota}^* \\ \boldsymbol{\iota}^{*\prime} & 0 \end{bmatrix} \begin{bmatrix} \boldsymbol{G}\dfrac{\partial \log \boldsymbol{z}}{\partial \log \boldsymbol{q}'} & \boldsymbol{G}\dfrac{\partial \log \boldsymbol{z}}{\partial \log \boldsymbol{y}'} \\ \dfrac{\partial \log R}{\partial \log \boldsymbol{q}'} & \dfrac{\partial \log R}{\partial \log \boldsymbol{y}'} \end{bmatrix}$$

$$= \begin{bmatrix} \boldsymbol{G}^{-1}\boldsymbol{H}^{*\prime} & \boldsymbol{I} \\ \dfrac{1}{\gamma}\boldsymbol{f}' & \boldsymbol{0} \end{bmatrix}, \tag{D.9}$$

which is the form which the fundamental matrix equation takes for the revenue maximizing firm. This can be solved in the same manner that (B.8) was solved for the cost minimizing firm. However, the equivalence of the Lagrange multiplier $\bar{\rho}$ to revenue in this case permits simplification as follows. Since $R = \Sigma_r\, y_r z_r$, we have

$$\frac{\partial \log R}{\partial \log \boldsymbol{y}'} = \boldsymbol{g}' + \boldsymbol{g}'\frac{\partial \log \boldsymbol{z}}{\partial \log \boldsymbol{y}'} = \boldsymbol{g}', \tag{D.10}$$

where we have used (D.8) in the second step, and

$$\frac{\partial \log R}{\partial \log \boldsymbol{q}'} = \boldsymbol{g}'\frac{\partial \log \boldsymbol{z}}{\partial \log \boldsymbol{q}'} = \frac{1}{\gamma}\boldsymbol{f}', \tag{D.11}$$

where we have used (D.7). Substitution of these results into (D.5) and (D.6) after premultiplication by $\boldsymbol{G}^{-1}$ yields

$$\boldsymbol{G}^{-1}(\boldsymbol{G}+\boldsymbol{H}^{**})\boldsymbol{G}^{-1}\boldsymbol{G}\frac{\partial \log \boldsymbol{z}}{\partial \log \boldsymbol{q}'} = \frac{1}{\gamma}\boldsymbol{\iota}^*\boldsymbol{f}' - \boldsymbol{G}^{-1}\boldsymbol{H}^{*\prime}, \tag{D.12}$$

$$\boldsymbol{G}^{-1}(\boldsymbol{G}+\boldsymbol{H}^{**})\boldsymbol{G}^{-1}\boldsymbol{G}\frac{\partial \log \boldsymbol{z}}{\partial \log \boldsymbol{y}'} = -\boldsymbol{I} + \boldsymbol{\iota}^*\boldsymbol{g}'. \tag{D.13}$$

Now premultiplication of (D.12) by $\bar{\boldsymbol{\Theta}}^*$ defined in (5.16) and use of (5.17) yields (5.20) directly; premultiplication of (D.13) by $\bar{\boldsymbol{\Theta}}^*$ similarly yields (5.19).

We write $\bar{\theta}_r^i$ as defined on the right side of (5.21) as

$$\frac{y_r z_r}{\partial R/\partial q_i}\frac{\partial \log z_r}{\partial \log q_i}\frac{1}{q_i}=\frac{Rg_r}{\bar{C}f_i}\frac{\partial \log z_r}{\partial \log q_i}=\frac{\gamma}{f_i}g_r\frac{\partial \log z_r}{\partial \log q_i},$$

where we have used (5.13) and (5.15) in the second and third steps. This shows that $\bar{\theta}_r^i$ is a multiple γ/f_i of $g_r\,\partial \log z_r/\partial \log q_i$, which is the (r, i)th element of (5.20). This shows that (5.22) and (5.23) hold.

D.3. The effects of using the input homogeneous production function

If we use the input homogeneous production function in (3.1) to explore the implications of cost minimization, we obtain in place of (3.2) and (3.3):

$$p_i q_i - \rho\frac{\partial h_Q}{\partial \log qi}=0, \tag{D.14}$$

$$\frac{\partial^2 L}{\partial \log q_i\,\partial \log q_j}=\delta_{ij}p_i q_i-\rho\frac{\partial^2 h_Q}{\partial \log q_i\,\partial \log q_j}. \tag{D.15}$$

Summation of (D.14) over i using (2.13) then leads to $\rho = C$, which should be compared to (5.3). Division of (D.15) by C yields the (i, j)th element of the matrix $\boldsymbol{F}-\boldsymbol{H}_Q$, which should be compared to (5.5). However, in contrast to the situation for (5.5), the constraint (2.22) implies $\boldsymbol{\iota}'(\boldsymbol{F}-\boldsymbol{H}_Q)\boldsymbol{\iota}=\boldsymbol{\iota}'\boldsymbol{F}\boldsymbol{\iota}=1$, which does not contradict the assumption that $\boldsymbol{F}-\boldsymbol{H}_Q$ is positive definite.

In a manner similar to that of section D.2, we take the derivative of (D.14) with respect to $\log p_j$ and combine for all i and j into the matrix equation

$$(\boldsymbol{F}-\boldsymbol{H}_Q)\frac{\partial \log \boldsymbol{q}}{\partial \log \boldsymbol{p}'}-\boldsymbol{f}\frac{\partial \log C}{\partial \log \boldsymbol{p}'}=-\boldsymbol{F}. \tag{D.16}$$

Differentiating with respect to log z_r we also obtain

$$(\boldsymbol{F}-\boldsymbol{H}_Q)\frac{\partial \log \boldsymbol{q}}{\partial \log \boldsymbol{z}'}-\boldsymbol{f}\frac{\partial \log C}{\partial \log \boldsymbol{z}'}=\boldsymbol{H}_Q^*. \tag{D.17}$$

As above, we also obtain from $C=\Sigma_i p_i q_i$:

$$\frac{\partial \log C}{\partial \log \boldsymbol{p}'}=\boldsymbol{f}'; \qquad \frac{\partial \log C}{\partial \log \boldsymbol{z}'}=\gamma \boldsymbol{g}', \tag{D.18}$$

so that (D.16) and (D.17) yield

$$\boldsymbol{F}^{-1}(\boldsymbol{F}-\boldsymbol{H}_Q)\boldsymbol{F}^{-1}\boldsymbol{F}\frac{\partial \log \boldsymbol{q}}{\partial \log \boldsymbol{p}'}=\boldsymbol{\iota}\boldsymbol{f}'-\boldsymbol{I}, \tag{D.19}$$

$$\boldsymbol{F}^{-1}(\boldsymbol{F}-\boldsymbol{H}_Q)\boldsymbol{F}^{-1}\boldsymbol{F}\frac{\partial \log \boldsymbol{q}}{\partial \log \boldsymbol{z}'}=\frac{1}{\gamma}\boldsymbol{\iota}\boldsymbol{g}'+\boldsymbol{F}^{-1}\boldsymbol{H}_Q^*. \tag{D.20}$$

Now, if we assume that $\boldsymbol{F}-\boldsymbol{H}_Q$ is positive definite, the implied matrix of price coefficients is

$$\boldsymbol{F}(\boldsymbol{F}-\boldsymbol{H}_Q)^{-1}\boldsymbol{F}. \tag{D.21}$$

Since $(\boldsymbol{F}-\boldsymbol{H}_Q)\boldsymbol{\iota}=\boldsymbol{f}$, we have $\boldsymbol{F}(\boldsymbol{F}-\boldsymbol{H}_Q)^{-1}\boldsymbol{F}\boldsymbol{\iota}=\boldsymbol{F}\boldsymbol{\iota}=\boldsymbol{f}$, which should be compared to (5.17); also we have $\boldsymbol{\iota}'\boldsymbol{F}(\boldsymbol{F}-\boldsymbol{H}_Q)^{-1}\boldsymbol{F}\boldsymbol{\iota}=1$, which should be compared to (5.18). Thus, (D.19) implies that

$$\boldsymbol{F}\frac{\partial \log \boldsymbol{q}}{\partial \log \boldsymbol{p}'}=-[\boldsymbol{F}(\boldsymbol{F}-\boldsymbol{H}_Q)^{-1}\boldsymbol{F}-\boldsymbol{f}\boldsymbol{f}']. \tag{D.22}$$

Comparison of this with (3.27) then yields

$$\boldsymbol{F}(\boldsymbol{F}-\boldsymbol{H}_Q)^{-1}\boldsymbol{F}=\psi(\boldsymbol{\Theta}-\boldsymbol{\theta}\boldsymbol{\theta}')+\boldsymbol{f}\boldsymbol{f}', \tag{D.23}$$

as asserted in fn. 7 in section 5.4. Thus, this matrix, like $\bar{\boldsymbol{\Theta}}^*$ in

Chapter 5, is normalized without the necessity of a normalizing coefficient and implies Divisia deflation of prices.

When we use the input homogeneous production function in the Lagrangian function for revenue maximization, we obtain $\bar{L}(z, \bar{\rho}) = \Sigma_r y_r z_r + \bar{\rho} h_Q(\boldsymbol{q}, z)$. The first-order condition is then

$$y_r z_r + \bar{\rho} \frac{\partial h_Q}{\partial \log z_r} = 0. \tag{D.24}$$

It is readily established along the lines of section 3.2 that

$$-\sum_{r=1}^{m} \frac{\partial h_Q}{\partial \log z_r} = \gamma = \frac{R}{\bar{\rho}}. \tag{D.25}$$

Thus, $\bar{\rho}$ now has the same interpretation as $\bar{C}$ in Chapter 5: shadow cost or the value of the marginal product of the input bundle. This is comparable to the interpretation of ρ in Chapter 3.

Using (D.25), we can write the matrix of second-order derivatives of the Lagrangian as

$$\frac{\partial^2 \bar{L}}{\partial \log z \, \partial \log z'} = R\left(\boldsymbol{G} + \frac{1}{\gamma} \boldsymbol{H}_Q^{**}\right). \tag{D.26}$$

We would like to assume that this matrix is negative definite, but we shall discover below that this assumption leads to a contradiction. We shall, in any case, assume that (D.26) is nonsingular.

We use (D.24), (D.25), $g_r = y_r z_r / R$, and (5.13) with $\bar{C}$ interpreted as $\bar{\rho}$, to obtain

$$g_r = -\frac{1}{\gamma} \frac{\partial h_Q}{\partial \log z_r}; \qquad f_i = \frac{\partial h_Q}{\partial \log q_i} \tag{D.27}$$

as expressions for the product and factor shares. Now we differentiate (D.24) with respect to $\log y_s$, divide by R, and combine the result for all r and s into

$$\left(\boldsymbol{G}+\frac{1}{\gamma}\boldsymbol{H}_Q^{**}\right)\frac{\partial \log \boldsymbol{z}}{\partial \log \boldsymbol{y}'}-\boldsymbol{g}\frac{\partial \log \bar{p}}{\partial \log \boldsymbol{y}'}=-\boldsymbol{G}. \tag{D.28}$$

Proceeding similarly, we differentiate (D.24) with respect to $\log q_i$, divide by R, and combine the result for all i and r as

$$\left(\boldsymbol{G}+\frac{1}{\gamma}\boldsymbol{H}_Q^{**}\right)\frac{\partial \log \boldsymbol{z}}{\partial \log \boldsymbol{q}'}-\boldsymbol{g}\frac{\partial \log \bar{p}}{\partial \log \boldsymbol{q}'}=-\frac{1}{\gamma}\boldsymbol{H}_Q^{*\prime}. \tag{D.29}$$

Differentiation of the production constraint with respect to $\log y_r$ and $\log q_i$ leads to

$$\boldsymbol{g}'\frac{\partial \log \boldsymbol{z}}{\partial \log \boldsymbol{y}'}=\boldsymbol{0}; \qquad \boldsymbol{g}'\frac{\partial \log \boldsymbol{z}}{\partial \log \boldsymbol{q}'}=\frac{1}{\gamma}\boldsymbol{f}'. \tag{D.30}$$

We combine (D.28), (D.29), and (D.30) into

$$\begin{bmatrix} -\boldsymbol{G}^{-1}\left(\boldsymbol{G}+\frac{1}{\gamma}\boldsymbol{H}_Q^{**}\right)\boldsymbol{G}^{-1} & \boldsymbol{\iota}^* \\ \boldsymbol{\iota}^{*\prime} & 0 \end{bmatrix}\begin{bmatrix} \boldsymbol{G}\frac{\partial \log \boldsymbol{z}}{\partial \log \boldsymbol{q}'} & \boldsymbol{G}\frac{\partial \log \boldsymbol{z}}{\partial \log \boldsymbol{y}'} \\ \frac{\partial \log \bar{p}}{\partial \log \boldsymbol{q}'} & \frac{\partial \log \bar{p}}{\partial \log \boldsymbol{y}'} \end{bmatrix}$$

$$=\begin{bmatrix} \frac{1}{\gamma}\boldsymbol{G}^{-1}\boldsymbol{H}_Q^{*\prime} & \boldsymbol{I} \\ \frac{1}{\gamma}\boldsymbol{f}' & \boldsymbol{0} \end{bmatrix} \tag{D.31}$$

which should be compared to (D.9). In one important respect it is similar to (B.8) because it cannot be simplified in the way that (D.9) was.

We define, for the scope of Appendix D, the coefficient β and the matrix $\boldsymbol{A}$ as

$$\beta = -\boldsymbol{g}'\left(\boldsymbol{G} + \frac{1}{\gamma}\boldsymbol{H}_Q^{**}\right)^{-1}\boldsymbol{g}, \tag{D.32}$$

$$\boldsymbol{A} = -\frac{1}{\beta}\boldsymbol{G}\left(\boldsymbol{G} + \frac{1}{\gamma}\boldsymbol{H}_Q^{**}\right)^{-1}\boldsymbol{G}. \tag{D.33}$$

Both (D.32) and (D.33) exist when (D.26) is nonsingular; if (D.26) were negative definite, we would then have $\beta > 0$ and $\boldsymbol{A}$ positive definite with elements summing to one. Using (D.32) and (D.33) we obtain the inverse of the leftmost partitioned matrix in (D.31):

$$\begin{bmatrix} -\boldsymbol{G}^{-1}\left(\boldsymbol{G} + \frac{1}{\gamma}\boldsymbol{H}_Q^{**}\right)\boldsymbol{G}^{-1} & \boldsymbol{\iota}^* \\ \boldsymbol{\iota}^{*\prime} & 0 \end{bmatrix}^{-1} = \begin{bmatrix} (\boldsymbol{A} - \boldsymbol{\alpha}\boldsymbol{\alpha}') & \boldsymbol{\alpha} \\ \boldsymbol{\alpha}' & -1/\beta \end{bmatrix}, \tag{D.34}$$

where

$$\boldsymbol{\alpha} = \boldsymbol{A}\boldsymbol{\iota}^*. \tag{D.35}$$

Now premultiplication of (D.31) by (D.34) leads to solutions for the derivatives of $\log z$:

$$\boldsymbol{G}\frac{\partial \log \boldsymbol{z}}{\partial \log \boldsymbol{q}'} = \frac{1}{\gamma}\boldsymbol{\alpha}\boldsymbol{f}' + \frac{\beta}{\gamma}(\boldsymbol{A} - \boldsymbol{\alpha}\boldsymbol{\alpha}')\boldsymbol{G}^{-1}\boldsymbol{H}_Q^{*\prime}, \tag{D.36}$$

$$\boldsymbol{G}\frac{\partial \log \boldsymbol{z}}{\partial \log \boldsymbol{y}'} = \beta(\boldsymbol{A} - \boldsymbol{\alpha}\boldsymbol{\alpha}'). \tag{D.37}$$

Comparison of (D.36) with (5.23) now indicates that

$$\bar{\boldsymbol{K}} = \boldsymbol{\alpha}\boldsymbol{\iota}' + \beta(\boldsymbol{A} - \boldsymbol{\alpha}\boldsymbol{\alpha}')\boldsymbol{G}^{-1}\boldsymbol{H}_Q^{*\prime}\boldsymbol{F}^{-1}. \tag{D.38}$$

Postmultiplication by $\boldsymbol{f}$, use of (2.23), and comparison with (5.33) then implies that $\bar{\boldsymbol{\theta}}^* = \boldsymbol{\alpha}$, so that $\boldsymbol{\alpha}$ is the vector of marginal shares of the outputs under revenue maximization. We consult (D.37) to find that we do indeed have Frisch deflation of output price changes when this approach is taken.

In addition to (D.36) and (D.37) we obtain expressions for the derivatives of $\log \bar{\rho}$ from the solution of (D.31):

$$\frac{\partial \log \bar{\rho}}{\partial \log \boldsymbol{q}'} = -\frac{1}{\beta\gamma}\boldsymbol{f}' + \frac{1}{\gamma}\boldsymbol{\alpha}'\boldsymbol{G}^{-1}\boldsymbol{H}_Q^{*\prime}, \tag{D.39}$$

$$\frac{\partial \log \bar{\rho}}{\partial \log \boldsymbol{y}'} = \boldsymbol{\alpha}'. \tag{D.40}$$

Equation (5.13), with $\bar{C}$ interpreted as $\bar{\rho}$, implies that

$$\frac{\partial \log R}{\partial \log \boldsymbol{q}'} = \frac{1}{\gamma}\boldsymbol{f}'. \tag{D.41}$$

Using (D.27) as well, we obtain $\partial \log R/\partial \log q_i = (1/\gamma)\, \partial h_Q/\partial \log q_i$. We take the derivative of this with respect to $\log q_j$, keeping other inputs and all output prices unchanged, to obtain $\partial^2 \log R/\partial \log q_i\, \partial \log q_j$ as the following expression:

$$-\frac{1}{\gamma}\frac{\partial h_Q}{\partial \log q_i}\frac{\partial \log \gamma}{\partial \log q_j} + \frac{1}{\gamma}\frac{\partial^2 h_Q}{\partial \log q_i\, \partial \log q_j} + \frac{1}{\gamma}\sum_{r=1}^{m}\frac{\partial^2 h_Q}{\partial \log q_i\, \partial \log z_r}\frac{\partial \log z_r}{\partial \log q_j}. \tag{D.42}$$

Using (D.27), this can be written in matrix form as

$$\frac{\partial^2 \log R}{\partial \log \boldsymbol{q}\, \partial \log \boldsymbol{q}'} = -\frac{1}{\gamma}\boldsymbol{f}\frac{\partial \log \gamma}{\partial \log \boldsymbol{q}'} + \frac{1}{\gamma}\boldsymbol{H}_Q + \frac{1}{\gamma}\boldsymbol{H}_Q^*\frac{\partial \log \boldsymbol{z}}{\partial \log \boldsymbol{q}'}. \tag{D.43}$$

From (D.25) we obtain $\partial \log \gamma/\partial \log \boldsymbol{q}' = \partial \log R/\partial \log \boldsymbol{q}' -$

$\partial \log \bar{p}/\partial \log \boldsymbol{q}'$, or, substituting from (D.39) and (D.41),

$$\frac{\partial \log \gamma}{\partial \log \boldsymbol{q}'} = \frac{1}{\gamma}\left(1+\frac{1}{\beta}\right)\boldsymbol{f}' - \frac{1}{\gamma}\boldsymbol{\alpha}'\boldsymbol{G}^{-1}\boldsymbol{H}_Q^{*\prime}. \tag{D.44}$$

Now substitution from (D.36) and (D.44) into (D.43) yields

$$\begin{aligned}\frac{\partial^2 \log R}{\partial \log \boldsymbol{q}\, \partial \log \boldsymbol{q}'} = &-\frac{1}{\gamma^2}\left(1+\frac{1}{\beta}\right)\boldsymbol{f}\boldsymbol{f}' \\ &+\frac{1}{\gamma^2}(\boldsymbol{f}\boldsymbol{\alpha}'\boldsymbol{G}^{-1}\boldsymbol{H}_Q^{*\prime} + \boldsymbol{H}_Q^{*}\boldsymbol{G}^{-1}\boldsymbol{\alpha}\boldsymbol{f}') \\ &+\frac{1}{\gamma}\boldsymbol{H}_Q + \frac{\beta}{\gamma^2}\boldsymbol{H}_Q^{*}\boldsymbol{G}^{-1}(\boldsymbol{A}-\boldsymbol{\alpha}\boldsymbol{\alpha}')\boldsymbol{G}^{-1}\boldsymbol{H}_Q^{*\prime}.\end{aligned} \tag{D.45}$$

Premultiplication of (D.45) by $\boldsymbol{\iota}'$ and postmultiplication by $\boldsymbol{\iota}$ with use of (2.22) and (2.23), then establishes that the sum of the elements of $\partial^2 \log \boldsymbol{R}/\partial \log \boldsymbol{q}\, \partial \log \boldsymbol{q}'$ is $-(1/\gamma^2)(1+1/\beta)$, or that

$$\frac{1}{\beta} = -1 - \gamma^2 \sum_{i=1}^{n}\sum_{j=1}^{n} \frac{\partial^2 \log R}{\partial \log q_i\, \partial \log q_j}, \tag{D.46}$$

which should be compared to (3.41). Since (D.41) implies $\Sigma_i\, \partial \log \boldsymbol{R}/\partial \log q_i = 1/\gamma$, we can equivalently write (D.46) as

$$\frac{1}{\beta} = -1 + \gamma \sum_{i=1}^{n} \frac{\partial \log \gamma}{\partial \log q_i}. \tag{D.47}$$

Now, note that this means that if the elasticity of scale is constant (i.e. if production is homogeneous), $\beta = -1$ is negative, in contradiction to the positive sign it should have if (D.26) is negative definite. If the elasticity of scale is not constant, then both the sign and the magnitude of the sum in (D.47) are uncertain, but obviously γ must increase rapidly with a proportionate increase in inputs for β to be positive.

We can compare (5.19) and (D.37) to obtain $\beta(\boldsymbol{A} - \boldsymbol{\alpha}\boldsymbol{\alpha}') =$

$-(\bar{\boldsymbol{\Theta}}^* - \boldsymbol{g}\boldsymbol{g}')$ or

$$\boldsymbol{A} = -\frac{1}{\beta}(\bar{\boldsymbol{\Theta}}^* - \boldsymbol{g}\boldsymbol{g}') + \boldsymbol{\alpha}\boldsymbol{\alpha}'. \tag{D.48}$$

When β is negative the first matrix on the right is a positive multiple of $\bar{\boldsymbol{\Theta}}^* - \boldsymbol{g}\boldsymbol{g}'$, which is negative semidefinite, while the second is positive semidefinite. Thus, $\boldsymbol{A}$ in general shares with $\bar{\boldsymbol{\Theta}}^*$ the characteristic of being indefinite. To show this, we premultiply by $\boldsymbol{\iota}^{*\prime}$ and postmultiply by $\boldsymbol{\iota}^*$; this yields $\boldsymbol{\iota}^{*\prime}\boldsymbol{A}\boldsymbol{\iota}^* = (\boldsymbol{\iota}^{*\prime}\boldsymbol{\alpha})^2 = 1$. For any vector $\boldsymbol{a} \neq 0$ which satisfies $\boldsymbol{a}'\boldsymbol{\alpha} = 0$, we have $\boldsymbol{a}'\boldsymbol{A}\boldsymbol{a} < 0$. This shows that the maverick root of $\bar{\boldsymbol{\Theta}}^*$ does not result from a peculiarity of the output homogeneous production function, but is an intrinsic feature of revenue maximization.

D.4. The derivatives of revenue

Shephard's lemma (2.31) for the revenue function can be written in vector form as $\partial R/\partial \boldsymbol{y} = \boldsymbol{z}$, which yields $\partial^2 R/\partial \boldsymbol{y}\,\partial \boldsymbol{y}' = \partial \boldsymbol{z}/\partial \boldsymbol{y}'$ after differentiation with respect to $\boldsymbol{y}'$. But $\partial \boldsymbol{z}/\partial \boldsymbol{y}' = R\boldsymbol{Y}^{-1}\boldsymbol{G}\,(\partial \log \boldsymbol{z}/\partial \log \boldsymbol{y}')\boldsymbol{Y}^{-1}$, so that (5.19) implies

$$\frac{\partial^2 R}{\partial \boldsymbol{y}\,\partial \boldsymbol{y}'} = -R\boldsymbol{Y}^{-1}(\bar{\boldsymbol{\Theta}}^* - \boldsymbol{g}\boldsymbol{g}')\boldsymbol{Y}^{-1}, \tag{D.49}$$

from which (6.13) follows. Differentiation of $\partial R/\partial \boldsymbol{y} = \boldsymbol{z}$ with respect to $\boldsymbol{q}'$ gives $\partial^2 R/\partial \boldsymbol{y}\,\partial \boldsymbol{q}' = \partial \boldsymbol{z}/\partial \boldsymbol{q}'$ and hence, using (5.23),

$$\frac{\partial^2 R}{\partial \boldsymbol{y}\,\partial \boldsymbol{q}'} = \boldsymbol{Y}^{-1}\bar{\boldsymbol{K}}\boldsymbol{P}, \tag{D.50}$$

where now $\boldsymbol{P}$ is the diagonal matrix which has the input prices p_i (when they are defined) or the marginal revenues $\partial R/\partial q_i$ (when the input prices are not defined) on the diagonal. This equation then yields (6.14).

We use (3.15) and (D.11) to write $\partial \log R/\partial \log q_i =$

$\partial h/\partial \log q_i$, and take the derivative with respect to $\log q_j$:

$$\frac{\partial^2 \log R}{\partial \log q_i\, \partial \log q_j} = \frac{\partial^2 h}{\partial \log q_i\, \partial \log q_j} + \sum_{r=1}^{m} \frac{\partial^2 h}{\partial \log q_i\, \partial \log z_r} \frac{\partial \log z_r}{\partial \log q_j}.$$

We use (2.17) and (2.19) to write the right-hand side of this in matrix form as $\boldsymbol{H} + \boldsymbol{H}^* \,\partial \log \boldsymbol{z}/\partial \log \boldsymbol{q}'$. Next, substitution from (5.19) yields

$$\frac{\partial^2 \log R}{\partial \log \boldsymbol{q}\, \partial \log \boldsymbol{q}'} = \boldsymbol{H} - \boldsymbol{H}^*\boldsymbol{G}^{-1}\bar{\boldsymbol{\Theta}}^*\boldsymbol{G}^{-1}\boldsymbol{H}^{*\prime}, \tag{D.51}$$

where we have used $\boldsymbol{H}^*\boldsymbol{G}^{-1}\boldsymbol{g} = \boldsymbol{H}^*\boldsymbol{\iota}^* = \boldsymbol{0}$ (see (2.27)).

Differentiation of $\partial R/\partial q_i = (R/q_i)\,\partial \log q_i$ with respect to q_j gives

$$\frac{\partial^2 R}{\partial q_i\, \partial q_j} = \frac{R}{q_i q_j}\left[\frac{\partial^2 \log R}{\partial \log q_i\, \partial \log q_j} + \frac{\partial \log R}{\partial \log q_i}\frac{\partial \log R}{\partial \log q_j} - \delta_{ij}\frac{\partial \log R}{\partial \log q_i}\right].$$

Using (5.13), (5.15), and (D.11) we can write this for all pairs (i, j) as

$$\frac{\partial^2 R}{\partial \boldsymbol{q}\, \partial \boldsymbol{q}'} = \frac{\gamma}{C}\boldsymbol{P}\boldsymbol{F}^{-1}\left[\frac{\partial^2 \log R}{\partial \log \boldsymbol{q}\, \partial \log \boldsymbol{q}'} + \frac{1}{\gamma^2}\boldsymbol{f}\boldsymbol{f}' - \frac{1}{\gamma}\boldsymbol{F}\right]\boldsymbol{F}^{-1}\boldsymbol{P}. \tag{D.52}$$

D.5. Derivation of the demand equations

We obtain $\Sigma_k\,(\partial^2 R/\partial q_i\, \partial q_k)(\partial q_k/\partial p_j) = \delta_{ij}$ by differentiating (5.37) with respect to p_j. We write this as

$$\sum_{k=1}^{n} \frac{\partial^2 R}{\partial q_i\, \partial q_k} q_k \frac{\partial \log q_k}{\partial \log p_j} = \delta_{ij} p_j.$$

Since $q_k = f_k C/p_k$, we can write this for all pairs (i, j) as

$$C\frac{\partial^2 R}{\partial \boldsymbol{q}\,\partial \boldsymbol{q}'}\boldsymbol{P}^{-1}\boldsymbol{F}\frac{\partial \log \boldsymbol{q}}{\partial \log \boldsymbol{p}'} = \boldsymbol{P}. \tag{D.53}$$

Now (5.40) permits us to define

$$-\bar{\psi}\bar{\boldsymbol{\Theta}} = \frac{1}{C}\boldsymbol{P}\left(\frac{\partial^2 R}{\partial \boldsymbol{q}\,\partial \boldsymbol{q}'}\right)^{-1}\boldsymbol{P}, \tag{D.54}$$

where $-\bar{\psi} = (1/C)\boldsymbol{p}'\,[\partial^2 R/\partial \boldsymbol{q}\,\partial \boldsymbol{q}']^{-1}\boldsymbol{p} < 0$ is chosen so that (5.42) holds. Note that this is equivalent to (6.15) once $\bar{\psi} = \gamma\psi^*$ is established. Premultiplication of (D.53) by $-\bar{\psi}\bar{\boldsymbol{\Theta}}\boldsymbol{P}^{-1}$ then establishes

$$\boldsymbol{F}\frac{\partial \log \boldsymbol{q}}{\partial \log \boldsymbol{p}'} = -\bar{\psi}\bar{\boldsymbol{\Theta}}. \tag{D.55}$$

Next we differentiate (5.37) with respect to y_r:

$$\frac{\partial^2 R}{\partial q_i\,\partial y_r} + \sum_{j=1}^{n}\frac{\partial^2 R}{\partial q_i\,\partial q_j}\frac{\partial q_j}{\partial y_r} = 0,$$

which implies

$$\frac{\partial \boldsymbol{q}}{\partial \boldsymbol{y}'} = -\left(\frac{\partial^2 R}{\partial \boldsymbol{q}\,\partial \boldsymbol{q}'}\right)^{-1}\frac{\partial^2 R}{\partial \boldsymbol{q}\,\partial \boldsymbol{y}'} = -\left(\frac{\partial^2 R}{\partial \boldsymbol{q}\,\partial \boldsymbol{q}'}\right)^{-1}\boldsymbol{P}\bar{\boldsymbol{K}}'\boldsymbol{Y}^{-1}, \tag{D.56}$$

where the last step is based on (D.50). We premultiply (D.56) by $(1/C)\boldsymbol{P}$, postmultiply by $\boldsymbol{Y}$, and use $f_i = p_i q_i/C$ and (D.54) to obtain

$$\boldsymbol{F}\frac{\partial \log \boldsymbol{q}}{\partial \log \boldsymbol{y}'} = \bar{\psi}\bar{\boldsymbol{\Theta}}\bar{\boldsymbol{K}}'. \tag{D.57}$$

Now (5.41) may be obtained by taking the differential of d(log $\boldsymbol{q}$), premultiplying by $\boldsymbol{F}$ and substituting from (D.55) and (D.57).

Appendix to Chapter 6

E.1. The derivatives of profit

When direct profit maximization is considered, both input and output prices must be considered independent variables, while the levels of use of inputs and production of outputs are dependent variables. Consequently, when we differentiate Shephard's lemma for outputs (2.34) with respect to y_s, we obtain $\partial^2\pi/\partial y_r\,\partial y_s = \partial z_r/\partial y_s$. Since $\partial z_r/\partial y_s = (z_r/y_s)\,\partial \log z_r/\partial \log y_s$, multiplication of this by $y_r y_s/R$ yields

$$\frac{y_r y_s}{R}\frac{\partial^2\pi}{\partial y_r\,\partial y_s} = g_r\frac{\partial \log z_r}{\partial \log y_s}. \tag{E.1}$$

Now, the left side of (E.1) is the (r, s)th element of the right side of (6.18), while the left side of (E.1) is the (r, s)th element of $\boldsymbol{G}\,\partial \log \boldsymbol{z}/\partial \log \boldsymbol{y}'$. Consulting (6.2) we observe that this matrix is $\psi^*\boldsymbol{\Theta}^*$, which establishes (6.18); alternatively, we can consult (C.7) to obtain the equivalence of $\boldsymbol{G}\,\partial \log \boldsymbol{z}/\partial \log \boldsymbol{y}'$ and $\psi^*\boldsymbol{\Theta}^*$.

Differentiation of (2.34) with respect to p_i similarly yields $\partial^2\pi/\partial y_r\,\partial p_i = \partial z_r/\partial p_i$, which is equivalent to

$$\frac{y_r p_i}{R}\frac{\partial^2\pi}{\partial y_r\,\partial p_i} = g_r\frac{\partial \log z_r}{\partial \log p_i}. \tag{E.2}$$

This, in conjunction with (6.2) or (C.9), then establishes (6.19).

Next we differentiate Shephard's lemma for inputs (2.33) with respect to p_j to obtain $\partial^2\pi/\partial p_i\,\partial p_j = -\partial q_i/\partial p_j$, which is equivalent to

$$-\frac{p_i p_j}{C}\frac{\partial^2\pi}{\partial p_i\,\partial p_j} = f_i\frac{\partial \log q_i}{\partial \log p_j}. \tag{E.3}$$

Now we consult (6.5) or (D.55) and (6.7) to obtain (6.20). Similarly, we differentiate (2.33) with respect to y_r to obtain

$$-\frac{p_i y_r}{C}\frac{\partial^2\pi}{\partial p_i\,\partial y_r} = f_i\frac{\partial \log q_i}{\partial \log y_r}, \tag{E.4}$$

and use either (6.5) or (D.57) and (6.7) to establish (6.21).

E.2. Properties of two measures of interaction

From (6.8) and $\mathrm{tr}(\boldsymbol{K}\bar{\boldsymbol{K}}) = \mathrm{tr}(\bar{\boldsymbol{K}}\boldsymbol{K})$ we obtain

$$\mathrm{tr}(\boldsymbol{K}\bar{\boldsymbol{K}}) = \mathrm{tr}(\bar{\boldsymbol{K}}\bar{\boldsymbol{\Theta}}\bar{\boldsymbol{K}}'\boldsymbol{\Theta}^{*-1}) = \mathrm{tr}(\boldsymbol{\Theta}^{*-1}\bar{\boldsymbol{K}}\bar{\boldsymbol{\Theta}}\bar{\boldsymbol{K}}'). \tag{E.5}$$

We consider the ith characteristic root of the matrix in the third member of (E.5), which satisfies

$$(\boldsymbol{\Theta}^{*-1}\bar{\boldsymbol{K}}\bar{\boldsymbol{\Theta}}\bar{\boldsymbol{K}}' - \lambda_i\boldsymbol{I})\boldsymbol{x}_i = \boldsymbol{0}, \tag{E.6}$$

where $\boldsymbol{x}_i$ is the corresponding characteristic vector. Premultiplying (E.6) by $\boldsymbol{\Theta}^*$, we obtain equivalently

$$(\bar{\boldsymbol{K}}\bar{\boldsymbol{\Theta}}\bar{\boldsymbol{K}}' - \lambda_i\boldsymbol{\Theta}^*)\boldsymbol{x}_i = \boldsymbol{0}. \tag{E.7}$$

Since the matrix $\bar{\boldsymbol{K}}\bar{\boldsymbol{\Theta}}\bar{\boldsymbol{K}}'$ is positive semidefinite and $\boldsymbol{\Theta}^*$ is positive definite, this means that $\lambda_i \geq 0$ holds for each λ_i. From the transpose of (6.8) we obtain $\boldsymbol{\Theta}^*\boldsymbol{K}'\boldsymbol{\iota} = \boldsymbol{\Theta}^*\boldsymbol{\iota}^* = \bar{\boldsymbol{K}}\bar{\boldsymbol{\Theta}}\boldsymbol{\iota}$, where we have used $\boldsymbol{K}'\boldsymbol{\iota} = \boldsymbol{\iota}^*$ (see (3.35)). When we also use $\bar{\boldsymbol{K}}'\boldsymbol{\iota}^* = \boldsymbol{\iota}$ (see (5.24)), we find that (E.7) is satisfied by $\lambda_1 = 1$ and $\boldsymbol{x}_1 = \boldsymbol{\iota}^*$.

Substitution from (6.9) into (E.7) yields

$$\left[\frac{1}{\psi^*}(\bar{\boldsymbol{\Theta}}^* - \boldsymbol{g}\boldsymbol{g}') + (1-\lambda_i)\boldsymbol{\Theta}^*\right]\boldsymbol{x}_i = \boldsymbol{0}.$$

Multiplication by -1 then yields

$$\left[-\frac{1}{\psi^*}(\bar{\boldsymbol{\Theta}}^* - \boldsymbol{g}\boldsymbol{g}') - (1-\lambda_i)\boldsymbol{\Theta}^*\right]\boldsymbol{x}_i = \boldsymbol{0}, \tag{E.8}$$

which also holds for the λ_i and $\boldsymbol{x}_i$ which satisfy (E.6) and (E.7). Since $-(1/\psi^*)(\bar{\boldsymbol{\Theta}}^* - \boldsymbol{g}\boldsymbol{g}')$ is positive semidefinite, it then follows that $1-\lambda_i \geq 0$. For $i \neq 1$, we have $\boldsymbol{x}_i'\boldsymbol{\iota}^* = 0$ and $-(1/\psi^*) \times (\bar{\boldsymbol{\Theta}}^* - \boldsymbol{g}\boldsymbol{g}')\boldsymbol{x}_i \neq \boldsymbol{0}$; consequently, for $i \neq 1$ we have $0 \leq \lambda_i < 1$.

Finally, we note that the trace in (E.5) equals the sum of the λ_i, while the rank of $\boldsymbol{K}\bar{\boldsymbol{K}}$, which satisfies

$$r(\boldsymbol{K}\bar{\boldsymbol{K}}) = r(\bar{\boldsymbol{K}}\boldsymbol{K}) = r(\bar{\boldsymbol{K}}\boldsymbol{\Theta}\bar{\boldsymbol{K}}'\boldsymbol{\Theta}^{*-1}) = r(\boldsymbol{\Theta}^{*-1}\bar{\boldsymbol{K}}\boldsymbol{\Theta}\bar{\boldsymbol{K}}'), \tag{E.9}$$

is equal to the number of nonzero λ_i's. This, with $\lambda_i < 1$ for $i \neq 1$, establishes (6.31).

To establish that (6.33) is non-negative, we consider vectors $\boldsymbol{x}$ which satisfy $\boldsymbol{x}'\boldsymbol{\iota}^* = 1$. If $\boldsymbol{x} = \boldsymbol{g}$, we have $\boldsymbol{x}'\bar{\boldsymbol{\Theta}}^{*-1}\boldsymbol{x} = 1$ from (5.17). If $\boldsymbol{x} \neq \boldsymbol{g}$, we have $\boldsymbol{x} = \bar{\boldsymbol{\Theta}}^*(\boldsymbol{\iota}^* + \boldsymbol{v})$, where $\boldsymbol{v} \neq \boldsymbol{0}$. Then

$$1 = \boldsymbol{\iota}^{*\prime}\boldsymbol{x} = \boldsymbol{\iota}^{*\prime}\bar{\boldsymbol{\Theta}}^*(\boldsymbol{\iota}^* + \boldsymbol{v}) = 1 + \boldsymbol{\iota}^{*\prime}\bar{\boldsymbol{\Theta}}^*\boldsymbol{v} \tag{E.10}$$

establishes that $\boldsymbol{\iota}^{*\prime}\bar{\boldsymbol{\Theta}}^*\boldsymbol{v} = \boldsymbol{g}'\boldsymbol{v} = 0$. But then

$$\begin{aligned}\boldsymbol{x}'\bar{\boldsymbol{\Theta}}^{*-1}\boldsymbol{x} &= (\boldsymbol{\iota}^* + \boldsymbol{v})'\bar{\boldsymbol{\Theta}}^*\bar{\boldsymbol{\Theta}}^{*-1}\bar{\boldsymbol{\Theta}}^*(\boldsymbol{\iota}^* + \boldsymbol{v}) \\ &= \boldsymbol{\iota}^{*\prime}\bar{\boldsymbol{\Theta}}^*\boldsymbol{\iota}^* + \boldsymbol{v}'\bar{\boldsymbol{\Theta}}^*\boldsymbol{v} \\ &= 1 + \boldsymbol{v}'\bar{\boldsymbol{\Theta}}^*\boldsymbol{v}.\end{aligned} \tag{E.11}$$

Since $\boldsymbol{g}'\boldsymbol{v} = 0$, $\boldsymbol{v}$ is an element of the vector subspace spanned by the characteristic vectors (relative to $\boldsymbol{G}$) of $\bar{\boldsymbol{\Theta}}^*$ which correspond to negative characteristic roots (see section D.1), and consequently $\boldsymbol{v}'\bar{\boldsymbol{\Theta}}^*\boldsymbol{v} < 0$. It then follows that $\boldsymbol{x}'\bar{\boldsymbol{\Theta}}^{*-1}\boldsymbol{x} < 1$, so if $\bar{\boldsymbol{\theta}}^* \neq \boldsymbol{g}$ in (6.33), then (6.33) is strictly positive.

Appendix to Chapter 7

The variance–covariance results stated in Sections 7.1 and 7.2 are obtained from the general result that if the marginal cost of information is small, the covariance matrix of the optimal decision distribution is a scalar multiple of the inverse of the Hessian matrix of the criterion function at the point of the full-information optimum. In the firm's case this criterion may be cost, revenue, or profit, but their optimization is subject to the production constraint $h(\boldsymbol{q}, \boldsymbol{z}) = 0$, whereas the general result stated above refers to an unconstrained optimum. To handle this problem, we solve the production constraint for the first input

$$q_1 = h_{e1}(\boldsymbol{q}_*, \boldsymbol{z}), \quad \text{where } \boldsymbol{q}_* = (q_2, \ldots, q_n)', \tag{F.1}$$

and for the first output

$$z_1 = h_{d1}(\boldsymbol{q}, \boldsymbol{z}_*), \quad \text{where } \boldsymbol{z}_* = (z_2, \ldots, z_m)'. \tag{F.2}$$

For interpretation of (F.1) and (F.2) see section 2.1.

F.1. Cost minimization

The firm's total cost can now be written

$$\boldsymbol{\Phi}_1(\boldsymbol{q}_*, z, p_1, \boldsymbol{p}_*) = p_1 h_{e1}(\boldsymbol{q}_*, z) + \boldsymbol{p}_*'\boldsymbol{q}_*, \tag{F.3}$$

where $\boldsymbol{p}_* = (p_2, \ldots, p_n)'$. We interpret $\boldsymbol{\Phi}_1$ as the firm's criterion for cost minimization, with $\boldsymbol{q}_*$ the vector of decision variables and z, p_1, and $\boldsymbol{p}_*$ the noncontrolled variables. The covariance matrix of the optimal decision distribution will then take the form

$$\mathscr{V}(\boldsymbol{q}_*) = k\left(\frac{\partial^2 \Phi_1}{\partial \boldsymbol{q}_* \, \partial \boldsymbol{q}_*'}\right)^{-1}, \tag{F.4}$$

where k is a positive scalar and $\partial^2 \Phi_1 / \partial \boldsymbol{q}_* \, \partial \boldsymbol{q}_*'$ is evaluated at the full-information cost minimum.

Minimizing (F.3) requires that the first derivative of $\Phi_1(\cdot)$ with respect to $\boldsymbol{q}_*$, which is $\partial \Phi_1 / \partial \boldsymbol{q}_* = p_1 \, \partial h_{e1} / \partial \boldsymbol{q}_* + \boldsymbol{p}_*$, be a zero vector,

$$\frac{\partial h_{e1}}{\partial \boldsymbol{q}_*} = -\frac{1}{p_1} \boldsymbol{p}_*, \tag{F.5}$$

and that $\partial^2 \Phi_1 / \partial \boldsymbol{q}_* \, \partial \boldsymbol{q}_*' = p_1 \, \partial^2 h_{e1} / \partial \boldsymbol{q}_* \, \partial \boldsymbol{q}_*'$ be positive definite. This equation shows that (F.4) can be written as

$$\mathscr{V}(\boldsymbol{q}_*) = \frac{k}{p_1}\left(\frac{\partial^2 h_{e1}}{\partial \boldsymbol{q}_* \, \partial \boldsymbol{q}_*'}\right)^{-1}. \tag{F.6}$$

We obtain $(\partial^2 h_{e1} / \partial \boldsymbol{q}_* \, \partial \boldsymbol{q}_*')(\partial \boldsymbol{q}_* / \partial \boldsymbol{p}_*') = -(1/p_1)\boldsymbol{I}$ by differentiating (F.5) with respect to $\boldsymbol{p}_*'$. This shows that $(\partial^2 h_{e1} / \partial \boldsymbol{q}_* \, \partial \boldsymbol{q}_*')^{-1} = -p_1(\partial \boldsymbol{q}_* / \partial \boldsymbol{p}_*')$, so that (F.6) becomes

$$\mathscr{V}(\boldsymbol{q}_*) = -k \frac{\partial \boldsymbol{q}_*}{\partial \boldsymbol{p}_*'}, \tag{F.7}$$

which specifies the covariance matrix of the $(n-1)$-element vector. Since we could have solved the production function for any of the q_i's in (F.1), symmetry and consistency considerations permit us to write the complete $n \times n$ result as

$$\mathscr{V}(\boldsymbol{q}) = -k \frac{\partial \boldsymbol{q}}{\partial \boldsymbol{p}'}. \tag{F.8}$$

The demand system (3.36) describes the change in $\boldsymbol{q}$, so we interpret (F.8) conditionally on current demand as $\mathscr{V}(\mathrm{d}\boldsymbol{q}\,|\,\boldsymbol{q}) = -k\, \partial\boldsymbol{q}/\partial\boldsymbol{p}'$. The system written with disturbance vector $\boldsymbol{\varepsilon}$ is

$$\boldsymbol{F}\,\mathrm{d}(\log \boldsymbol{q}) = \gamma \boldsymbol{K}\boldsymbol{G}\,\mathrm{d}(\log \boldsymbol{z}) - \psi(\boldsymbol{\Theta} - \boldsymbol{\theta}\boldsymbol{\theta}')\,\mathrm{d}(\log \boldsymbol{p}) + \boldsymbol{\varepsilon}. \tag{F.9}$$

Since the expectation of the decision distribution is the full-information optimum, it follows that the mean of $\boldsymbol{\varepsilon}$ is a zero vector. The vector of left-hand variables in (F.9) is $\boldsymbol{F}\,\mathrm{d}(\log \boldsymbol{q}) = (1/C)\boldsymbol{P}\,\mathrm{d}\boldsymbol{q}$ and consequently the matrix of derivatives $\partial\boldsymbol{q}/\partial\boldsymbol{p}'$ is equal to $-\psi C\boldsymbol{P}^{-1}(\boldsymbol{\Theta} - \boldsymbol{\theta}\boldsymbol{\theta}')\boldsymbol{P}^{-1}$. Thus, we have

$$\begin{aligned}\mathscr{V}\left(\frac{1}{C}\boldsymbol{P}\,\mathrm{d}\boldsymbol{q}\right) &= \frac{1}{C^2}\boldsymbol{P}(-k)[-\psi C\boldsymbol{P}^{-1}(\boldsymbol{\Theta} - \boldsymbol{\theta}\boldsymbol{\theta}')\boldsymbol{P}^{-1}]\boldsymbol{P}\\ &= \frac{k\psi}{C}(\boldsymbol{\Theta} - \boldsymbol{\theta}\boldsymbol{\theta}').\end{aligned}$$

Since $\boldsymbol{\varepsilon}$ is the random part of $\boldsymbol{F}\,\mathrm{d}(\log \boldsymbol{q})$, this confirms (7.2) with σ^2 specified as k/C.

F.2. Revenue maximization

We now use (F.2) to write minus revenue as

$$\Phi_2(\boldsymbol{z}_*, \boldsymbol{q}, y_1, \boldsymbol{y}_*) = -y_1 h_{d1}(\boldsymbol{q}, \boldsymbol{z}_*) - \boldsymbol{y}_*'\boldsymbol{z}_*, \tag{F.10}$$

where $\boldsymbol{y}_* = (y_2, \ldots, y_m)'$, and $\boldsymbol{z}_*$ is now the vector of decision variables. Since Φ_2 is minus revenue, we are to minimize it; consequently the same procedure we used before is applicable. The first-order condition is that $\partial\Phi_2/\partial\boldsymbol{z}_* = -y_1\,\partial h_{d1}/\partial\boldsymbol{z}_* - \boldsymbol{y}_*$ is a zero vector,

$$\frac{\partial h_{d1}}{\partial \boldsymbol{z}_*} = -\frac{1}{y_1}\boldsymbol{y}_*, \tag{F.11}$$

and the second-order condition is that $\partial^2\Phi_2/\partial z_* \, \partial z'_* = -y_1 \, \partial^2 h_{d1}/\partial z_* \, \partial z'_*$ be positive definite. Since the covariance matrix of the optimal decision distribution is $\mathcal{V}(z_*) = k(\partial^2\Phi_2/\partial z_* \, \partial z'_*)^{-1}$ for some positive k, we can then write

$$\mathcal{V}(z_*) = -\frac{k}{y_1}\left(\frac{\partial^2 h_{d1}}{\partial z_* \, \partial z'_*}\right)^{-1}. \tag{F.12}$$

We differentiate (F.11) with respect to y'_* to obtain $(\partial^2 h_{d1}/\partial z_* \, \partial z'_*)(\partial z_*/\partial y'_*) = -(1/y_1)\boldsymbol{I}$, which shows that

$$(\partial^2 h_{d1}/\partial z_* \, \partial z'_*)^{-1} = -y_1 \, \partial z_*/\partial y'_*.$$

We substitute this result into (F.12) and use symmetry and consistency considerations to extend the result to

$$\mathcal{V}(z) = k\,\frac{\partial z}{\partial y'}. \tag{F.13}$$

As before, we interpret this conditionally as $\mathcal{V}(\mathrm{d}z \mid z) = k \, \partial z/\partial y'$. We add $\bar{\boldsymbol{\varepsilon}}^*$ to the system of supply equations (5.25):

$$\boldsymbol{G} \, \mathrm{d}(\log z) = \frac{1}{\gamma} \bar{\boldsymbol{K}}\boldsymbol{F} \, \mathrm{d}(\log \boldsymbol{q}) - (\bar{\boldsymbol{\Theta}}^* - \boldsymbol{g}\boldsymbol{g}') \, \mathrm{d}(\log \boldsymbol{y}) + \bar{\boldsymbol{\varepsilon}}^*. \tag{F.14}$$

The vector of left-hand variables is $\boldsymbol{G} \, \mathrm{d}(\log z) = (1/R)\boldsymbol{Y} \, \mathrm{d}z$, so that $\partial z/\partial y'$ is $-R\boldsymbol{Y}^{-1}(\bar{\boldsymbol{\Theta}}^* - \boldsymbol{g}\boldsymbol{g}')\boldsymbol{Y}^{-1}$ and therefore

$$\begin{aligned}\mathcal{V}\left(\frac{1}{R}\boldsymbol{Y} \, \mathrm{d}z\right) &= \frac{1}{R^2}\boldsymbol{Y}[-kR\boldsymbol{Y}^{-1}(\bar{\boldsymbol{\Theta}}^* - \boldsymbol{g}\boldsymbol{g}')\boldsymbol{Y}^{-1}]\boldsymbol{Y} \\ &= -\frac{k}{R}(\bar{\boldsymbol{\Theta}}^* - \boldsymbol{g}\boldsymbol{g}').\end{aligned}$$

Since $\bar{\boldsymbol{\varepsilon}}^*$ is the random part of $\boldsymbol{G} \, \mathrm{d}(\log z)$, this confirms (7.11) with σ^2 interpreted as $k\gamma/R$.

F.3. Profit maximization

We use (F.1) to write minus profit as

$$\Phi_3(\boldsymbol{q}_*, \boldsymbol{z}, p_1, \boldsymbol{p}_*, \boldsymbol{y}) = p_1 h_{e1}(\boldsymbol{q}_*, \boldsymbol{z}) + \boldsymbol{p}_*' \boldsymbol{q}_* - \boldsymbol{y}'\boldsymbol{z}, \tag{F.15}$$

where the decision variables are now the elements of both $\boldsymbol{q}_*$ and $\boldsymbol{z}$. The covariance matrix of the optimal decision distribution is thus

$$\mathscr{V}\begin{pmatrix}\boldsymbol{q}_*\\ \boldsymbol{z}\end{pmatrix} = k\begin{bmatrix}\partial^2\Phi_3/\partial\boldsymbol{q}_*\,\partial\boldsymbol{q}_*' & \partial^2\Phi_3/\partial\boldsymbol{q}_*\,\partial\boldsymbol{z}'\\ \partial^2\Phi_3/\partial\boldsymbol{z}\,\partial\boldsymbol{q}_*' & \partial^2\Phi_3/\partial\boldsymbol{z}\,\partial\boldsymbol{z}'\end{bmatrix}^{-1}. \tag{F.16}$$

We equate the first derivatives of $\Phi_3(\cdot)$ with respect to $\boldsymbol{q}_*$ and $\boldsymbol{z}$ to zero,

$$\begin{bmatrix}\partial h_{e1}/\partial\boldsymbol{q}_*\\ \partial h_{e1}/\partial\boldsymbol{z}\end{bmatrix} = \frac{1}{p_1}\begin{bmatrix}-\boldsymbol{p}_*\\ \boldsymbol{y}\end{bmatrix}, \tag{F.17}$$

and require that the matrix of second derivatives of $\Phi_3(\cdot)$ with respect to the same variables be positive definite. Since this matrix is a multiple p_1 of the corresponding matrix of $h_{e1}(\cdot)$, we can write (F.16) as

$$\mathscr{V}\begin{pmatrix}\boldsymbol{q}_*\\ \boldsymbol{z}\end{pmatrix} = \frac{k}{p_1}\begin{bmatrix}\partial^2 h_{e1}/\partial\boldsymbol{q}_*\,\partial\boldsymbol{q}_*' & \partial^2 h_{e1}/\partial\boldsymbol{q}_*\,\partial\boldsymbol{z}'\\ \partial^2 h_{e1}/\partial\boldsymbol{z}\,\partial\boldsymbol{q}_*' & \partial^2 h_{e1}/\partial\boldsymbol{z}\,\partial\boldsymbol{z}'\end{bmatrix}^{-1}. \tag{F.18}$$

Next we differentiate (F.17) with respect to $(-\boldsymbol{p}_*'\ \boldsymbol{y}')$:

$$\begin{bmatrix}\partial^2 h_{e1}/\partial\boldsymbol{q}_*\,\partial\boldsymbol{q}_*' & \partial^2 h_{e1}/\partial\boldsymbol{q}_*\,\partial\boldsymbol{z}'\\ \partial^2 h_{e1}/\partial\boldsymbol{z}\,\partial\boldsymbol{q}_*' & \partial^2 h_{e1}/\partial\boldsymbol{z}\,\partial\boldsymbol{z}'\end{bmatrix}\begin{bmatrix}-\partial\boldsymbol{q}_*/\partial\boldsymbol{p}_*' & \partial\boldsymbol{q}_*/\partial\boldsymbol{y}'\\ -\partial\boldsymbol{z}/\partial\boldsymbol{p}_*' & \partial\boldsymbol{z}/\partial\boldsymbol{y}'\end{bmatrix} = \frac{1}{p_1}\boldsymbol{I}. \tag{F.19}$$

It follows from (F.18) and (F.19) that the covariance matrix of $\boldsymbol{q}_*$ and $\boldsymbol{z}$ equals k times the partitioned matrix immediately to the left of the equal sign in (F.19). The complete result is

$$\mathscr{V}\begin{pmatrix} \boldsymbol{q} \\ \boldsymbol{z} \end{pmatrix} = k \begin{bmatrix} -\partial \boldsymbol{q}/\partial \boldsymbol{p}' & \partial \boldsymbol{q}/\partial \boldsymbol{y}' \\ -\partial \boldsymbol{z}/\partial \boldsymbol{p}' & \partial \boldsymbol{z}/\partial \boldsymbol{y}' \end{bmatrix}. \tag{F.20}$$

As before, we interpret this conditionally. Since this is profit maximization, we add the disturbance vectors $\boldsymbol{\varepsilon}^*$ to (4.7) and $\bar{\boldsymbol{\varepsilon}}$ to (5.41):

$$\boldsymbol{G}\,\mathrm{d}(\log \boldsymbol{z}) = \psi^* \boldsymbol{\Theta}^*[\mathrm{d}(\log \boldsymbol{y}) - \boldsymbol{K}'\,\mathrm{d}(\log \boldsymbol{p})] + \boldsymbol{\varepsilon}^*, \tag{F.21}$$

$$\boldsymbol{F}\,\mathrm{d}(\log \mathbf{q}) = -\gamma\psi^* \bar{\boldsymbol{\Theta}}[\mathrm{d}(\log \boldsymbol{p}) - \bar{\boldsymbol{K}}'\,\mathrm{d}(\log \boldsymbol{y})] + \bar{\boldsymbol{\varepsilon}}. \tag{F.22}$$

Thus, $\boldsymbol{\varepsilon}^*$ is the conditionally random part of $\boldsymbol{G}\,\mathrm{d}(\log \boldsymbol{z}) = (1/R)\boldsymbol{Y}\,\mathrm{d}\boldsymbol{z}$ and $\bar{\boldsymbol{\varepsilon}}$ is the random part of $\boldsymbol{F}\,\mathrm{d}(\log \boldsymbol{q}) = (1/C)\boldsymbol{P}\,\mathrm{d}\boldsymbol{q}$. Also, we have $\partial \boldsymbol{z}/\partial \boldsymbol{y}' = R\psi^* \boldsymbol{Y}^{-1}\boldsymbol{\Theta}^*\boldsymbol{Y}^{-1}$, $\partial \boldsymbol{z}/\partial \boldsymbol{p}' = -R\psi^*\boldsymbol{Y}^{-1}\boldsymbol{\Theta}^*\boldsymbol{K}'\boldsymbol{P}^{-1}$, $\partial \boldsymbol{q}/\partial \boldsymbol{p}' = -C\gamma\psi^*\boldsymbol{P}^{-1}\bar{\boldsymbol{\Theta}}^{-1}\boldsymbol{P}^{-1}$, and $\partial \boldsymbol{q}/\partial \boldsymbol{y}' = \gamma C\psi^*\boldsymbol{P}^{-1}\bar{\boldsymbol{\Theta}}\bar{\boldsymbol{K}}'\boldsymbol{Y}^{-1}$, so that

$$\mathscr{V}\begin{pmatrix} \bar{\boldsymbol{\varepsilon}} \\ \boldsymbol{\varepsilon}^* \end{pmatrix} = \mathscr{V}\left(\begin{bmatrix} (1/C)\boldsymbol{P} & \mathbf{0} \\ \mathbf{0} & (1/R)\boldsymbol{Y} \end{bmatrix} \begin{bmatrix} \mathrm{d}\boldsymbol{q} \\ \mathrm{d}\boldsymbol{z} \end{bmatrix}\right)$$

$$= \begin{bmatrix} \frac{1}{C}\boldsymbol{P} & \mathbf{0} \\ \mathbf{0} & \frac{1}{R}\boldsymbol{Y} \end{bmatrix} \begin{bmatrix} C\gamma\psi^*\boldsymbol{P}^{-1}\bar{\boldsymbol{\Theta}}\boldsymbol{P}^{-1} & C\gamma\psi^*\boldsymbol{P}^{-1}\bar{\boldsymbol{\Theta}}\bar{\boldsymbol{K}}'\boldsymbol{Y}^{-1} \\ R\psi^*\boldsymbol{Y}^{-1}\boldsymbol{\Theta}^*\boldsymbol{K}'\boldsymbol{P}^{-1} & R\psi^*\boldsymbol{Y}^{-1}\boldsymbol{\Theta}^*\boldsymbol{Y}^{-1} \end{bmatrix}$$

$$\times \begin{bmatrix} \mathbf{0} & \frac{1}{R}\boldsymbol{Y} \\ \frac{1}{C}\boldsymbol{P} & \mathbf{0} \end{bmatrix} \tag{F.23}$$

which yields, using $R = \gamma C$,

$$\mathscr{V}\begin{pmatrix} \bar{\boldsymbol{\varepsilon}} \\ \boldsymbol{\varepsilon}^* \end{pmatrix} = \frac{k}{C}\begin{bmatrix} \gamma\psi^*\bar{\boldsymbol{\Theta}} & \psi^*\bar{\boldsymbol{\Theta}}\bar{\boldsymbol{K}}' \\ \psi^*\boldsymbol{\Theta}^*\boldsymbol{K}' & (\psi^*/\gamma)\boldsymbol{\Theta}^* \end{bmatrix}. \tag{F.24}$$

We interpret k/C as σ^2, so that the two diagonal blocks immediately imply (7.13) and (7.4). The two off-diagonal blocks are the transposes of each other in view of (6.8), and therefore confirm (7.14).

To confirm (7.2) in the case of profit maximization we substitute (F.21) into (F.9) to obtain (6.3) with a disturbance vector $\boldsymbol{\varepsilon} + \gamma \boldsymbol{K}\boldsymbol{\varepsilon}^*$ added to it. Since the resulting system is equivalent to (F.22), we can equate the disturbance vectors

$$\bar{\boldsymbol{\varepsilon}} = \boldsymbol{\varepsilon} + \gamma \boldsymbol{K}\boldsymbol{\varepsilon}^*. \tag{F.25}$$

Next we use (F.24) with $k/C = \sigma^2$ in

$$\begin{aligned}\sigma^2\psi^*\boldsymbol{\Theta}^*\boldsymbol{K}' &= \mathscr{E}(\boldsymbol{\varepsilon}^*\bar{\boldsymbol{\varepsilon}}') = \mathscr{E}[\boldsymbol{\varepsilon}^*(\boldsymbol{\varepsilon} + \gamma\boldsymbol{K}\boldsymbol{\varepsilon}^*)'] \\ &= \mathscr{E}(\boldsymbol{\varepsilon}^*\boldsymbol{\varepsilon}') + \sigma^2\psi^*\boldsymbol{\Theta}^*\boldsymbol{K}',\end{aligned}$$

which implies $\mathscr{E}(\boldsymbol{\varepsilon}^*\boldsymbol{\varepsilon}') = \boldsymbol{0}$ so that given the normality of $\boldsymbol{\varepsilon}$ and $\boldsymbol{\varepsilon}^*$ they are independent. Also, we have

$$\begin{aligned}\sigma^2\gamma\psi^*\bar{\boldsymbol{\Theta}} &= \mathscr{E}(\bar{\boldsymbol{\varepsilon}}\bar{\boldsymbol{\varepsilon}}') = \mathscr{E}[(\boldsymbol{\varepsilon} + \gamma\boldsymbol{K}\boldsymbol{\varepsilon}^*)(\boldsymbol{\varepsilon} + \gamma\boldsymbol{K}\boldsymbol{\varepsilon}^*)'] \\ &= \mathscr{E}(\boldsymbol{\varepsilon}\boldsymbol{\varepsilon}') + \sigma^2\gamma\psi^*\boldsymbol{K}\boldsymbol{\Theta}^*\boldsymbol{K}',\end{aligned}$$

which together with (6.10) implies $\mathscr{E}(\boldsymbol{\varepsilon}\boldsymbol{\varepsilon}') = \sigma^2\psi(\boldsymbol{\Theta} - \boldsymbol{\theta}\boldsymbol{\theta}')$ and thus confirms (7.2).

In a similar way, we substitute (F.22) into (F.14) to obtain (6.6) with a disturbance vector $\bar{\boldsymbol{\varepsilon}}^* + (1/\gamma)\bar{\boldsymbol{K}}\bar{\boldsymbol{\varepsilon}}$ added. We equate this system to (F.21) to obtain

$$\boldsymbol{\varepsilon}^* = \bar{\boldsymbol{\varepsilon}}^* + \frac{1}{\gamma}\bar{\boldsymbol{K}}\bar{\boldsymbol{\varepsilon}}. \tag{F.26}$$

Now we use (F.24) in

$$\begin{aligned}\sigma^2\psi^*\bar{\boldsymbol{\Theta}}\bar{\boldsymbol{K}}' &= \mathscr{E}(\bar{\boldsymbol{\varepsilon}}\boldsymbol{\varepsilon}^{*\prime}) = \mathscr{E}\left[\bar{\boldsymbol{\varepsilon}}\left(\bar{\boldsymbol{\varepsilon}}^* + \frac{1}{\gamma}\bar{\boldsymbol{K}}\bar{\boldsymbol{\varepsilon}}\right)'\right] \\ &= \mathscr{E}(\bar{\boldsymbol{\varepsilon}}\bar{\boldsymbol{\varepsilon}}^{*\prime}) + \sigma^2\psi^*\bar{\boldsymbol{\Theta}}\bar{\boldsymbol{K}}',\end{aligned}$$

so that $\mathscr{E}(\bar{\boldsymbol{\varepsilon}}\bar{\boldsymbol{\varepsilon}}^{*\prime})=\mathbf{0}$ and $\bar{\boldsymbol{\varepsilon}}$ and $\bar{\boldsymbol{\varepsilon}}^*$ are independently distributed given their normality. Also, we have

$$\sigma^2\frac{\psi^*}{\gamma}\boldsymbol{\Theta}^* = \mathscr{E}(\boldsymbol{\varepsilon}^*\boldsymbol{\varepsilon}^{*\prime}) = \mathscr{E}\left[\left(\bar{\boldsymbol{\varepsilon}}^* + \frac{1}{\gamma}\bar{\boldsymbol{K}}\bar{\boldsymbol{\varepsilon}}\right)\left(\bar{\boldsymbol{\varepsilon}}^* + \frac{1}{\gamma}\bar{\boldsymbol{K}}\bar{\boldsymbol{\varepsilon}}\right)'\right]$$

$$= \mathscr{E}(\bar{\boldsymbol{\varepsilon}}^*\bar{\boldsymbol{\varepsilon}}^{*\prime}) + \sigma^2\frac{\psi^*}{\gamma}\bar{\boldsymbol{K}}\bar{\boldsymbol{\Theta}}\bar{\boldsymbol{K}}'$$

which, with (6.9), implies $\mathscr{E}(\bar{\boldsymbol{\varepsilon}}^*\bar{\boldsymbol{\varepsilon}}^{*\prime}) = -(\sigma^2/\gamma)(\bar{\boldsymbol{\Theta}}^* - \boldsymbol{g}\boldsymbol{g}')$ confirming (7.11) for profit maximization.

References

[1] Allen, R. G. D. *Mathematical Economics*. Second edition (first edition 1956). London: Macmillan & Co. Ltd., 1959.

[2] Allen, R. G. D. *Macro-Economic Theory*. New York: St. Martin's Press, Inc., 1968.

[3] Anderson, T. W. *An Introduction to Multivariate Statistical Analysis*. New York: John Wiley & Sons, Inc., 1958.

[4] Applebaum, E. "Testing Neoclassical Production Theory." *Journal of Econometrics*, 7 (1978), pp. 87–102.

[5] Arrow, K. J. and F. H. Hahn. *General Competitive Analysis*. San Francisco: Holden-Day, Inc., 1972.

[6] Bailey, M. J. "Price and Output Determination by a Firm Selling Related Products." *American Economic Review*, 44 (1954), pp. 82–93.

[7] Barbosa, F. de H. *Rational Random Behavior: Extensions and Applications*. Doctoral Dissertation, The University of Chicago, 1975.

[8] Barnett, W. A. "Theoretical Foundations for the Rotterdam Model." *Review of Economic Studies*, 46 (1979), pp. 109–130.

[9] Barten, A. P. "Consumer Demand Functions Under Conditions of Almost Additive Preferences." *Econometrica*, 32 (1964), pp. 1–38.

[10] Baumol, W. J. "On the Proper Cost Tests for Natural Monopoly in a Multiproduct Industry." *American Economic Review*, 67 (1977), pp. 809–822.

[11] Baumol, W. J., E. E. Bailey and R. D. Willig. "Weak Invisible Hand Theorems on the Sustainability of Multiproduct Natural Monopoly." *American Economic Review*, 67 (1977), pp. 350–365.

[12] Becker, G. S. *Economic Theory*. New York: Alfred A. Knopf, 1971.

[13] Beringer, C. "Estimating Enterprise Production Functions from Input–Output Data on Multiple Enterprise Farms." *Journal of Farm Economics*, 38 (1956), pp. 923–930.

[14] Berndt, E. R. and L. R. Christensen. "The Translog Function and the Substitution of Equipment, Structures, and Labor in U.S. Manufacturing 1929–68." *Journal of Econometrics*, 1 (1973), pp. 81–113.

[15] Blair, R. D. and A. A. Heggestad. "The Impact of Uncertainty upon the Multiproduct Firm." *Southern Economic Journal*, 44 (1977), pp. 136–142.

[16] Brown, A. and A. Deaton. "Surveys in Applied Economics: Models of Consumer Behaviour." *Economic Journal*, 82 (1972), pp. 1145–1236.

[17] Burgess, D. F. "A Cost Minimization Approach to Import Demand Equations." *Review of Economics and Statistics*, 56 (1974), pp. 225–234.

[18] Burgess, D. F. "Duality Theory and Pitfalls in the Specification of Technologies." *Journal of Econometrics*, 3 (1975), pp. 105–121.

[19] Burmeister, E. and S. J. Turnovsky. "The Degree of Joint Production." *International Economic Review*, 12 (1971), pp. 99–105.

[20] Carlson, S. *A Contribution to the Pure Theory of Production*. Doctoral Dissertation, The University of Chicago, 1936. Later published in a slightly revised form as *A Study on the Pure Theory of Production*, first edition 1939, n.p. Reissued, New York: Augustus M. Kelley Publishers, 1969.

[21] Chetty, V. K. "Econometrics of Joint Production: A Comment." *Econometrica*, 37 (1969), p. 731.

[22] Christensen, L. R. and W. H. Greene, "Economies of Scale in U.S. Electric Power Generation." *Journal of Political Economy*, 84 (1978), pp. 655–676.

[23] Christensen, L. R., D. W. Jorgenson and L. J. Lau. "Transcendental Logarithmic Production Frontiers." *Review of Economics and Statistics*, 55 (1973), pp. 28–45.

[24] Clemens, E. W. "Price Discrimination and the Multi-Product Firm." *Review of Economic Studies*, 19 (1950–51), pp. 1–11.

[25] Clements, K. W. "The Theory of the Firm and Multisectoral Supply Analysis." Report 7818 of the Center for Mathematical Studies in Business and Economics, The University of Chicago, 1978.

[26] Crum, W. L. "The Statistical Allocation of Joint Costs." *Journal of the American Statistical Association*, 21 (1926), pp. 9–26.

[27] Dayan, D. "Behavior of the Firm Under Regulatory Constraint: A Reexamination." Copy supplied by author.

[28] Dhrymes, P. J. "On the Theory of the Monopolistic Multiproduct Firm Under Uncertainty." *International Economic Review*, 5 (1964), pp. 239–257.

[29] Dhrymes, P. J. and B. M. Mitchell. "Estimation of Joint Production Functions." *Econometrica*, 37 (1969), pp. 732–736.

[30] Divisia, F. "L'indice monétaire et la théorie de la monnaie." *Revue d'Economie Politique*, 39 (1925), pp. 980–1008.

[31] Ferguson, C. E. *The Neoclassical Theory of Production and Distribution*. Cambridge University Press, 1969.

[32] Frisch, R. *New Methods of Measuring Marginal Utility*. Tübingen: J. C. B. Mohr, 1932.

[33] Frisch, R. *Theory of Production*. Chicago: Rand McNally & Company, 1965.

[34] Graaff, J. de V. "Income Effects and the Theory of the Firm." *Review of Economic Studies*, 18 (1950–51), pp. 79–86.

[35] Hall, R. E. "The Specification of Technology with Several Kinds of Output." *Journal of Political Economy*, 81 (1973), pp. 878–892.

[36] Hanoch, G. "Homotheticity in Joint Production." *Journal of Economic Theory*, 2 (1970), pp. 423–426.

[37] Hasenkamp, G. *Specification and Estimation of Multiple-Output Production Functions*. Berlin, Heidelberg, and New York: Springer-Verlag, 1976.

[38] Hasenkamp, G. "A Study of Multiple-Output Production Functions: Klein's Railroad Study Revisited." *Journal of Econometrics*, 4 (1976), pp. 253–262.

[39] Henderson, J. M. and R. E. Quandt. *Microeconomic Theory*. Second edition (first edition 1959). New York: McGraw-Hill, Inc., 1972.
[40] Hicks, J. R. *Value and Capital*. Second edition (first edition 1939). Oxford: Clarendon Press, 1946.
[41] Hirota, M. and K. Kuga. "On an Intrinsic Joint Production." *International Economic Review*, 12 (1971), pp. 87–98.
[42] Hotelling, H. "Edgeworth's Taxation Paradox and the Nature of Demand and Supply Functions." *Journal of Political Economy*, 40 (1932), pp. 577–616.
[43] Houthakker, H. S. "Additive Preferences." *Econometrica*, 28 (1960), pp. 244–257; errata, 30 (1962), p. 633.
[44] Hughes, J. P. "Factor Demand in the Multi-Product Firm." *Southern Economic Journal*, 45 (1978), pp. 494–501.
[45] Jorgenson, D. W. and L. J. Lau. "The Duality of Technology and Economic Behaviour." *Review of Economic Studies*, 61 (1974), pp. 181–200.
[46] Klein, L. R. "The Use of Cross-Section Data in Econometrics with Application to a Study of Railroad Services in the United States." Mimeographed report of the National Bureau of Economic Research, 1947.
[47] Klein, L. R. *A Textbook of Econometrics*. Second edition (first edition 1952). Englewood Cliffs, N.J.: Prentice-Hall, Inc., 1974.
[48] Laitinen, K. "Measurement of Real Income." Report 7846 of the Center for Mathematical Studies in Business and Economics, The University of Chicago, 1978.
[49] Laitinen, K. "Why Is Demand Homogeneity So Often Rejected?" *Economics Letters*, 1 (1978), pp. 187–191.
[50] Laitinen, K. and H. Theil. "Supply and Demand of the Multiproduct Firm." *European Economic Review*, 11 (1978), pp. 107–154.
[51] Lau, L. J. "Profit Functions of Technologies with Multiple Inputs and Outputs." *Review of Economics and Statistics*, 54 (1972), pp. 281–289.
[52] Makower, H. and W. J. Baumol. "The Analogy Between Producer and Consumer Equilibrium Analysis." *Economica*, 17 (1950), pp. 63–80.
[53] Mauer, W. A. and T. H. Naylor. "Monopolistic–Monopsonistic Competition: The Multi-Product, Multi-Factor Firm." *Southern Economic Journal*, 31 (1964–65), pp. 38–43.
[54] McFadden, D. "Cost, Revenue, and Profit Functions." In: *Production Economics: A Dual Approach to Theory and Applications*, M. Fuss and D. McFadden, eds. Amsterdam: North-Holland Publishing Company, 1978.
[55] Mundlak, Y. "Specification and Estimation of Multiproduct Production Functions." *Journal of Farm Economics*, 45 (1963), pp. 433–445.
[56] Naylor, T. H. "A Kuhn–Tucker Model of the Multi-Product, Multi-Factor Firm." *Sourthern Economic Journal*, 31 (1965), pp. 324–330.
[57] Nerlove, M. *Estimation and Identification of Cobb–Douglas Production Functions*. Amsterdam: North-Holland Publishing Company, 1965.
[58] Panzar, J. C. and R. D. Willig. "Economies of Scale in Multi-Output Production." *Quarterly Journal of Economics*, 91 (1977), pp. 481–493.

[59] Panzar, J. C. and R. D. Willig. "Free Entry and the Sustainability of Natural Monopoly." *Bell Journal of Economics*, 8 (1977), pp. 1–22.
[60] Pfouts, R. W. "The Theory of Cost and Production in the Multi-Product Firm." *Econometrica*, 29 (1961), pp. 650–658.
[61] Pfouts, R. W. "Multi-Product Firms vs. Single-Product Firms: The Theory of Cost and Production." *Metroeconomica*, 16 (1964), pp. 51–66.
[62] Pfouts, R. W. "Some Cost and Profit Relationships in the Multi-Product Firm." *Southern Economic Journal*, 39 (1973), pp. 361–365.
[63] Powell, A. A. and F. H. G. Gruen. "The Constant Elasticity of Transformation Production Frontier and Linear Supply System." *International Economic Review*, 9 (1968), pp. 315–328.
[64] Rao, P. "A Note on Econometrics of Joint Production." *Econometrica*, 37 (1969), pp. 737–738.
[65] Reder, M. W. "Inter-Temporal Relations of Demand and Supply Within the Firm." *Canadian Journal of Economics and Political Science*, 7 (1941), pp. 25–38.
[66] Sakai, Y. "Substitution and Expansion Effects in Production Theory: The Case of Joint Production." *Journal of Economic Theory*, 9 (1974), pp. 255–274.
[67] Samuelson, P. A. "Prices of Factors and Goods in General Equilibrium." *Review of Economic Studies*, 21 (1953), pp. 1–20.
[68] Samuelson, P. A. "The Fundamental Singularity Theorem for Non-Joint Production." *International Economic Review*, 7 (1966), pp. 34–41.
[69] Sharkey, W. W. and L. G. Telser. "Supportable Cost Functions for the Multiproduct Firm." *Journal of Economic Theory*, 18 (1978), pp. 23–37.
[70] Shephard, R. W. *Cost and Production Functions*. Princeton University Press, 1953.
[71] Shephard, R. W. *Theory of Cost and Production Functions*. Princeton University Press, 1970.
[72] Stigler, G. J. "The Economics of Information." *Journal of Political Economy*, 69 (1961), pp. 213–225.
[73] Stigler, G. J. "Information in the Labor Market." *Journal of Political Economy*, 70 (1962), Supplement, pp. 94–105.
[74] Stigler, G. J. *The Theory of Price*. Third edition (first edition 1942). New York: The Macmillan Company, 1966.
[75] Takayama, A. *Mathematical Economics*. Hinsdale, Illinois: The Dryden Press, 1974.
[76] Theil, H. *Principles of Econometrics*. New York: John Wiley and Sons, Inc., 1971.
[77] Theil, H. "The Theory of Rational Random Behavior and Its Application to Demand Analysis." *European Economic Review*, 6 (1975), pp. 217–226.
[78] Theil, H. *Theory and Measurement of Consumer Demand*. Two Volumes, Amsterdam: North Holland Publishing Company, 1975–76.
[79] Theil, H. "The Independent Inputs of Production." *Econometrica*, 45 (1977), pp. 1303–1327.
[80] Theil, H. *The System-Wide Approach to Microeconomics*. University of Chicago Press, 1980.

[81] Theil, H. and K. Laitinen. "A Parametrization of the Multiproduct Firm." Report 7803 of the Center for Mathematical Studies in Business and Economics, The University of Chicago, 1978.

[82] Theil, H. and K. Laitinen. "Maximum Likelihood Estimation of the Rotterdam Model Under Two Different Conditions." *Economics Letters*, 2 (1979), pp. 239–244.

[83] Uzawa, H. "Production Functions with Constant Elasticities of Substitution." *Review of Economic Studies*, 29 (1962), pp. 291–299.

[84] Vinod, H. D. "Econometrics of Joint Production." *Econometrica*, 36 (1968), pp. 322–336.

[85] Vinod, H. D. "Canonical Ridge and Econometrics of Joint Production." *Journal of Econometrics*, 4 (1976), pp. 147–166.

[86] Weaver, R. D. "Returns to Scale for Multiple Product, Non-Homothetic Production." Staff Paper No. 8, College of Agriculture, Pennsylvania State University, 1978.

[87] Weldon, J. C. "The Multi-Product Firm." *Canadian Journal of Economics and Political Science*, 14 (1948), pp. 176–190.

Index